Postcolonial Bollywood and Muslim Identity

Production, Representation, and Reception

NADIRA KHATUN

OXFORD
UNIVERSITY PRESS

Great Clarendon Street, Oxford, OX2 6DP,
United Kingdom

Oxford University Press is a department of the University of Oxford.
It furthers the University's objective of excellence in research, scholarship,
and education by publishing worldwide. Oxford is a registered trade mark of
Oxford University Press in the UK and in certain other countries

© Nadira Khatun 2024

The moral rights of the author have been asserted

First Edition published in 2024

Published in the United States of America by Oxford University Press
198 Madison Avenue, New York, NY 10016, United States of America

British Library Cataloguing in Publication Data

Data available

Library of Congress Control Number: 2023943783

ISBN 978-0-19-889101-7

DOI: 10.1093/oso/9780198891017.001.0001

Printed and bound in India by
Replika Press Pvt. Ltd.

For Maa, Dada (brother) and Saptarshi

Preface
By Mujibur Rehman

It is almost impossible to challenge the formulations of Amartya Sen on identity which he has argued as multidimensional.[1] One wonders why often one dimension of a person's identity becomes salient and invariably becomes a source of dispute. This remains a legitimate question to raise again and again. No definite closure on this as yet. I wonder if we could ever have had closure, yet it is necessary to wrestle with it again. For instance, we may dismiss this purely as a result of a human mind's confused naivety, but then too many puzzles could be swept under the carpet with such explanations. And science or its pursuits or scientific mind cannot be declared dead!

While religious identity of any kind has been generally contentious, Muslim identity seems to be disproportionately so in recent years, both domestically and globally, for varied reasons. Globally, some would argue that the 9/11 attack on the Twin Towers is the dividing line. In a similar vein, the demolition of Babri Masjid on 6 December 1992—particularly in the wider context of the Bhartiya Janata Party (BJP)'s electoral dominance—has caused such a shift in the Indian context. Scholarships are also there that demonstrate the genesis of Islamophobia beyond these specific incidents at the Indian as well as global level. Generally speaking, scholars have spent lots of valuable energy exploring the reasons behind this in recent years. What is remarkable about this intellectual enquiry is that it has not only acquired speed and variety but it has become truly interdisciplinary.

This book by Nadira Khatun is robust evidence of such an effort. It seeks to explore the issues of Muslim representation in the particular context of Bollywood films. Close reading of the text will convince any reader that this is an outcome of many years of research. Its journey began as a doctoral research and has gone through qualitative transformations over

---

[1] Amartya Sen (2015) *Identity and Violence: Illusions of Destiny*. Penguin,.

the years with several rounds of research during her post-PhD life, including her life as a professional academic. She has interviewed mainly three categories of people associated with Bollywood: (1) filmmakers, (2) film critics, and (3) audiences to prepare its content. She has done a very impressive job on this count.

The conclusion that she arrives at with painstaking research is not particularly pleasant. It shows enormous bias towards the Muslim identity since the early days of Bollywood film, which dates back to colonial times. This negativity about Muslim identity, as her research indicates, is not uniform, and it has varied with the changing context of Indian politics. In the post-Independence India or Nehruvian India (say until the rise of the BJP in the late 1980s), there were efforts to build harmonious relationships between two major communities of India: Hindus and Muslims. However, political trends seem to be quite different in the Indian context in recent years. What seems to be apparent is the conflict between Hindus and Muslims—and considerable state indifference to deal with such conflicts. In part, this could be blamed for representation issues that Dr Khatun has raised with tremendous intellectual prowess.

One prominent claim that Dr Khatun makes is the organic relationship between state ideology and Bollywood filmmaking, which is seemingly the reason for Islamophobic films in recent years. Say, for example, *The Kashmir Files* and many others. There are some obvious questions that we might raise in this context. For instance, if the Bollywood films are all driven by state ideology and possess enormous propaganda value, how should we explain the transformation of India's secular state character to its increasingly Hindu majoritarian avatar? Indeed, there are influential explanations about this transition apparent in the writings of Christophe Jaffrelot,[2] Thomas Bloom Hansen,[3] Mujibur Rehman,[4] and others. However, there is no such persuasive explanation from the research on film studies or Bollywood in particular. One wonders if there is a different

[2] Christophe Jaffrelot (1998) *The Hindu Nationalist Movement in India*. New York: Columbia University Press; also see Christopher Jaffrelot, Angana Chatterjee, and Thomas Bloom Hansen (Eds.) (2019) *Majoritarian State*. New Delhi: HarperCollins; Also a review by Shaikh Mujibur Rehman, 'Rule by a Majority', in *Frontline*, 29 September 2019.

[3] Thomas Bloom Hansen (2021) *The Law of Force: The Violent Heart of Indian Politics*. New Delhi: Aleph.

[4] Mujibur Rehman (Ed.) (2018) *Rise of Saffron Power: Reflections on Indian Politics*. New Delhi: Routledge.

argument or at least varied nuances of similar argument emerge owing to the work on the Bollywood film. Put differently, why was it Bollywood has failed to strengthen secular character of Indian society when it had the opportunity to do so? In my view, while we may have differences of opinion about the power of Bollywood or its potential, to argue that it alone has such a power might be a bit of an exaggeration. It means it is necessary to recognize that Bollywood alone is not enough to reflect on the politics of representation.

This takes us to the next question, which is the relationship between politics or more specifically electoral politics and Bollywood. Seen purely from the way Bollywood actors have fared in India's electoral theatre, the record seems to be mixed. Moreover, there is more encouraging evidence in the regional film industries. Take, for example, N.T. Ramarao or M.G. Ramachandran in Andhra Pradesh or Tamil Nadu respectively. In Bollywood, there is hardly any parallel of these film personalities of regional films. For instance, Bollywood's biggest political superstar Amitabh Bachchan was not particularly a great success or rather a flop in the Indian political theatre. Some of these case studies do raise a legitimate question about the power of Bollywood as a propaganda machine. It works in some ways and does not work in other instances. Recent work by Parth Chatterjee's *I am the People*,[5] written in the context of populism, presents interesting perspectives on this debate.

Dr Nadira Khatun, however, does raise a very valid question, which is about stereotyping of Muslims, and its negative portrayal. In a number of Bollywood movies such an attempt was made, for instance, *Roja*, *Fanna*, *Mission Kashmir*, *Black Friday*, *New York*, *A Wednesday*, *Sarfarosh*, etc. It is tempting to conclude that some of these movies and their box office success might have helped perpetuate a Muslim militant image. At the same time it has not worked for the alternative secular, tolerant image, particularly in the era when Muslim militancy was not a regular headline in India or elsewhere. Say, for instance, during the period ranging from the 1950s to 1970s. Kashmir militancy was a late 1980s development.

As Prakash Jha suggests according to the interview by Dr Khatun, in most cases the stories are driven by the market. But then market is not an

---

[5] see Partha Chatterjee (2019) *I am the People*. New Delhi: Permanent Black; also see my review published in *Frontline* on 9 April 2021.

innocent institution. Take, for example, the extraordinary success of *The Kashmir Files* and compare and contrast it with the spectacular box office failures of movies based on the lives of Narendra Modi or Bala Saheb Thackeray. Deep interrogation is needed to make sense of what is unfolding in India.

In her attempt to explain and use the idea of representation, Dr Khatun has deployed the works of scholars belonging to Frankfurt School, British Cultural Studies, French Structuralists, and post-structuralists with great sophistication and skill. Dr Khatun has creatively used the scholarship of various genres to advance her argument. She has almost come to resolve the issue of misrepresentation of Muslim identity in Bollywood. In some fundamental ways, she agrees with what Edward Said used to argue on the role of the American media. One comes across a parallel about this in Indian Bollywood. In a discussion, noted filmmaker Mahesh Bhatt told me how the Urdu subtitles gradually disappeared from the Hindi films, while they used to be an almost indispensable part of the film's life in the 1950s and 1960s.

What appears to be a Muslim question is neither limited to Bollywood nor to India anymore. It has global dimension today. There is a need for more works of this kind to fight the stereotypes. On the global dimension, I think Anne Norton, in her book *On the Muslim Question* (2013), has posed the puzzle in a beautiful manner in its preface. This is how she raises the concerns of the Muslim Question:

> The Muslim questions remains the great question for the West. The perversities of that question remain. Muslims are still marked as a danger to freedom of speech, yet speech by Muslims and in defence of Muslims is still most heavily censored speech. Muslims are still given scripts that they must read.[6]

Dr Shaikh Mujibur Rehman is a faculty at Jamia Millia Central University, New Delhi, India. He is the author of a forthcoming book, *Shikwa-e-Hind: The Political Future of Indian Muslims*, to be published by Simon and Schuster, New Delhi.

---

[6] Anne Norton (2013) *On the Muslim Question*. Princeton, NJ: Princeton University Press.

Acknowledgements

This book comes at the end of six and half years of labour, and during this period and throughout this time, my family, friends, and peers kept me going. Since the monograph is a continuation of my PhD work, I am grateful to the Tata Institute of Social Sciences (TISS), Mumbai, for providing me with the intellectual space that is every academic's dream. Most importantly, this monograph would not have reached this stage without the visiting assistant professor position in the Department of Communication Studies and Multimedia at McMaster University, Hamilton. I am immensely grateful to Dr Faiza Hirzi for creating the visiting scholar position, which provided me with ample time and resources to write, rewrite, and restructure the manuscript. I also thank Lorraine Bell for making my initial days at McMaster easier by setting up library access and office space. I want to express my gratitude to the Vice Chancellor of XIM University, Fr Antony R. Uvari, SJ, and the former Dean of the School of Communications of that time, Fr Donald D'Silva, for their support, encouragement, and approval of a year-long sabbatical for the visiting fellow position at McMaster University. I am thankful to Fr Alwyn Rodrigues and Fr E.A. Augustine, SJ, for their encouragement.

I want to express my deep and sincere gratitude to my Ph.D. supervisor, N. Jayaram, for his supervision, guidance, and advice. He agreed to guide me when I was going through the most difficult time finding a supervisor for my doctoral work. Your comments have always been very insightful and detailed, with suggestions on style, content, as well as wider relevance of the work. I wish to express my warm and sincere thanks to Abdul Shaban. I especially want to thank Prof Shaban for his enthusiastic support of the project, his engagement responses, and his extremely productive questions. He has always pushed me to explore the theoretical framework and theoretical implications of this work. Above all, and the most needed, he provided me with constant support throughout this work. His wide knowledge and logical way of thinking have been of great value to me. I have learnt a lot from him these past few years, not just the academic work, but also the values of life.

I am immensely thankful to Mujibur Rehman, political scientist and academician, for writing the preface of this book. His critical insights of political history at the beginning of the book indeed strengthened and justified my further argument. Beyond writing just the preface, he was always there for critical, insightful *addas*.

I am grateful to all the participants in this research. I am most thankful to the filmmakers—Javed Akhtar, Shyam Benegal, Rensil D'Silva, Kabir Khan, Soojit Sircar, Amit Khanna, Mahesh Bhatt, Vinay Shukla, Haider Ali, Kamlesh Pandey, Shibani Bathija, Ashutosh Gowariker, who gave me their valuable time in spite of their busy schedules. Apart from filmmakers, I am most indebted to the film critic Rajiv Masand. In my initial stage of fieldwork, he was the first person who gave me the contacts of many prominent film critics and filmmakers. I started my fieldwork with those contacts. I am immensely thankful to my friend and colleague, Faiz Ullah, who provided me with the initial contacts of the film critics. I am also grateful to the film critics Mayank Shekhar, Rauf Ahmed, Shiladitya Sen, Nasreen Kunni Kabir, and Nandini Ramnath. Moreover, the responses of the academicians and critical thinkers like Teesta Setalvad, Ram Puniyani, Asghar Ali Engineer, Sitara Shabnam (name changed), Kaifiya Fatehma (name changed), and Irfan Engineer helped me to strengthen my argument in this study.

I must mention the students at the School of Communications, XIM University, for their indirect support, encouragement, and the class discussion on critical social issues, which primarily led me to formulate certain arguments presented in the book differently. I would especially like to thank my dear students Basyukta Basuprava, Aditya Mohapatra, and Megha Misra for providing me with the contacts of the audiences whom I interviewed to refurnish and update the empirical data presented in the book. I am also thankful to the audience who spent their time watching the films which were relevant to my study. I must acknowledge and remember the constant motivation and encouragement of Nadarajah Manickam and Abhnay Dey to finish the manuscript.

Another important person for whom the book has reached its final stage is Moutushi Mukherjee, the ex-commissioning of the book. At certain times she has gone beyond her defined job roles to help me out and to make the process smooth and comfortable for a first-time author like me. I am extremely thankful to my current commissioning editor Natasha Sarkar for always being there to clarify my thousands of doubts. Most importantly, I must thank Barun Sarkar, the production manager of OUP India, for his overall support, cooperation, and advice at every step. Two anonymous reviewers have been kind enough to provide me with numerous insightful and helpful constructive suggestions. The constructive criticism and ideas have improved this book. I am grateful to Binita Roy for carefully proofreading the final version of the manuscript.

I am happy to mention Sreeja Burman, a graphic design artist who happened to be my student, who gladly accepted my proposal to do a few illustrations for the book, and my partner Saptarshi Kundu for agreeing to co-design the cover page of the book.

I would gladly remember the love and support that all my ex-colleagues from TISS extended to me on this journey. Special thanks to Premlatha, Sohini, Jaya, Tina, Ketoki, Rincy, Benedict, Bidu, Sahana, Melody, Debu, Meghadeepa, Barsha, Mohan, and Fiaz for making the whole experience a wonderful one. You became members of my extended family. I especially must thank Diviya, who was always there for my every academic help which was required while conducting the research.

This book would not be in existence if TISS did not provide the opportunity to a subaltern student like me to pursue doctoral research in one of the premier social science research institutes in India. During my stay at TISS, when the formative ideas of this book were initially taking shape, I got immense help from the staff at the Sir Dorabji Tata Memorial Library, TISS. Thank you, Poornima and Vidya, and all at the Research and Development section. A special thanks to Sribatsa Pradhan, the librarian of XIM University, for always being so helpful even at the time I was not physically present on campus.

My parents are the ones who sincerely raised me with their caring and gentle love. Without their encouragement and understanding, it would have been impossible for me to finish this work. My Maa, who is a constant source of strength and affection. My brother, Mossarrap Hossain Khan, is the person who instilled the fundamentals of learning by showing me the joys of intellectual pursuits ever since I was a child. He was the first person to inspire me to write this book. I must thank Mary Ann Chacko, who is more than a sister. She was always there for my mental and academic strength. Thank you to my sister (Dilara) and brother-in-law (Altaf Hussain) for being my mental strength. I want to thank my mother-in-law and father-in-law for their constant support and encouragement.

At home, Saptarshi showed extraordinary patience and continued to cheer me on; he showered me with love when I was at my crankiest worst. He was there in every stage of this study, and his unconditional mental support and encouragement when I was upset. Thanks to him for always being there to do my last-minute formatting work. I could never have done this without his unconditional support.

Sections of Chapter 1 were presented as an academic paper in a doctoral synopsis at Keele University, United Kingdom, on 8 November 2013, as a guest lecture at the Department of Peace Studies, McMaster University, Hamilton, on 2 November 2021. A section of Chapter 3 appeared in the special issue of the *Journal of Religion and Film*, 22(3), Article 8 (December 2018), presented as a seminar paper at the 2018 International Conference on Religion and Film, sponsored by the *Journal of Religion and Film* and hosted by the University of Toronto, Canada, from 2–5 May 2018, presented at the I World Cinema International Conference on "Cinema of India" held at the University Complutense of Madrid scheduled 15–16 June 2021. A section of Chapter 4 appeared as a book chapter in Dr Santosh Kumar Biswal (Eds.), *Social and Cultural Dynamics of Indian Cinema*, Pennsylvania: IGI Global Press (July 2020). Chapter 5 is a modified and enlarged version of a paper that appeared in the *Journal of Arab and Muslim Media Research*, 9(1), April 2016, presented a paper at the conference on 'Identity in Times of Change' held at School of Social Sciences, the University of Manchester, United Kingdom, on 7 June 2019.

The chapters have all been completely reworked and restructured to turn the prior ideas into a comprehensive monograph in the context of the current sociopolitical landscape.

Table of Contents

Figures

Abbreviations

ACP	Assistant Commissioner of Police
BBC	British Broadcasting Corporation
BJP	Bharatiya Janata Party
BSF	Border Security Force
CAA	Citizenship (Amendment) Act, 2019
CAB	Citizenship (Amendment) Bill, 2019
CBFC	Central Board of Film Certification, India
CBSE	Central Board of Secondary Education, India
CDA	Critical discourse analysis
CE	Common Era
CIA	Central Intelligence Agency, USA
COVID-19	Coronavirus disease
DCP	Deputy Commissioner of Police
IMDB	Internet Movie Database, online database of information related to films
IRA	Irish Republican Army
IPTA	Indian People's Theatre Association
ISI	Inter-Services Intelligence, Pakistan
JEM	Jaish-e-Mohammed, Pakistan
JKLF	Jammu and Kashmir Liberation Front
JNU	Jawaharlal Nehru University
MCOCA	The Maharashtra Control of Organised Crime Act, 1999
MG	Minimum guarantee system (in film distribution)
MNC	Multinational Corporation
MNS	Maharashtra Navnirman Sena
MP	Member of Parliament
NDA	National Democratic Alliance
NFDC	National Film Development Corporation of India
NRC	National Register of Citizens, India
OBC	Other Backward Castes
OTT	Over the Top, means of providing television/film content over the Internet
POTA	Prevention of Terrorism Act, 2002
RAW	Research and Analysis Wing, India
RSS	Rashtriya Swayamsevak Sangh
SC	Scheduled Caste

SRK	Shah Rukh Khan, Indian Actor
SSP	Senior Superintendent Police
ST	Scheduled Tribe
TADA	The Terrorist and Disruptive Activities (Prevention) Act, 1987
TV	Television
ULFA	United Liberation Front of Asom
UK	United Kingdom
USA	United States of America
VHP	Vishva Hindu Parishad
YUVA	Youth for Unity and Voluntary Action, a non-profit organization

Introduction: Muslims in Postcolonial Bollywood: Theoretical debates and Methodological Positions

'For a long time, we have not made any film on the Partition; on that mayhem with huge, humongous grand part of Indian history. Perhaps Indian cinema did not have the language; we don't have the syntax to deal with [that]; so we just pretended that it has never happened. And there was total silence in Hindi Cinema vis-à-vis this chapter of Indian history.'
—Javed Akhtar (Personal interview, 24 March 2014)

I was interviewing Javed Akhtar—a successful and renowned lyricist, poet, and screenwriter of Bollywood, and also an Indian political activist—for the empirical data of this book. He replied to my question concerning the reiteration of stereotypical Muslim representation in postcolonial Bombay Hindi cinema or contemporary Bollywood cinema. He is right in pointing out how Bombay Hindi cinema or Bollywood cinema has conveniently overlooked the most complex and controversial issues of independent India, and the Partition[1] is one of them.

[1] British India was split into two sovereign dominions in 1947: Pakistan and India. Today, the Islamic Republic of Pakistan and the People's Republic of Bangladesh make up the Dominion of Pakistan, while the Dominion of India is now known as the Republic of India. Two provinces, Bengal and Punjab, were split depending on the majority of Muslims or non-Muslims in each district during the partition. Urvashi Butalia writes, 'In the space of a few months, about twelve million people moved between the new, truncated India and the two wings, East and West, of the newly created Pakistan. By far the largest proportion of these refugees—more than ten million of them—crossed the western border which divided the historic state of Punjab, Muslims

Postcolonial Bollywood and Muslim Identity. Nadira Khatun, Oxford University Press. © Oxford University Press 2024.
DOI: 10.1093/oso/9780198891017.003.0001

India witnessed a number of communal events in post-Independence India such as multiple riots throughout the country at different times. There were some major communal riots which took place and had an impact across the country due to heavy media coverage. The most prominent incident of communal violence are riots in the course of the India–Pakistan Partition in 1947, the 1984 anti-Sikh riots,[2] the riots that took place post-Babri Masjid demolition in 1991–1992,[3] the post-Godhra riots in Gujarat in 2002,[4] Muzaffarnagar in UP in

travelling west to Pakistan, Hindus and Sikhs east to India. Slaughter sometimes accompanied and sometimes prompted their movement; many others died from malnutrition and contagious disease. Estimates of the dead vary from 200,000 (the contemporary British figure) to two million (a later Indian estimate) but that somewhere around a million people died is now widely accepted. As always there was widespread sexual savagery: about 75,000 women are thought to have been abducted and raped by men of religions different from their own (and indeed sometimes by men of their own religion).' Butalia, U. (2017) *The Other Side of Silence: Voices from the Partition of India.* UK: Penguin.

[2] Following the assassination of Prime Minister Smt. Indira Gandhi on 31 October 1984 by her two Sikh security guards, Sikhs and their properties came under attack in Delhi and other cities across the nation. Beginning on the evening of 31 October 1984, there were violent incidents in Delhi. The Sikhs and their properties were subjected to brutal assault over the course of the next two days. Numerous Sikhs were murdered. Others suffered injuries. Large-scale property looting and burning took place. See Justice Nanavati Commission Report. (2005) *Justice Nanavati Commission of Inquiry (1984 Anti-Sikh Riots).* [Pdf] Government of India. Available at https://www.mha.gov.in/sites/default/files/Nanavati-I_eng_0.pdf. 'Official figures claim that almost 3000 people were killed.' Jeffery, R. and Hall, I. (2020) Post-conflict Justice in Divided Democracies: The 1984 Anti-Sikh Riots in India. *Third World Quarterly,* 41(6), pp. 994–1011.

[3] Hindu right-wing organizations ran a number of initiatives at the end of the 1980s and the beginning of the 1990s to successfully mobilize and earn support from the public. These campaigns mostly relied on anti-Muslim propaganda. The Ayodhya movement was the most successful of these' endeavours. The Hindu right wing gained their first significant triumph with the destruction of the Babri Masjid on 6 December 1992 when the volunteers and cadres of the Sangh Parivar destroyed the historic building, popularizing the idea that Ayodhya is where the Hindu God Rama was born. Paola Bacchetta (2000) mentions that 'As news of the mosque demolition spread throughout India, riots broke out between Hindus and Muslims in several major cities. A striking feature of the riots was the alleged use of sexuality and violence against individuals to signify domination. Muslim women were allegedly raped (National Women's Conference 1993), Muslim men castrated, over one thousand left dead in the first month alone.' Bacchetta, P. (2000) Sacred Space in Conflict in India: The Babri Masjid Affair. *Growth and Change,* 31(2), p. 257.

[4] The Godhra riots of 2002 are a turning point in Indian politics. The Sabarmati Express was allegedly attacked by some Muslims on 27 February 2002, at Gujarat's Godhra railway station. Hindu pilgrims who had just left Ayodhya, the scene of the Babri Masjid-Ram Janmabhoomi controversy, were among the passengers. The incident led to widespread attacks on Muslims in Ahmadabad and other regions of Gujarat, which were justified as acts of retaliatory cruelty. Paul Brass (2004) mentions, 'where widespread killings, mostly of Muslims, were carried out on a scale, and with a ferocity, reminiscent of the genocidal massacres that occurred during the partition of the Punjab in 1947, and with the apparent involvement—by several eyewitness accounts—of ministers in the government itself, under the leadership of Bharatiya Janata Party (BJP) Chief Minister Narendra Modi' [The Gujarat pogrom of 2002. *therearenosunglasses.*

2013,[5] the Delhi riots during CAA (Citizenship (Amendment) Act, 2019)–NRC (National Register of Citizens)[6] movement in New Delhi in 2020, and sporadic incidents of lynching in the last decade. Apart from the 1984 anti-Sikh riots, all other major communal conflicts mentioned above involved Hindus and Muslims. While on the one hand we have witnessed a spate of communal violence, on the other hand India, along with other nations, saw the emergence of terrorism committed in the name of Islam in the last three decades. Most interestingly, the above-mentioned incidents of communal violence never acquired an important space in Bollywood as mentioned by Javed Akhtar, but Islamic terrorism became an overexploited genre in Bollywood cinema. Thus, Bollywood has represented Muslims through a selective ideological lens and often overlooked situating them in landmark Indian sociopolitical historical events.

---

wordpress.com, 26 March. Available at https://therearenosunglasses.wordpress.com/2008/12/01/the-gujarat-pogrom-of-2002/

[5] According to the report by Prof. Mohan Rao et al., 'The overwhelming weight of evidence points towards the fact that Muslims have disproportionately been at the receiving end of the communal orgy that swept Muzaffarnagar during the months of September and October 2013 in terms of loss to life and property and displacement of people from their homes and villages. As per the information available from the SSP (Senior Superintendent Police's) office a total of 52 people died in the communal disturbances of which 37 were Muslims and 15 were Hindus ... While deaths among the Hindus took place in the violence that ensued the Jat Mahapanchayat at Nangla Mandaur on 8th September, the Muslim deaths have taken place in different villages over a period of time in much more planned attacks. None of the Jat deaths were the result out of violence generally directed against Hindus, but were of the Jats who were returning form the Mahapanchayat and who deliberately provoked the Muslims while passing through their areas/villages. There are no reports of Jats and the Hindus otherwise living in these areas/villages being attacked by Muslims. As per unofficial sources as many as 100,000 Muslims had been displaced from their homes while by the time of our visit the government acknowledged that 50,955 persons had been displaced who were accommodated in 11 relief camps.' Rao, Mohan, et al. (2013) *Communalism and the Role of the State: An Investigation into the Communal Violence in Muzaffarnagar and its Aftermath.* [pdf] Economic and Political Weekly. Available at https://www.epw.in/system/files/pdf/2014_49/2/Muzaffarnagar%20Report%20-%20Final%20(1).pdf

[6] The Government of India passed the Citizenship (Amendment) Act (CAA) on 12 December 2019. The Act was followed by the proposals of the National Register of Citizens (NRC). While reporting columnist N.D Jayaprakash mentions, 'Strong anti-CAA rallies recently erupted across the nation, and now these protestors are being charged for orchestrating the 2019 riots in Delhi. Thirteen Hindus and forty Muslims were among the 53 deaths in these clashes, which disproportionately affected the minority community. The destruction of religious structures (14 mosques, a dargah, but no temple) is another illustration of the type of targeted violence that took place.' Jayaprakash, N.D. (2020) Delhi Riots 2020: There Was a Conspiracy, But Not the One the Police Alleges. *The Wire*, 15 July. Available at https://thewire.in/communalism/delhi-riots-2020-there-was-a-conspiracy-but-not-the-one-the-police-alleges

Islam is a monotheistic religion centred on the philosophies enunciated in the Quran, a text that its followers, known as Muslims, believe to be a verbatim replication of God's words. It is the world's second major religion in terms of the number of followers. According to Pew Research Centre, a global demographic study of more than 200 nations, there were 1.57 billion Muslims of all ages in the world in 2009, accounting for 23 per cent of the total global population of 6.8 billion. Over 300 million Muslims or one-fifth of the world's Muslim population reside in nations where Islam is not the majority religion. Similarly, more Muslims live in China than in Syria, and more Muslims live in Russia than in Jordan and Libya combined (Pew Research Centre, 2009). These Muslim minority communities are frequently quite large. India, for example, has the world's third-largest Muslim population. According to the 2011 Census in India, there are 172.2 million Muslims in the country, accounting for 14.2 per cent of the overall population (Registrar General of India, 2011).

Muslims are all adherents of Islam, but neither in India nor any other place on earth are they considered as a homogeneous group. The number of Muslims who have migrated to India from Muslim-dominated nations like Arabia and other nations is very low. The majority of Muslims in India are descended from lower-caste Hindus who were once labelled as untouchables. Furthermore, many troops and administrative officials started their families with Hindus across the country during the rule of the Mughals[7] (1526–1857). As a result, the majority of Muslims in India are converted to Islam and still observe the longstanding traditions and rituals of the region that their ancestors had been performing for centuries. We can notice a strong Mughal influence in multiple Indian cultural arenas—architecture, food, music, musical instruments, sartorial practices—once Islamic dominion began to take hold in India towards the end of the twelfth century CE. The Mughals did not only contribute to Indian culture but also began to follow the existing culture of the land as well.

---

[7] Between the sixteenth and nineteenth centuries, the Mughal Empire, an Islamic early modern empire, ruled over a large portion of South Asia. The empire lasted for around 200 years, extending from the western borders of the Indus River basin, northwest Afghanistan, and Kashmir in the north, to the highlands of modern-day Assam and Bangladesh in the east, and the Deccan Plateau in South India (Stein, 2010); modern countries of India, Bangladesh, Pakistan, and Afghanistan. Stein, B. (2010) *A History of India (Vol. 9)*. John Wiley and Sons.

Religious principles and rituals alone cannot define a community's identity. Rather, it is dependent on a number of elements, the most important of which is cultural variables. Despite the fact that Muslims are diverse, traditional media portrays them as a monolithic group. As a result, they are assigned an essentialized identity as 'the Muslim community' and are even lumped together as 'Indian Muslims'. Nowhere is a more essentialized and homogenized portrayal of Muslims more prevalent and pervasive than in popular cinema. Muslims are always associated with a few religio-cultural components, such as the Urdu language, biryani, and meat as a food habit, sartorial practices like wearing the skull cap, *burqa*, and *Patani* dress. As a result, they appear to be homogenized. But the truth is that Muslims around the nation observe different diets, language, and sartorial choices.

Given that these portrayals have all-encompassing ramifications on Muslims and their everyday life, films are a crucial source of data for constructing a frame of reference. The homogenized portrayal of Muslims in films is not new, nor is it exclusive to Bollywood cinema. *The Terrible Turkish Executioner*, a 1904 French film, 'provides one of the earliest narrative depictions of the Middle East on film ... It contains a series of narrative elements that can be found in most films made subsequently in Hollywood about the Middle East and its Muslim inhabitants, be they Turks, Arabs, or Iranians' (Eisele, 2002: 68). Jack Shaheen claims that Hollywood has stereotypically portrayed Arab Muslims with frequent usage of the 'black beard, headdress, dark sunglasses' (2003: 172). Moreover, there are certain elements in the backdrop, such as 'a limousine, harem maidens, oil wells, camels' (Shaheen, 2003) which add to that homogenous portrayal of Arab Muslims. The inaccurate notion of Arabs as 'brute murderers, sleazy rapists, religious fanatics, oil-rich dimwits, and abusers of women' (Shaheen, 2003: 172) owes its origin to depictions in popular films. As Hollywood films are now watched in every country on the planet, 'Arab images [depicted in them] influence not just worldwide viewers, but also international filmmakers' (Shaheen, 2003: 174).

Similarly, Muslims have traditionally been portrayed in Bombay Hindi films or contemporary Bollywood as 'Others', right from the origin of the film industry. 'The representation of the Muslim as "Other" has in fact been a long-term trend within the discourse of popular Hindi Cinema' (Kavoori and Punathambekar, 2008: 135). The purpose of this book is to examine how Muslims are portrayed in Hindi films, the reason behind representing them in a particular way and how they are perceived by the audiences who watch them. In the early era of the Indian film industry, during the post-Independence period, Muslim characters were mostly based on Mughal court life; therefore, few typical symbols like language, sartorial practices, and body language were assigned to the Muslim protagonists. The audiences of those films formed an imagined image of Muslims, and that image was in absolute contrast to the real image of Indian Muslims at that time. This type of depiction is termed as the formation of the 'exotic Other' (Kavoori and Panathambekar, 2008). Other than that, films made soon after Independence portrayed Muslim protagonists as 'sane, sensible, good, and devout ... specially those written by progressive writers' (Benegal, 2007: 230). During this Nehruvian period, Bombay Hindi cinema was considered to be the nationalized film institution; it tried to uphold the rich culture and tradition of India through film texts. Edward Johnson defines the films of the period as exhibiting 'the splendour of pre-Raj India, the costumes, nobility, and drama were presented with an emotional thrust that did much to re-establish Indian national esteem' (cited in Durah, 2006: 176).

In the 1970s, 'a distinct change in the characterization of Muslims started emerging in the Bollywood films. The characters though for some time continued to remain aristocratic [and] were pushed towards hedonist pursuits' (Mujtaba, 2012). Fareed Kazmi writes:

> the characterization of Muslims is delineated in terms of abstractions. They emerge as stereotypes represented by well-defined signs of speech, appearance, dress, social and religious practice ... ignored are the real-life men and women with distinct class positions, social backgrounds and individual disposition. (Kazmi, cited in Kaori and Panathambekar, 2008: 140)

The exotic image of Muslims matched stereotypes in culture, region, and socioeconomic class, yet there were Muslims from non-Urdu speaking backgrounds, aristocratic mansion dwellers, but regular farmers, labourers, and artisans, but they weren't represented very often. Through all these above-mentioned symbols and attributes, a 'stereotypical and mythical image' (Islam, 2007: 405) of Muslims re-emphasized the identity of the 'Muslim Other'. Another intriguing trend in the late 1970s and early 1980s was the portrayal of Mumbai's underworld figures; since then, Muslim characters in Bollywood films have also become negative. In this regard, Shyam Benegal points out, 'while the films of the Nehruvian era reflected the "tolerant" secularism of the state (with all its attendant problems and anxieties), the 1970s and 1980s saw the emergence of an alternative politics of minority representation with the rise of the "new cinema"' (2007: 225).

From the early 1990s, there was a slew of events and developments—the rise of aggressive Hindu right-wing politics, the destruction of the Babri Masjid on 6 December 1992, India and Pakistan's nuclear tests in 1998, terrorist strikes on the Pentagon and a section of the World Trade Towers in New York and Washington—that had huge impact on Bollywood film texts. Since that time, Bollywood has been depicting Muslims and Islam based on unchallenged assumptions and prejudices. Muslims started getting represented as rioters. 'After the nuclear test by India and Pakistan, patriotism bordering on anti-Pakistani jingoism [became] a major theme of popular Hindi cinema' (Benegal, 2007: 237). A symbiotic connection emerged between Kashmir, Pakistan, and Muslims. Moreover, films have been made about serial bomb explosions in India and overseas and that has reduced Muslim identity to being merely *jihadi* terrorists. Considering this, Fiske and Hartley write, 'The media experts are selecting and sending out the message they would like to receive. Of course, the picture does not appear to be so fluid as we watch: there are preferred meanings inherent in every message' (Fiske and Hartley, cited in Kazmi, 1999: 13).

Theoretical Perspectives

As I will deconstruct the representation of Muslims in Bollywood text in this book, first I will theorize the notion of representation through the lens of cultural studies. The process of combining symbols to produce meaning is termed as 'representation'. The most pioneering scholars such as Frankfurt School media researchers, British Cultural theorists, and French structuralists and post-structuralists argued that culture is a social construct that is produced through representation. Representation is the process of communicating meaning through any medium, particularly the mass media, using elements of 'reality' including people, places, things, events, cultural identities, and other non-material notions. These representations could be spoken, written, still, or moving images. Due to the dominance of visual signs and our own representation in every part of life in the twentieth and twenty-first century, moving images have emerged as the primary means of mass communication. According to Lisa Taylor and Andrew Wills (1999), no representation is free from an ideological position because the process requires signs to be selected and combined together to create meaning about an object. I argue that film and media houses select and merge certain types of signs for a kind of ideological construct to justify a particular version of social reality. It becomes more evident from the writings of Taylor and Wills who further mention that 'no cultural representation can offer access to "truth" about what is being represented, but what such representations do provide is an indication about how power relations are organized in a society, at certain historical moments' (1999: 40). It gets more noticeable from the changing pattern of Muslim representation in Bombay Hindi cinema or Bollywood that those representations are always aligned to the sociopolitical power relation and power structure of Indian society. Therefore, in this book, I explore how Bollywood represented Muslim identities; rather how during the production and consumption processes, it is being constructed. In this regard, I will outline several concepts that have affected theoretical viewpoints on identity representation and I will divide the theoretical understanding of representation and identification into three categories: Muslim identity representation, political economy of Bollywood behind the construction of such identities, and audience consumption of those texts.

Construction of 'Muslim' Identity in Postcolonial Bollywood

One of the most important and well-known theories on the formation of Muslim identity is the Orientalist discourse through different forms of media platforms. The key theorists of the discourse include Daniel

Norman (1960), Edward Said (1981, 1996), and Ziauddin Sardar (1992), although Said is the pioneer in this field. Orientalism, according to Said, is a 'style of thought based upon an ontological and epistemological distinction made between "the Orient" and (most of the time) "the Occident"' (1978: 02), where Western civilization is superior than Eastern civilization (specifically Muslims in the Middle East). Orientalism began to grow as a significant intellectual theoretical discourse around at the end of the eighteenth century, and more notably at the turn of the nineteenth century, expressing contradictory images of the 'East'. According to Said, the West sought to define the Orient as 'the Others' in order to legitimize exploitation of the economy, imperial desires, and colonial rule, and there was also a political motivation to transmit Oriental knowledge. Said further says that, in the postmodern electronic world, 'there has been a reinforcement of the stereotypes by which the Orient is viewed' (Said, 1978: 26). A similar scenario to Said's theory of portraying Muslims as Others in the Western media exists in the Indian media, particularly Indian Hindi films. In Hindi cinema, Muslims are shown as Others in essentially all the genres. Certain cultural emblems are used to denote the 'Muslim identity' of 'Others', some of which are superfluous and redundant. To paint a stereotypical and misleading picture of Islam, these symbols—which include attire, dietary practices, and social etiquette—linked to Muslims, similar to what the Western media did in the case of the Middle East. For example, Shahid Amin, a subaltern historian, showed after examining some advertisements that Muslims were most often identified using Turkish caps, and not just any cap. Muslims are identified as foreigners by certain cultural markers, and these identifiers are occasionally exploited and are used to impose an identity on Muslims that goes beyond the nation-state they might belong to. Amin mentions:

This stereotypical image on the billboard is not a real-life image: it is officially reproduced on such posters in the supposed interests of nation-building. The result is a paradox: although Indians are not used to a Turkish cap in their midst, it is a prominent sign of the Indian Muslim in national integration posters. In other words, the national advertisement asks us to recognize an image which we do not encounter within the geographical confines of our nation-state. (2005: 6–7)

Though Amin analysed advertisements to define the characteristics of the 'Muslim identity' as constructed by non-Muslims, I argue that in Hindi cinema Muslims are also burdened with some cultural markers, such as the 'beard', 'skull cap', '*burqa*', '*hijab*', '*Pathani* outfit', and Aligarh-cut salwar kameez to construct their identity as 'Others'. Said (1978) had stated previously a pattern of 'us' Europeans representing 'them' non-Europeans that led to the hegemony of European culture. He mentions that there is

> a collective notion identifying 'us' Europeans as against all 'those' non-Europeans, and indeed it can be argued that the major component in European culture is precisely what made that culture hegemonic both in and outside Europe: the idea of European identity as a superior one in comparison with all the non-European peoples and cultures. (Said, 1978: 7)

Knowledge, representation, and the formation of knowledge as well as how knowledge is obtained are all intertwined with issues of power, class, and materiality, according to Said. He examines how Islam and Muslims are portrayed in Western media and recounts how the United States' media continues to skew Middle Eastern imagery (Said, 1996). A comparable episode took place in Central Europe, where Slobodan Milosevic used the same approach, using 'the mass media to drive the majority population into a frenzy by depicting it as being under siege by the minority population' (Rajgopal, 2011: 238). Illustrating the case of Hollywood cinema, Jack Shaheen (2001) pointed out that issues such as a lack of representation of ordinary Muslims or their contrary derogatory portrayals might serve to perpetuate prejudices that already exist.

As mentioned by Edward Said, the notion of power is intricately connected to knowledge and, therefore, the most powerful group or the dominant class of a society determines the mechanics of depicting specific groups in a particular manner. Madhava Prasad (1998) and Fareed Kazmi (1999) used the Althusser Ian concept of ideological 'interpellation' and the Gramscian concept of 'hegemony' to propose interpretations of Bollywood films. Prasad adopts the ideology of Marxist theory, which explains the 'universalization of the particular interests of a class's

(1998: 8). He incorporates Gramsci's notion of hegemony and Althusser's conception of 'ideology' into Marxian theory and argues:

> In a social formation characterized by an uneven combination of modes of production only formally subordinated to capital, where political power is shared by a coalition of bourgeoisie, rural rich and the bureaucratic elite, the explanatory scheme in question functions as a disavowal of modernity, an assurance of the permanence of the state of formal subsumption. Such an assurance can only be ideological in nature, operating on an unconscious plane as a guarantee of national identity. It runs counter to the drive, on another level, towards modernization and the establishment of bourgeois hegemony. (1998: 7)

In his subsequent arguments, he claims that the numerous discourses and institutions of the earlier era were rendered obsolete by the discourse of bourgeois hegemony. Hindu nationalism has appropriated the precarious national project in an effort to 're-establish political unity on a communal foundation' (Prasad, 1998: 9) demonstrating the widening of the political spectrum. *Ideology of the Hindi Film*, a study by Prasad, situates Hindi films in India to be the 'site of ideological production' (1998: 9).

According to Fareed Kazmi (1999), Indian Hindi cinema is a significant 'cultural and ideological force'. The media is not only a mirror of social reality, but it also helps to create it. He uses the Gramscian concept of 'hegemony' to describe how Hindi films gain cultural significance and garner support for a particular interpretation of social reality over others. He claims:

> Conventional cinema works by reflecting and expressing the 'popular element', its feelings, precepts, and 'common sense'. It operates by transforming elements at large in the culture—not through inventing or imposing arbitrary materials on a stunned and passive audience. This model helps us to understand that while conventional cinema certainly plays a role in securing legitimization of ruling class ideas, it does not do this by luring the masses in to these ideas—with or without the unwitting complicity of their own unconscious processes. Conventional cinema works by appropriating meaningful elements already extant in the culture at large—as its 'raw materials'—and transforming them

in such a way that they express ruling class hegemonic principles. (1999: 72)

In Bollywood films, Muslims have been shown as the 'Other' and stereo-typed, but in the last few decades, Muslims have become the enemy of the nation and are shown as those terrorizing the nation-state. According to several scholars, from the early 1990s, Hindutva nationalism had a significant impact on the unfavourable image of Muslims. Maidul Islam (2007, 2018), Ira Bhaskar and Richard Allen (2009), Fareed Kazmi and Sanjeev Kumar (2011), S.S. Rajgopal (2011), Amit Rai (2003), Sanjeev Kumar (2013), Ronie Patrick (2013), N. Hussein and S. Hussein (2015), and Roshni Sengupta (2020) have studied multiple facets of the recent Bollywood texts and reveal that Muslims are characterized stereotypic-ally at multiple levels through the depiction of language use, behaviour, sartorial choices, food habits, masculine patriarchy, women without agency, *tawaifs*, orthodox households, the roles of gangsters, dons, ter-rorists, Pakistanis, or are shown as benevolent and loyal to the nation. In the last two decades, the negative images of Muslims have become more dominant than ever before. All these scholars argue that Hindutva or Hindu nationalist groups exploited the media, particularly films, to create terror in the minds of the majority to make them perceive that they are being threatened by minority communities. The roles of terrorists (je-hadis), extremists, underworld dons, and anti-social elements are com-monly used to depict Muslims. Madhu Kishwar, an Indian writer who studied the psyche of Indians, mentions:

> Hindus harbour deep-seated fears of Muslims because they believe them to be innately cruel and violent. Their regular meat eating versus the vegetarianism of many Hindus and the fact that many of the butcher community people are Muslims, feeds into the stereotype of Muslims as *Kasai's* (killers). (Cited in Rajgopal, 2011: 238)

Thus, the Hindutva movement used deep-seated anti-Muslim senti-ment to bring the majority of the populace together. This technique of polarizing people was based on the tumultuous history of the subcon-tinent. Citizens had a strong fear of Muslim invaders during the Middle Ages, such as Mahmud, the Sultan of Gazin, who annually plundered northern India. Hindu nationalists concocted similar scenarios to make it appear as though the crisis had occurred recently (Rajgopal, 2011). Rajgopal further points out that cinema mirrored selective 'behaviours and values associated [with] certain social groups as the norm, while marginalizing those of others' (Rajgopal, 2011: 241). In his empirical investigation, Prakash Louis (2000) demonstrates how Rashtriya Swayamsevak Sangh (RSS) attempted to bring a communal colour to history books. Furthermore, the BJP (Bharatiya Janata Party)-led administration twisted history in order to instil communal consciousness in the young minds.

Cinema became an essential instrument for propagating the notion of nationalism in the postcolonial nation-state. Be it sexual, religious, or ethnic identity, the gap in Indian society has never been more visible than it has been in the past few years. However, despite this, Indian Hindi films have always painted a monolithic picture of the country and projected a 'certain essence of "Indianess"' (Rajagopal, 2011: 240). The Indian diaspora is the most receptive of this kind of portrayal. If Hindu culture and tradition is to be portrayed as a national culture, I argue that Others must be portrayed as either less or differently. Muslims are represented as attempting to harm the nation, while victims are the representatives of the majoritarian group. As a result, Hindus are projected as the society's norm, whereas Muslims are seen as the 'disrupter of the norm, hence perceived them as "Other"' (Rajagopal, 2011: 241).

The concept of a self-conscious and aggressive nationalism in Bollywood films is allied to Imagined Communities, a foundational work by Benedict Anderson (1983). The idea of nationalism was first presented in cinema during the silent era, but cultural appropriation didn't begin until the advent of talkies, according to Anderson. Though the medium could not mobilize the nation, it provided citizens a new orientation. Gradually, film evolved into the main propaganda weapon in the hands of nation-builders. Similarly, Bombay Hindi cinema or Bollywood texts always correlated with state ideology. Initially, Bollywood upheld Nehruvian socialism, but in the later years it started aligning to the right-wing politics of the country. Most importantly, we have observed a number of instances in recent times when political dialogues are echoed in the most celebrated Bollywood texts or Bollywood dialogues are being used in the political context. For example, the most celebrated strategy of the Modi-led government is the 'surgical strike'—whether the term is used in the context of demonetization or of attacks launched in Pakistan-administrated Kashmir across the Line of Control to hit terrorist sites in 2016. This same concept is further glorified by Bollywood through multiple texts such as *Tanhaji* or *Uri: The Surgical Strike*. On the other hand, a dialogue—How is the *Josh* (energy)?—from the film *Uri: The Surgical Strike* was used by the ministers multiple times in different occasions to boost morale among people. Therefore, it can be claimed that Bollywood is playing a key role in propagating state ideology and is acting as a 'state apparatus'. Bollywood was utilized recently to propagate the notion of nationalism and construct cultural identity; this 'imagined nationhood' is theorized by Benedict Anderson in his book *Imagined Communities: Reflections on the Origin and Spread of Nationalism* (1983). In this context, Shobha Rajgopal argues, 'Indian mainstream cinema too perfected propaganda to an art form. A plethora of Indian films demonstrate this process through their representation of the Indian family threatened by menacing Islamic terrorists' (2011). There are several films such as *Sooryavanshi*, *Uri*, *Neerja*, *Sarbjit*, *Roja*, *Baby*, *A Wednesday*, *Mission Istanbul*, *Black Friday*, *Fanaa*, *The Attacks on 26/11*, *Agent Vinod*, *Mumbai Meri Jaan*, *Sarfarosh*, *Kurbaan*, *Mission Kashmir*, *Shikandar*, and *New York*, which substantiate Rajgopal's argument.

One other important argument to note here is that the probable reason behind aligning cultural state with state ideology is due to common consensus of the people during that particular time period. Therefore, we notice a chronological change in ideology depicted in film texts depending on the country's politics. The political economy of Indian film production is based on private ownership, corporatization, and consumption and is not financed and manufactured by the public body. Thus, individual producers, banners, and studios are fully accountable for Hindi film production. The involvement of big national and international corporate conglomerates is a relatively new phenomenon. The primary objective of the industry is to make a profit. According to Prakash Jha, a national award-winning independent director and producer:

Today when I'm making a film, I have to think of its market compatibility so that it can be released in theatres. Nobody has the money to complete a film today unless he gets money from the market. And if

I am competing in the market then I have to work as the market works. (Cited in Kazmi, 1999: 51)

Being a profit-making industry, financing and producing a film in the Bombay film industry has undergone multiple changes. Because Bombay was utilized as an access point to the Indian mainland during the British colonial time, the city became an industrial powerhouse. 'Bombay allowed film technology to take root and flourish as capital from other industrial and commercial activity flowed into filmmaking' (Ganti, 2004: 7). In the 1920s and 1930s, studio culture was quite popular. Originally, studios were responsible for the entire expenses of filmmaking, and they utilized their own technicians and artists. New Theatre in Calcutta, Imperial Film Company in Bombay, Prabhat Film Company in Pune, and Bombay Talkies were the most well-known film studios at the time. Distribution and exhibition were handled by different groups of distributors.

The Second World War had a negative impact on studio culture in the Bombay film industry, resulting in the emergence of a new generation of independent producers. According to the Film Enquiry Committee's report, in 1939 there were 94 producers who produced 167 pictures, and in 1948 there were 211 producers who produced 264 movies (Prasad, 1998). 'Wartime shortages in basic goods and commodities led to thriving black market and, by 1944, war profiteers increasingly laundered their illegal earnings by investing in film production' (Ganti, 2004: 20). Consequently, filmmaking expenditures began to rise, and studios found themselves unable to compete with lone producers. Because independent producers gave far more financial assistance than studios, the new black market economy enticed stars away from the studio culture. Both qualified and unqualified individuals with money made films. The prominent stars were 'lured away with the offers of huge sums' (Prasad, 1998: 39), and stars acquired influence over the production process. Star power played a role in their films' success.

In *Producing Bollywood* (2012), Tejaswini Ganti offers a comprehensive description of the importance of the 'basic political economy of Hindi cinema by illustrating the role and significance of distributors and exhibitors' (Ganti, 2012: 176). Before the existence of corporate producers and media conglomerates around 2003, producers were completely reliant on distributors to market their products (Ganti, 2012). There are several types of distribution systems in use in the business, the most popular of which is the 'minimum guarantee system', often known as 'MG'. Distributors pay 30 to 40 per cent of the film's cost upfront, with the remainder due when the prints are delivered. They also cover the costs of copyrights, publicity, and theatre leases. In exchange, they extract as much profit as possible after the film's release (Ganti, 2012). According to Madhav Prasad, MG is a 'system ... akin to the "putting out system" of early capitalism where production is subservient to distributor's capital which is advanced to producers' (1998: 40). Because of the primary motive of profit-making that has existed from the initial period of the Indian film industry, it has always conformed to state ideology, mainly to be accepted by the majority of the audiences, who determine if a film is a 'hit' (financially successful) or a 'flop' (financially unsuccessful). Judith Mayne mentions, 'Spectatorship is not just the relationship that occurs between the viewer and the screen, but also and especially how that relationship lives on once the spectator leaves the theatre' (1993: 2–3). To make the film appreciated by the majority of people, on the one hand these films utilize state ideology; on the other hand, they incorporate certain identifiable elements which people can easily associate with. Consequently, Bollywood film texts have been supportive of the philosophies of ruling parties and promoted a stereotypical image of society. These homogenized representations of different elements of society create a space for building 'imagined communities', as the print media did in nineteenth-century Europe (Anderson, 1983). In this book, I shall examine how postcolonial Bollywood texts historically represented Muslims and in the process constructed a homogenized image of the religious identity.

This book seeks to capture the changing image of Muslims in popular Bollywood films over the last seven decades. In Hindi films, Muslims have traditionally been portrayed through the lens of religion. Narratives associated with that specific religious identity were adapted based on the sociopolitical and economic settings of the country at the time of any film's making. In their seminal work on the cinematic portrayal of Muslims by Amit Rai (2003); Maidul Islam (2007); Ira Bhaskar and Richard Allen (2009); Roshni Sengupta (2013, 2020); Fareed Kazmi and Sanjeev Kumar (2011); S.S. Rajgopal (2011); Ronie Patrick (2013); Sanjeev Kumar (2013); and Meeraj Mubarki (2014) have addressed the issues of history, narrative style, Muslim identity, and Muslim characterization in Bollywood cinema. This book joins an increasing corpus of scholarship on Muslim representation in postcolonial Bollywood cinema that draws upon prior concerns and difficulties about narrative style and politics of representing Muslims but expands the focus to include issues of Muslim film genres, the chronological shift in the portrayal of Muslims depending on the nation's politics, particularly backed by empirical data. In this book, I have divided representation of Muslims into different genres and critically looked at how they evolved gradually based on the country's contemporary politics. The arguments are backed by theoretical discourse as well as empirical data. Because there have been many changes in the Indian sociopolitical landscape, analysis and arguments would be incomplete if we do not take into account the changing perceptions of audiences.

Filmmakers, Film Critics, Audiences, and Images of Muslims

This book is also part of the growing qualitative research about Bollywood film texts representing Muslims, filmmaking practices, and audience perception. It seeks to elaborate Bollywood by identifying the complex sociopolitical contexts of film texts, production processes, and diverse perceptions of audiences depending on their socioeconomic and cultural backgrounds. I try to acquire insights into the subjective views of various stakeholders (filmmakers, film critics, and audiences) and their use of cinematic space to manufacture the sense of reality, as we are primarily dealing with the illusive realm of perceptions.

Through different points of view, a qualitative method is utilized to deal with the complexities of Bollywood films, which include variables such as portrayal of Muslims, modification in the representation of Muslims over the previous seven decades, and the impact of critical sociopolitical shifts in India on the Bollywood cinematic space. Via in-depth interviews, the research presented here attempts to capture these notions through the understandings of the audience, film critics, and filmmakers on the specified issues connected to either film texts concerning Muslims or the politics of making those texts. The inductive trait of qualitative research helped me to understand the topic from an open-ended, pointed per-spective rather than through a narrow lens of hypothesis. Consequently, I have developed notions, perceptions, and understanding from the pat-terns that were derived through the data. Furthermore, because of the qualitative research approach, I have been able to apply a flexible study design, which is essential for a media researcher because audiences are not constant for all of the movies that portray Muslims.

The section on methodology has been grouped into five seg-ments: finding the study's specific participants, research site, data col-lecting procedures, data analysis methods, and research ethics. In terms of methodology, as mentioned earlier, I utilized a qualitative approach to examine Muslim representations in Hindi films by interpreting them as cultural texts. Apart from that, via in-depth interviews, I was able to record the perspectives of select audiences (25), film critics (8), and filmmakers (13). Although many other regional films address the chosen research topic, the study is only focused on Bollywood cinema because Muslims have enormous screen presence there and Bollywood movies have a pan-Indian appeal.

Research Site

I chose Mumbai as my primary research site to examine the interaction between the 'maker and consumer' of Bollywood film because the current study is about Bollywood and its business which is mostly Mumbai cen-tric. Major offices of film production companies can be found in Mumbai, which is where the majority of Indian Bollywood films are developed. In order to interview the filmmakers, Mumbai was chosen as the primary location of my research. The most widely used language in Mumbai is Hindi. As a result, it was easier to identify audience members with whom I could interact and with whom language was not a barrier. Additionally, Mumbai is home to a number of academic and social scientific institutes that enabled me to meet with academics working in comparable fields like communalism and secularism and incorporate their viewpoints into my research. In addition, Mumbai's numerous media organizations made it easier for me to connect with well-known film critics. Filmmakers were evidently easily accessible in Mumbai.

Participants

The participants in this study came from a variety of backgrounds and worked in an array of sectors. In-depth interviews were conducted individually with each participant. Three groups are distinguished among them: (1) The audience, which consists of viewers of particular films which are important for this study. They have all been personally interviewed in order to better understand how viewers perceive Muslim images and the evolution of representation in Bollywood movies. The participants' articulations regarding representational change and Muslim images have been attempted to be recorded; (2) Film critics made up the second group. I aimed to capture the filmmaking and cinema text critical viewpoint. The complexities of filmmaking and audience viewpoints were explained by cinema critics; (3) The third category consisted of filmmakers who are either directly involved in producing Muslim films or who offer a general overview of how the Hindi film business operates.

Procedure of Data Collection

This book is a continuation of my doctoral work. The initial data collection procedure began in July 2012. India has witnessed a lot of changes in the sociopolitical space since then. Moreover, filmmaking and film viewing have also changed due to technological advancements in these years; therefore, I have collected another round of data with a new set of audiences and some more filmmakers to understand the new changes in filmmaking practices and patterns of film consumption. The whole procedure was carried out in two stages: first, the participants were either contacted through emails or over the phone, where they were given an overview of the study's aim as well as some background information about myself. The second stage entailed visiting these people and conducting interviews with them. For the recent interviews in 2020 and 2021, I had to conduct them using video-calling facilities due to the Covid-19 pandemic restrictions and because I was based in Canada for one year in 2021. A snowballing method was used to contact the participants, who were chosen purposively. I began by interviewing the audience, then moved on to interviewing the critics, and at last spoke with the filmmakers. While the majority of the interviews were conducted in open spaces like offices and cafes, some were conducted in the participants' residences. Since this was a qualitative study, there was no set amount of time allotted for each interviewee to speak. Instead, they were allowed to talk for as long or as little as they wanted. Throughout the data collection process, an interview guide (see Appendix 1) was maintained on hand, and field notes were collected.

The participants. As mentioned, the first category for this inquiry is audiences who are purposefully chosen. Audiences are the key factor to determining whether a film is considered mainstream, parallel, or middle cinema. Understanding their perception was one of the important factors to know how they perceive Muslim representation. Individual interviews were conducted with participants who were viewers of the selected films either having Muslim protagonists or Muslim-related themes.

On the basis of an interview guide, I sought to investigate the respondents' viewpoints, convictions, and experiences of viewing those cinematic spaces. It was mostly a reciprocal conversation, and I leveraged my research background to promote interaction with participants, but I did not compel anyone to reply on any point. Non-verbal activities and background signals, such as the participants' facial expressions and gestures, the circumstances, and so on, were also observed and documented. Questions were posed based on the responses of the respondents. I recorded the interviews with an audio recorder. I attempted to record the viewpoint of audiences with the 'lowest common denominator', often known as the mass audience in media studies.

Participants of various age groups (youth, adults, and the elderly) and genders were interviewed. For the first group, made up of audience members, I have used purposive sampling with the intention of reaching out to diverse identities (gender, religion, caste, region, class, etc.) and backgrounds (socioeconomic) to maximize the chances of being selected. For in-depth understanding of this study, I had a certain identifying axis (such as gender, age, etc.) in mind that we want to frame our questions around accordingly. Information was gathered from twenty participants, ten of whom were academics, two engineers, four activists, and four manual labourers. The informants were purposefully chosen in the first round based on personal connections as the major criterion was to attract audience members who had seen Muslim-themed films. Audiences primarily belong to Mumbai, except two participants who belong to Kashmir. I have conducted interviews with audiences primarily from Mumbai because I wanted to capture people's perceptions from diverse backgrounds. Mumbai as a cosmopolitan city fulfilled this criterion very well. Therefore, it was easier for me to collect data from diverse identities of audience from a single place. Moreover, I have followed theoretical sampling to select my audience; therefore, I collected data until the time I received repetitively same answers. I have deliberately chosen participants from Kashmir because there is an important section in this book which discusses films based on Kashmir or Kashmiris. So I wanted to include the subjective position of Kashmiris on Bollywood texts based on Kashmir as much as I wanted views of audiences who belong to other parts of India. Most interestingly, I got very different perspectives from the participants belonging to Kashmir and to Mumbai on the same kind of films.

The film critics. I was having a talk on my doctoral project with a colleague who is an academician. He had worked as a journalist for some time in a media house. He was ready to help me with the contact information of film critics who are associated with other media houses. Within a few days he gave me the contact details of approximately eight of the most renowned film journalists in the country who work for various well-recognized media houses. I contacted all of them, but only three of them responded positively. The remaining five cited reasons such as a lack of time, a reluctance to speak with an academic, distance, and so on. I was able to make a few additional relationships with distinguished film reviewers with the help of the three critics who agreed to talk to me. I gathered replies from eight film critics in total. Seven of them were from Mumbai and worked for media organizations, while one participant was employed in a local Bengali daily in Kolkata. The Appendix has a brief biography of each of these cinema critics.

The filmmakers. This is the category that I found the most challenging to tackle. During their interview with me, one of the film critics offered me the contact information of a number of filmmakers. I was able to make a few additional contacts as a result of those connections. I have interviewed those filmmakers who are either actively involved in the production of cinema based on Muslims or have a comprehensive understanding of the overall Bollywood industry. In the Appendix, a brief profile of each filmmaker has been provided. Through the snowball sampling, I was able to reach out to Javed Akhtar (lyricist, Indian political activist, and screenwriter), Shoojit Sircar (director and producer), Shyam Benegal (director and screen writer), Kabir Khan (director, screenwriter, and cinematographer), Shibani Bhatija (screenwriter), Mahesh Bhatt (film writer, producer, and director), Kamlesh Pandey (film writer), Ashutosh Gowarikar (director, actor, writer, and producer), Vinay Shukla (film writer, producer, and director), Amit Khanna (lyricist and producer), Haider Ali (actor and screenwriter), Rensil D'Silva (director, screenplay writer, ad filmmaker), and Satish Munda (film writer and director). After multiple attempts to contact them to get appointments for the interviews, I got the appointment over the phone and, in some instances, through e-mails. I was able to get the contact details for a few additional directors, although some of them didn't reply. There were some filmmakers who replied but withdrew from the interviews.

Observations on Data Collection

During the data-collecting phase, there were three significant challenges. The first challenge was gaining access to the audiences who had watched films in the genres that focus on Muslims. The major part of my analysis was intended to be drawn from the audience's perception of watching those films which I deal with in my study, but once I started my data collection I learned that locating audiences who had watched those specific films was challenging. Apart from that, only a few people are aware of modern Muslim films, and they could not speak much about Muslim films released much earlier. Some of the viewers had seen the movie a long time back, and could simply recall the plot or the romantic angle, but not the film's details. As a result, there are certain interviews in the data which I was unable to utilize since they did not pertain to information about the film's Muslim image, political, or historical context. Finally, I asked select members of the audience to watch specific films so that I might interview them afterwards. However, as a result of this, the audience not only watched the films, but also read critiques into them, which I could tell from their well-prepared responses. Another issue I encountered during my interviews with people from disadvantaged socioeconomic backgrounds was that they lacked the time to see a film through to the end. I tried to interview house helps, daily manual workers, and security personnel of a residential society. They didn't have enough money to go to the theatres and watch each of the films I wanted to review. Furthermore, they couldn't afford to watch an entire film on a television set at home since they had no time to do so. Workers in India's unregulated labour market are required to work every day of the week, including holidays. As a result, I was unable to suggest that they join me in viewing films.

The second concern was interviewing and connecting to filmmakers who were out of reach for an individual without any industry connection. Rajiv Masand, a film critic, provided me with a couple of their connections. Despite the fact that I could contact them using customized mobile text messaging and email to discuss my study, the first response rate was poor and delayed. Few of the filmmakers responded right away, but because they did not have defined working hours, therefore I had to wait a long time to meet with them. Because the Hindi film business is unlike any other corporate entity, it does not have consistent working hours. Furthermore, I had to take re-appointments at least more than three times with some filmmakers owing to their frequently shifting work schedules. The other significant issue I faced with filmmakers was that they were always on the go—for shooting, site hunting, and vacations. There are times when I would initiate a discussion and they would agree to engage in the research, but they would have to go abroad after some time, resulting in a communication gap. I had to begin the dialogue over and reintroduce myself and the topic after each pause. Due to their hectic and unpredictable work schedules, the interviews did not take place in a few cases even after numerous attempts on my part and a favourable response from the filmmaker.

The final major obstacle was conducting interviews as an insider. I had to introduce myself to the participants before approaching them. After I revealed my own identity of being Muslim, I saw that a few informants, especially the audience, were cautious about their choice of words and ideological position. It was sometimes hard to determine the actual viewers' perspective on social reality and screen text.

Data Analysis

The emphasis of this book is on discourses of Muslim representation in Bollywood film texts. I used critical discourse analysis as the methodological technique for the deconstruction of the texts representing Muslims and I treat 'texts as active in constructing a social reality by offering definitions and categorizations which are linked to wider social and cultural structures, relations and processes. These conceptualizations are not neutral; they are linked to institutional power structures and practices and are therefore value-laden' (Aapola, 1997: 50). In this book, I want to locate the Bollywood texts representing Muslims in the larger sociopolitical context of power structures. Therefore, by using critical discourse analysis, I shall analyse how narratives are framed, how readers are situated related to the texts they consume, and how the use of language encourages the viewer to make particular interpretations of the text, in addition to the text's style and structural pattern (Berger, 2016: 261). Sinikka Aapola further mentions: 'Certain versions of the world are presented as legitimate in hegemonic discourses, while others may be silenced or challenged' (1997: 50). The same notion can be employed to the discourses of Muslim representation. I want to locate how Bollywood has highlighted certain types of perspectives and ignored some remarkable happenings through films where Muslim characters are made to play important roles. Cameron and Panovic's (2014) chapter on critical discourse analysis in the book *Working with Written Discourse*, mentions:

> Critical discourse analysis (CDA) [which] is an approach that highlights the social, ideological and political dimension of discourse. Its practitioners regard discourse in the same way as critical social theorists like Foucault ... as something that does not just describe a preexisting reality, but actively shapes our understand of reality. (66)

Using the same analytical framework, I try to dismantle accepted hegemonic narratives regarding religion, nationalism, culture, and gender. By analysing the films, we may also comprehend major social, cultural, and political developments in the portrayal of Muslims in postcolonial Bollywood cinema.

ATLAS.ti: Analysis of In-Depth interviews. I recorded the interviews on tape or online, and none of the interviewees voiced any opposition to the recording process. Afterwards the interviews were transcribed verbatim and if necessary they were translated later. The transcribed and translated data was organized into themes, and ATLAS.ti (qualitative data analysis software) was used for thematic analysis. The codes were created from the data first, then utilized to create sub-themes, and finally themes were developed from the sub-themes.

From the discourse analysis of film texts and analysis of in-depth interviews, the following four themes emerged:

(1) A chronological change in Muslim portrayal in Bollywood.
(2) The power of history and politics behind this chronological change
(3) Film industry mechanism and political economy of Bollywood.

Ethical Issues

In the last two decades, the question of Muslim identity has become a focal point of debate and discussion as well as a very complex and controversial one because of India's changing sociopolitical landscape. Some participants requested that their names and identities be changed after one of them spoke about his own experience during the 1992 riots. Due to the need for anonymity, all audience identities in this study are pseudonyms. Participants had all the liberty to exit the conversation at any time. Moreover, a few Muslim film critics were cautious in their interactions with me. 'If people comment on sensitive issues, they [Shiv Sena] can come and bang [on] his/her house', one of the film critics said.

Structure of this Book

Except for the Introduction and Conclusion, the book is divided into five chapters. Examining the involvement of Muslims in making Hindi films, the first chapter titled 'Role of Muslims in Filmmaking' is a historical account of Muslims' position in producing Bollywood texts. Depending on the representational schemes of films representing Muslims, the book has been split into a further four chapters, which discuss the following Muslim film genres: 'Muslim Historical Genre and Muslims in Historical Genre: From Diplomat Warriors to Barbarian Outsiders' (Chapter 2); 'The Muslim Social Genre: From Exotic Exclusive to Ordinary Inclusive' (Chapter 3); 'The Muslim Political Genre: From Anti-Pakistani Jingoism to Islamophobia' (Chapter 4); and 'The Muslim Modern Genre: From Allegiant to Secular' (Chapter 5).

The first chapter shows how Muslims have had a significant role in the Indian Hindi film industry since its inception over a century ago. They have significantly influenced the construction of those images and are also prominently depicted in Bollywood. In this chapter, I discuss how the involvement of Muslims was also influenced by the political landscape of the nation.

In Chapter 2 I discuss how Muslim Historical films are a separate genre primarily because of their accounts of magnificent past legends and renowned personalities. On the contrary, the recent genre of Historical films represents Muslim rulers through the prism of aggressive Hindu nationalist discourse. I shall discuss and critically look at the sharp distinction between representing Muslims in the Historical genre and in the Muslim Historical genre in this chapter. Most of the Muslim Historical films in the post-Independence period, so-called Nehruvian era of the 1950s to 1960s), were based on the secular Mughal rulers and focused on the exoticism of those rulers. The films in this genre and the participants of my empirical study hint that Muslims were positively stereotyped at this time. On the other hand, contemporary historical films are inspired by iconic Muslim historical figures, myths, and events to create an 'enemy image' of 'outsiders' who have been marked with specific 'political signs'. Here I argue that by adopting an anti-Islamic stance, contemporary historical films in Bollywood have become a powerful weapon for fostering nationalism. The chapter shows how most recent Bollywood films such as *Panipat* (2019), *Kesari* (2019), and *Tanhaji* (2020) are suitably aligned with the saffronized version of historical narratives. These films adopt a right-wing political stance to construct 'evil images' of Muslim 'foreigners' and give currency to the idea of Hindu nationalism.

In Chapter 3 I discuss the Muslim Social genre, a subsection of the broader genre 'The Social', wherein films showcase everyday household narratives and romantic tales. The Muslim Social genre alludes to films that describe Islamicate culture. This genre flourished mostly in the 1950s and 1960s, and reflected an idealized Muslim world where *nawabs*, indulging in hedonistic pursuits, lived in grandeur with their aristocratic idiosyncrasies intact. The secular ideology of the state was additionally reflected in the films of this genre, which enunciated the conflict between the modern (refinement, learning, progress) and tradition (respect, pride, dedication). Muslim Social films typecasted Muslims using multiple cultural elements such as language, culture, place, and socioeconomic status. Some films that released sometime later belong to the same genre, such as *Garam Hawa* (1973), *Salim Langde Pe Mat Ro* (1989), *Mammo* (1994), *Ishqiya* (2010), and *Dedh Ishqiya* (2010), which fortunately are not about *nawabs* and courtesans, but show a community expressing its concerns on different issues.

In Chapter 4 I discuss the Muslim Political genre. Towards the end of the 1980s and the beginning of the 1990s, India witnessed the forceful rise of the Hindu right-wing movement. As the foremost schema was to formulate a national identity, Bollywood began showing a monolithic depiction of the nation, undermining the diverse (gender-based, religious, and cultural) identities existing in that same nation. As a result, new changes could be noticed in the Bollywood cinematic space. To create a sense of national unity at the time of Hindutva nationalism, Bollywood filmmakers were inspired to formulate 'enemy images' of 'outsiders', who were set apart as 'Others' using explicit 'political signs'. The 1990s likewise saw the ascent of movies that represented terrorists. I refer to them as 'Terroristic films' (Khatun, 2016). Filmmaker Mani Ratnam's *Roja* (1992), based on Kashmiri militants, opened the floodgates for such films. Bollywood's depictions of Kashmir can be categorized into two primary groups: pre-1989 and post-1989. An abrupt change in the representation of Kashmiris can be noticed from 1989, when the problem of insurgency increased. Additionally, at the time of Hindutva nationalism, in contemporary Bollywood we notice that Muslim women generate a sense of national unity by sacrificing their own husbands and brothers. The most widely known films on the geopolitics of Kashmir are *Fiza* (2000), *Faana* (2006), and *Raazi* (2018), all of which espoused the statist position that Kashmir is an essential part of India. The female protagonists of these films, Fiza, Fanaa, and Sehmat Khan, kill their brothers or husbands to demonstrate their loyalty to the nation and to protect the Indian nation from the evil Islamic terrorist or Pakistanis. The core arguments in these films are based on a dichotomy between the 'good' and the 'bad' Muslim (Mamdani, 2004). I also argue that these texts transmit the notion of nationalism by constructing dualistic characters: Muslim men are portrayed as a threat to the nation, whereas Muslim women are portrayed as the true nationalists who guard the homeland from traitors such as Islamic extremists. The 9/11 terrorist attacks have left a permanent mark on world politics and many movies in Hollywood as well as Bollywood were made on the subject of terrorism. There are many films such as *Yun Hota Toh Kya Hota* (2006), *Kurbaan* (2009), *My Name Is Khan* (2010), *Ek Tha Tiger* (2012), *Agent Vinod* (2012), and *Tiger Zinda Hai* (2017), which have depicted geopolitical conflicts and international terrorism. In the last two decades, Bollywood also produced films that celebrate xenophobic right-wing ideology by representing the anti-Pakistan theme. In such films, the juxtaposition of Pakistani–terrorist–Muslim was loosely done. This has been exacerbated by the fact that India and Pakistan have been engaged in many cross-border conflicts, such as in 1948, 1965, and 1971. The most violent of such conflicts was the Kargil War of 1999. Thus, it is no coincidence that in the period between 1997 and 2007 Bollywood released a number of war films including *Border* (1997), *Sarfarosh* 1999), *Maa Tujhe Salam* (2002), *Pukar* (2000), *Gadar* (2001), *LOC* (2003), *Deewaar* (2004), *Ab Tumhare Hawale Watan Saathiyo* (2004), *Lakshya* (2004), *Sarhad Paar* (2006), *1971* (2007), *The Ghazi Attack* (2017), and *Uri: The Surgical Strike* (2019).

I shall look at the Muslim Modern genre in Chapter 5 and analyse Muslim characters in order to deconstruct them. The representation of Muslims in contemporary film narratives attempts to move away from formula-based stereotypical depictions of Muslims, where the only two options to portray them were as 'exotic' or 'wicked' in relation to the nation-state. Interestingly, in this genre Muslim characters are not presented through the prism of religion. However, it has to be noted that although these Muslim characters are not shown as enemies of the state or as anti-nationals, they do have to prove their nationalism and demonstrate their patriotism, loyalty, and innocence in the course of the film. By tracing all these films where Muslims play the role of pivotal characters— *Chak De! India* (2007), *Iqbal* (2005), *Raazi* (2018), *Mulk* (2018), and *War* (2019)—we find that Muslims are destined to show their loyalty to the state. However, in films such as *Dhoom 3* (2013), *Sultan* (2016), *Kedarnath* (2018), *Gully Boy* (2019), and *Gulabo Sitabo* (2020) we find that Muslims are not presented through the prism of religion and people encounter daily social and economic challenges like other citizens. In the majority of these films, even the term 'Muslim' is not mentioned in relation to the characters.

A Personal Note

Before delving into the chapters, I would like to provide an account of encountering the subject line of this book and its connection to my personal life. While Bollywood has become a metaphor for society in the twentieth and twenty-first centuries, it still incorporates imagination and fantasy. Cinema is utilized as a representational tool. Indian popular films provide vital insights into people's beliefs and actions, as well as the social context in which they live. It enables people to comprehend important aspects of their culture, such as religious revivalism, law and order, and the fortunes of Indian minorities, particularly Muslims. I intend to begin my book by addressing my own identity as a Muslim, and then contextualize the depiction of Muslims in Indian Hindi film.

Like hundreds of other Muslim families in India, I grew up in a Hindu-dominated region in rural West Bengal. I was brought up much like my other friends and my parents used to wear traditional Bengali clothes. My father still dresses in *dhoti* and *kurta*,[8] while my mother drapes her *sari* (a long piece of cloth) in the Bengali way. She also wears a *bindi*,[9] a Hindu identification symbol (probably to assimilate with her neighbourhood). Furthermore, our food habits are quite similar to traditional Bengali cuisine, where fish and rice predominate. The only distinction in terms of cultural practices that I remember from my youth was that we celebrated

---

[8] *Dhoti* and *kurta* are Bengali traditional clothes which used to be considered as superior, sophisticated attire for the Bengali *bhadralok* (gentlemen). Guha, A. (2016) West Bengal Elections: Unchanged amidst Change. *Economic and Political Weekly*, pp. 69–71.

[9] The *bindi* is usually a mark worn by men and women who are engaged in Hindu traditional and ritual activities. Though it has a big traditional association, a *bindi* has been commodified as a cosmetic product, but it still has a vast cultural significance in modern India. Antony, M.G. (2010) On the Spot: Seeking Acceptance and Expressing Resistance through the Bindi. *Journal of International and Intercultural Communication*, 3(4), pp. 346–68.

more festivals than our neighbours, such as Eid-al Fitr and Shab-e-Barat. The Bengali cultural practices never interfered with our religious practices even though my mother strictly followed the rituals and practices of Islam.

As I grew older, I began to notice an unusual discrepancy between my family and the portrayal of Muslims on screen, either in television or in films. Furthermore, I started sensing the strange dichotomy in India of accepting Muslim stars in Bollywood but not Muslim citizens of the country by the majority groups in India. Bollywood film stars, particularly the 'Khans', are idolized in India, and having the same family surname, even I was admired by my peers in school. They used to believe that I was fortunate enough to share the same surname 'Khan' with some of the country's most well-known actors. My family, however, was not as fortunate as the film stars. My mother was always apprehensive of being refused when she offered meals to a member of the majority group, who discriminate against eating food prepared by Muslims as it is assumed that we consume beef as part of our daily diet. Because eating beef is such a taboo among Hindus, since I was a child, people from different age groups asked me numerous times whether my family ate the meat. I was so young at the time that I had no idea why people were so interested in learning about beef consumption. As a gesture of admiration (I supposed this judging from their tone), people often told me during my graduation and university years, 'You don't look like a Muslim'. What does a Muslim look like? Despite the fact that my family and even extended family members are devout believers of Islam's five pillars,[10] we have never donned the *burqa*, headscarf, or skull cap (typical markers of Muslim identity that we frequently notice on the screen). Thousands of Muslims, I believe, in India do not express their symbolic identification as Muslims, yet a homogenized picture of Muslim identity is still produced and disseminated by popular media. The identity of Muslims and Islam was constructed by various forms of mass media and not by a group of individuals who wear Islamic symbols (*burqa*, skull cap, etc.).

---

[10] *Shahadah* (witnessing the oneness of God and the prophethood of Muhammad), *Salat* (regular observance of the five prescribed daily prayers), *Zakah* (almsgiving), *Sawn* (fasting), and *Hajj* (pilgrimage to Mecca) (oxfordislamicstudies.com).

During the British colonial period, the identity of the Muslim 'Other' existed because it was beneficial to the colonial strategy of divide and rule, and subsequently to effect India's partition and for the establishment of Pakistan. After the demolition of the Babri Masjid in India three decades ago, the concept of 'Otherness' has grown more complex. Though the tragedy had no direct influence on our lives, I recall my father telling my mother about how the Rashtriya Swayamsevak Sangh (RSS) and other right-wing groups stated that Muslims must go to Pakistan. He, on the other hand, never took that as a threat. My parents were probably confident that they would never have to leave their homeland.

After the attack on the World Trade Towers in 2001, Muslims and Islam as a religion became enemies of the world. The identification of being 'Other' was changed to 'Enemy' as a result of this incident. Apart from that, after the Babri mosque demolition, there were a series of explosions orchestrated by terrorists that took place in various regions of India. In 2008, I moved to Mumbai for an integrated MPhil–PhD programme, and that year, Mumbai was the site of India's most devastating terrorist assault. Despite the fact that the attack was carried out by a gang of Pakistani terrorists, Indian Muslims and their Islamic identity was jeopardized. Terrorists planned and carried out the bombings in the name of jihad, hence their motivations were linked to Islam. As a result, many forms of media began portraying Islam as the cruellest of all religions. This was evident to me in 2011 when I was looking for rented accommodation in Mumbai as my family was relocating. When I informed the owners about my Muslim identity, they gave me a strange reaction. Several brokers refused to help me find me an apartment as soon as they learnt my surname. Finally, due to my husband's Hindu background, I was able to obtain an apartment in a cosmopolitan neighbourhood. Now, in contemporary India, the new policies and amendments brought by the current government are raising concerns. We see a number of controversial policies, laws, verdicts, Acts, and state activities such as the Citizenship (Amendment) Act, 2019 (Constitutional Amendment); the abrogation of Article 370 of the constitution (the article gave special status to the inhabitants of Kashmir, the only Muslim-dominated territory in the country); and the anti-religious conversion law (targeting the alleged conspiracy theory of 'Love Jihad'). The anti-religious conversion law known as the Freedom of Religion Bill, 2020, which makes religious conversion solely for the purpose of marriage illegal, has been approved as an Ordinance by the Madhya Pradesh cabinet, following two other states, Uttar Pradesh and Himachal Pradesh (Vishwanath, 2021). Belonging to an inter-religious marriage, a sense of threat lingers within me. On the other hand, it is fascinating and interesting for me to note that the representation of Muslims in Bollywood has undergone changes based on the sociopolitical situation of the times, as we will see in greater detail in the subsequent chapters.

I hope this book provides an understanding of the imaginary world of complex identities of Muslims in Bollywood cinema and no one will ever say to me, 'You're different and you don't look like a Muslim'.

1

Role of Muslims in Filmmaking

Figure 1.1 Director Imtiaz Ali behind the camera
Source: Nadira Khatun; illustration by Sreeja Burman.

This chapter examines the history of Hindi cinema, paying particular attention to its sociopolitical history and with a critical focus on the representational scheme of Bollywood films when it comes to the depiction of Muslim identity. I shall explore how politics has historically

Postcolonial Bollywood and Muslim Identity. Nadira Khatun, Oxford University Press. © Oxford University Press 2024.
DOI: 10.1093/oso/9780198891017.003.0002

occupied a crucial role in formulating the identity and determining the existence of Muslims in Indian Hindi cinema: a key in this has been the contribution of Muslims in filmmaking. Throughout the 110-year-old history of the Hindi film industry, Muslims have not only been often represented in movies, they have also been an integral part of film production. However, despite this, one can argue that the existence and impact of Muslims in Indian Hindi films has not been very significant; this is notwithstanding the active involvement of Muslims in the making of Bombay film texts, be it by penning Urdu dialogues and lyrics; contributing to filmmaking or executing through acting; or, of course, by composing or directing music. For example, film scholar Tejeswini Ganti writes, 'not only are Muslims comparatively well represented within [Bollywood's] ranks in the form of writers, lyricists, composers, producers, and directors, but that some of the most popular film stars of Hindi cinema, both male and female, have been Muslims' (cited in Kavoori and Punathambekar, 2008: 133). Historically, thus, the Mumbai film industry is perceived as a very secular space where people from different religions work together without conflict. The participation of Muslims in the Bombay film industry can be traced back to four different eras: (a) pre-Partition and pre-Independence; (b) post-Independence; (c) prior to and post the demolition of the Babri Masjid and the initiation of the liberalization era; and (d) the Narendra Modi-led government period.

Contribution of Muslims in the Origin and Growth of the Mumbai Film Industry

After the cinematography show by Lumierè Brothers in Novelty Theatre, Bombay (now Mumbai), on 14 July 1896 (Barnouw, 1963), the city became the centre of Indian filmmaking primarily for two reasons. First, because of its financial base 'Bombay allowed for film technology to take root and flourish as capital from other industrial and commercial activity flowed into filmmaking' (Ganti, 2004: 7). The second aspect was that Bombay provided the creative infrastructure to the filmmakers 'as it was the centre of Parsi Film Theatre, a commercial theatre movement originating in the mid-nineteenth century sponsored by the Parsi traders

who were the dominant business community in the Bombay Presidency'
(Ganti, 2004: 7). From its initial days, Muslims contributed in multiple
ways to filmmaking by popularizing Islamicate culture, costume, language, music, and so on. As directors, lyricists, screenplay writers, chore-
ographers, and composers Muslims reached the pinnacle of success in
the Bombay film industry, which from the beginning occupied a position of great importance in the emergence of filmmaking in India. This
has led many to frequently hail the Bombay film industry as an inclusive
and secular space for the marginalized minority community. Mayank
Shekhar, a film critic, had the following to say in a personal interview:

> I think Bollywood or Indian popular Hindi cinema is lot better than
> Indian society, it's a lot more liberal, it's a lot more encompassing or
> secular than the people [of the country] are ... If you look at the end of
> production, I think there is no possibility whatsoever of any discrimin-
> ation in Bollywood when it comes to religion. (Personal interview, 14
> January 2013)

The Hindi film industry in Bombay started from the 1940s to represent Muslim ethos, primarily North Indian culture. Mukul Kesavan
(1994: 246), following Marshall G.S. Hodgson (1974: 57–9), termed
these films as 'Islamicate'. According to this definition, 'Islamicate' is
not all about the religion, Islam, itself, rather it says, 'the social and cultural complex historically associated with Islam and the Muslims, both
among Muslims themselves and even when found among non-Muslims'
(Hodgson, 1974: 59). The usage of such Muslim ethos predominantly
consisted of the usage of cultural elements such as language, food habits,
sartorial choices, and music that were mainly influenced by the 'Pathan'.
During the pre-Independence era, the north Indian urban space was
dominated by Muslim populations. Muslims in northern India com-
prised the entire social structure: from 'royalty and aristocracy, a landowning (*zamindari*) class as well as the beginnings of an educated
middle class, a petty bourgeoisie and to lower classes' (Dwyer, 2006: 98).
Of these, the north Indian Muslim bourgeoisie and aristocratic classes
of the early nineteenth century inspired filmmakers in Bombay. The
grandeur of Mughal kings and *nawabs* was also the major source of

inspiration for many of the north Indian filmmakers who started to come into the limelight in the 1940s. Amit Khanna, ex-chairman of Reliance Entertainment, says:

> The culture of north India, especially U.P. [Uttar Pradesh, earlier the United Provinces], dominated other cultures of India as Hindi films were mostly made by north Indians. They started to create a shared culture through Hindi cinema. (Personal interview, 24 March 2014)

Two of the areas in which the influence of Islamicate culture on Bollywood films was most prominent were costume design and make-up. Islam as a religion does not prescribe a specific dress code; rather it differs in practitioners from region to region. In the genre of Muslim Historical and Social films, Islamicate culture has been closely linked with the Mughal court through the usage of clothes. In other genres of film, Islamicate culture has been indicated by showing the majority of Muslim men as wearing kurta–pyjama along with skullcaps. This form of kurta–pyjama can be described as somewhat resembling a frock coat and loose or tight trousers.[1] Muslim men and women following Islam do not adhere to any standard attire. But, in popular perception, the dress that is most identified with Muslim women in India—especially in the north and north-west—is the salwar kameez or Punjabi suit. Muslim women have also often been shown wearing scarfed headdresses and *burqas*, outfits often connected to Islam. However, it is important to note here that the *burqa* has been used in Hindi films over the years to not just depict Muslim women: it is employed as a useful tool for hiding identities, by both Hindu and Muslim characters; in other films such as *Chaudhvi ka Chand* (1961), the *burqa* leads to much confusion and misery; even men strategically use the *burqa* to conceal themselves and their wrongful acts—in *Well Done Abba* (2009)

---

[1] Jawaharlal Nehru, India's first prime minister after India's Independence in 1947, is a famous icon who adopted this fashion. To establish the relation between political figures and class consciousness, Ruby Sircar mentions, 'While Gandhi tried to avoid the caste system by dictating the way he dressed, other politicians, such as class-conservative Jawaharlal Nehru or practical politician Vallabhbhai Jhaverbhai Patel, knowingly did. Both were connected to courtly India and bourgeois urban classes as well as nineteenth-century colonial developments in folk costumes, and wore sherwanis or *achkan* (coats) and *churidars* (jodhpurs) as a way to be connected to existing power elites'. Sircar, R. (2019) Rewriting, Adapting, and Fashioning National Styles in India. *Fashion and Postcolonial Critique*, pp. 156–169.

a robber dresses in a *burqa* to evade the police. Shyam Benegal, the director of *Well Done Abba*, had this to say about the *burqa*:

> I think the custom of wearing *burqa*... is not very interesting. That's why
> I have used the dress sometimes to create a comedy scene. (Personal
> interview, 29 June 2013)

Besides costume design, another major aspect of Hindi cinema that made extensive use of Islamicate culture was dialogue. In 1931 when talkies were introduced in the Bombay film industry, it became apparent that the language of dialogue to be used could pose a potential problem. In India as a multilingual country, and in a cosmopolitan city like Bombay, no one language could be said to have supremacy. So it was difficult for filmmakers to determine the language to be used (Dwyer, 2006). There was no standardized version of spoken Hindi that would lend itself to easy usage by filmmakers. It is at this point that Hindi filmmakers adopted Urdu—a supposedly Muslim language—as a means of onscreen communication. This was also aided by the presence of many well-known and talented Urdu writers and poets in Bombay around that time. A number of these Urdu writers had migrated to Bombay from across north India during the 1930s and 1940s, where they worked for various Urdu newspapers such as *Mussavar* and *Karawan*. At the same time, they also started working in the city's film industry as dialogue writers, lyricists, and scriptwriters. Rupleena Bose points out:

> At a time when the language in cinema was predominantly Urdu, the
> world of publishing was closely linked with the film industry, causing
> a steady exchange of ideas and themes expressed by the writers of
> those times. Writers like Saadat Hasan Manto, Krishan Chandar, Ismat
> Chughtai and Shahid Latif who were eminent writers were also a part of
> the film industry of 1930s and 1940s. (Bose, 2009: 62)

A significant number of the Urdu writers were members of the Progressive Writers' Movement[2]—who went on to become members of

---

[2] This was formed in 1936 in Lucknow. The Urdu name of this literary movement was *Anjuman Taraqqi Pasand Musannifin*. Hussain, G. (2022). Ethnonationality of Caste in

the well-known Indian People's Theatre Association[3]—and greatly influenced the content of Hindi films. Writers associated with this movement rejected the then popular genres of the mythological and historical romance, instead urging filmmakers to make realistic films. The writers propagated the ideology of the movement, which promoted the philosophy of social justice and equality in pre-Partition British India. 'Writers like Saadat Hasan Manto, Ali Sardar Jafri, Rajinder Singh Bedi, Sahir Ludhianvi, Kaifi Azmi, Khwaja Ahmed Abbas and others brought a politically left-wing and overtly secular outlook to the films they were associated with' (Needham and Rajan, 2007: 230). However, the early attempts of these writers were unsuccessful at the box office as audiences at that time could not accept the views of the movement, which were considered 'radical' at that time.

Much like in the popularization of the Urdu language in Hindi films, Muslims have made enormous contributions in the field of music in the Bombay film industry. Here we have to keep in mind that just as in the case of Islamic attire, there is no one specific genre of Islamic music because Islam is multiethnic and multilingual. In the Indian context, there is nothing called Muslim musical genre or a genre created by Muslim artists. As pointed out by Rachel Dwyer, 'Indian classical music was centred around the courts [it was] often associated with Islamicate culture; though being, again, in no way "Islamicate"' (Dwyer, 2006: 108). In recognition of his contributions to the fields of classical and semi-classical ghazal music, Gazal Talat Mehmood was awarded the Padma Bhushan (which is based on another genre of Urdu poetry). Mohammed Rafi, Hariharan, Jagjit Singh, and Pankaj Udhas are significant ghazal performers. The 'high' and 'popular' Muslim cultures come together in this framework of music and dialogue. Amirbai Karnataki, Samshad Begum, Mahammad Rafi, Talat Mehmood, Khursheed Bano, and Suraiya are the

Pakistan: Privileged Caste Morality in Sindhi Progressive Literature and Politics. *Critical Sociology*, 48(1), pp. 127–149.

[3] According to Nandi Bhatia, 'In 1942, a group of progressive writers who recognized the potential of popular theatre as an effective weapon in the fight for national liberation from British imperialism and from fascism and in the struggles of peasants, workers, and other oppressed classes formed a group called the Indian People's Theatre Association (IPTA)'. Bhatia, Nandi (2010). *Acts of Authority/Acts of Resistance: Theater and Politics in Colonial and Postcolonial India*. University of Michigan Press, p. 76.

most prominent singers from the early years of Hindi cinema. Ghulam Haider, the music director, honoured talents such as Noorjehan[4] and Lata Mangeshkar.

Moreover, Sufi music is significantly linked to Islamic culture and has also been an integral part of Bollywood films since decades. For example, *qawwali*, a genre of Sufi music, is extensively utilized in Bombay cinema. Haidar Ali has long been associated with the Bombay film industry as his parents Pramila and Kumar were actively involved in the Bombay industry. Pramila was the stage name of Esther Victoria Abraham, a Jewish Indian actress, model, and the first female film financier in the Hindi cinema business. Kumar (actual name Syed Hasan Ali Zaidi) was an actor who starred in films such as *Mughal-e-Azam*, *Shri 420*, and *Watan*. As he has long been associated directly or indirectly with the Bollywood film industry, Haidar Ali was in a unique position to explain the connection between Islam and Sufism and how Sufism influenced India's Hindu culture. He says:

> From different parts of the world people have migrated to India—such as Persians, Turks, Mughals. Lodhi and Mughals came and became part of India. Sufism arrived in India with them and became very much part of the Hindu ethos ... The qawwali form is basically devotional. It was not only love; it was a love for the god, for the supreme. It's more like *aban*, *bhajan*, *kirtan* (spiritual prayers). (Personal interview, 5 April 2014)

The inclusion of qawwali performances was in the form of standalone shows or it was common for two groups of singers to perform against each other in Hindi cinema during the 1940s (Zubedi and Sarrazin, 2016). The style of incorporating qawwali in films is popularly referred to as 'filmi qawwali', the main purpose of which is entertainment. Its rising success is due to the introduction of Sufi music by Bollywood. Another major reason is the contribution of the iconic Pakistani qawwal star Nusrat Fateh Ali Khan, who revolutionized qawwali music making

---

[4] Noorjehan first appeared in movies and later became famous for the music of *Khazanchi* (1941), written and composed by Ghulam Haider. Haider and Noorjehan both moved to Pakistan after Partition.

it highly popular among north Indian audiences (Nayyar, 1988). Nusrat Fateh Ali Khan also composed a number of songs for Bollywood films. A number of filmmakers have been and continue to be inspired by Nusrat Fateh Ali Khan's qawwalis. Rachel Dwyer, a film researcher, notes that occasionally they 'modify the lyrics to remove any spiritual meaning, although some echo of a higher love remains for some listeners' (Dwyer, 2006: 110): 'Kinne sona' becomes 'Kitna sona' in *Raja Hindustani* (1996, dir. Dharmesh Darshan) and 'Mast' is turned into an item song in *Mohra* (1994, dir. Rajiv Rai). Music directors such as Anu Malik, Rahat Fateh Ali Khan, and A.R. Rahman have used qawwalis directly in Bollywood. Recently too there have been songs in films which take inspiration from Sufi music; for example, 'Kabira' (reference to Saint Kabir) in *Yeh Jawaani Hai Deewani* (2013) and the song 'Deewani Mastaani' from the periodical drama *Bajirao Mastaani* (2015), which resonate with Sufi expression (Rajan, 2018). Bollywood has also come up with a new style, which is a fusion of qawwali and Western pop-rock music. For instance, we have Kavita Seth's 'Tumhi Ho Bandhu' from *Cocktail* (2012), and 'Jeete Hai Chal' in *Neerja* (2016) that contains similar elements (Sen, 2017).

On the other hand, female qawwali artists have also made a significant impact on Bollywood cinema. Their popularity in Bollywood may be attributed to the 'uniqueness' that is associated with female practitioners of qawwali. One of the earliest references to qawwali performed by women can be traced back to the song 'Ahen na bharin shikwe na kiye' from *Zeenat* (1945). Later there were multiple films such as *Mughal-E-Azam* (1960) where a form of qawwali as competitive duet was showcased. There were films like *Barasat Ki Raat* (1960) and *Nikaah* (1982), which portray female singers participating in a competitive performance between two groups. In recent times, Pakistani artist Abida Parveen, a qawwal, has amassed great popularity as someone who is popular for *sufiyana kalaam* (a form of Sufi poetry sung in a vernacular language with local instrumentation) (Abbas, 2002). Moreover, there is another artist, Reshma, 'a folk singer who has entered this male-dominated playing field in Qawwali with her *sufiyana kalaam* influenced songs such as *Dama Dam Mast Kalandar*, and *Hai O' Rabba nahion lagda dil mera* amongst others. However, neither of them perform *Qawwali* in its traditional format' (Qureshi, 1999).

Hindi cinema's most enduring and significant association with Muslims has been through lyricists and scriptwriters. Lyricists who have drawn inspiration from the genre *nazm* are Agha Kashmiri, Kaifi Azmi, Gulzar, Akhtar Mirza, Saadat Hossan Manto, Shakeel Badayuni, the most popular writers Salim Khan and Javed Akhtar of Bombay Hindi cinema (Dwyer, 2006). In the early cinema era of the 1930s and 1940s, there was evidence of a true cultural convergence when film dialogues were written in Persianized Urdu. Young Muslim poets and authors like Sahir Ludhianvi and Majrooh Sultanpuri offered Hindi films a new degree of sophistication and depth in the 1950s and 1960s (Ahmed, 1992). Even now, the idiomatic expressions 'Allah' and 'Bismillah' are popular in dialogue and music (Ahmed, 1992).

Politics in Engaging Muslims in the Pre- and Post-Partition Period Bombay Films

As already stated, in the early period of Bombay cinema, Parsi theatre was the major contributor of actors and writers. Also, Parsi theatre had played a substantial role in film production and distribution until the 1930s, and they were owned by three prominent studios, namely Imperial Film, Wadia Movietone, and Minerva Movietone. Ardeshir Irani, a Parsi, directed the very first Indian talkie, *Alam Ara* (1931). On the other hand, though there were a fair number of Muslim industrialists from Gujarat such as the Khojas and Memons who could finance the films of the time but only a very few Muslims were engaged in the early days of filmmaking. That 'the industry has a disproportionate number of Muslim stars, producers, directors, stunts, in fact at all levels, is only true of the Indian cinema after this point' in Rachel Dwyer's observation (Dwyer, 2006: 99). Until the introduction of talkies, just a few Muslims were involved in important roles in the Bombay filmmaking world.

On 15 August 1947, India attained freedom from British colonialism but India was fragmented, and Pakistan was founded as a separate nation. The Partition (and later the formation of the third nation Bangladesh) had a profound effect on the Indian sociopolitical realm, especially on the matter of identity of Indian Muslims, who lost the collective weight of their 800-year-old history in the country. The veteran Muslim League leader Chaudhry Khaliquzzaman lamented that the two-nation theory which ultimately led to the Partition 'proved positively injurious to the Muslims in India, and on a long view basis to Muslims everywhere' (cited in Puri, 1993). After 1947, the Muslim community did not have the traditional position of power and prestige in India and lost a significant amount of respect in the eyes of the majority Hindu community because of the role of some Muslims in the fragmentation of the country.

In many respects, 1947 saw the birth of a new community. Jawaharlal Nehru asserted a secular democratic foundation for the Indian nation-state, and therefore destabilized communal polarization in the newly in-dependent India. If we look back, we will see that the political parties of the 1950s formed a strong ideological foundation for the nation—with the major opposition being the socialists and the Congress to the left of the centre. Moreover, there existed other ideologies in the political land-scape such as liberal capitalism of the Swatantra Party, Marxism of the communist party, and assertive nationalism of the Bhartiya Jana Sangh (Puri, 1993: 2142). There were only a few political parties, such as the Muslim League in Kerala and the Akali Dal of Punjab, which barred asso-ciates of other religious identities.

In the post-Independence India, though Muslims faced many inse-curities, their anxieties were soothed by the Indian Constitution, which offered the fundamental rights and minority rights that ascertained the basic principles of secularism and democracy in the country. Moreover, the insecurities of the Muslims in a divided India were reassured by the leadership of three stalwarts, Maulana Abul Kalam Azad, Rafi Ahmad Kidwai, and Sheikh Abdullah. The idea of a composite Indian nationalism was offered spiritual recognition by Azad's reading of the Quran and Islam and its arguments were reconciled with the desire for Muslim identity. On the other hand, Kidwai could connect with non-Muslims with much ease. In the 1950s, the Muslim community lost the leadership of these leaders and thereafter things changed. According to the Indian political com-mentator and human rights activist Balraj Puri, 'So far as Muslim asser-tion is concerned, it was pronounced on three main issues which emerged as symbols of the Muslim identity, namely, Aligarh Muslim University, Urdu language and Muslim Personal Law' (1993: 2143).

In the pre- and post-Partition period, Urdu-speaking Muslims from North and Central India had actively participated in the Muslim politics of India. Though Urdu is frequently used as a symbol of composite culture, it was the issue of linguistic identity that gave rise to the very first organized division between the Hindu and Muslim elites in late nineteenth-century India. Indian reformist-writer and social activist Asghar Ali Engineer mentions, 'Persian was replaced by English at higher courts and by Urdu at lower ones' (1991: 1036). Maharaja Kishan Prashad of Benaras and several others started claiming that the court language be Hindi written in Devnagri, while Sir Syed Ahmad Khan and many others persisted with using Urdu written in Persian script. However, the then political and social elite, irrespective of their religious identity, spoke the same language, that is, Urdu, and maintained the same cultural milieu more or less. Many of those who embraced the demand for Urdu language were Muslims, and those who favoured Hindi were Hindus. It should be recalled that it was not just a matter of cultural and linguistic identity; it was also a question of livelihood. Gradually, Hindi was acknowledged as the court language of the state without demanding the assertions of Urdu (Engineer, 1991). In the film industry, Urdu came into prominence after the introduction of talkies (as will be explained later in the chapter). People specializing in the Urdu language (lyricists, directors, dialogue writers) were soon in demand. A significant number of Urdu-speaking Muslims who were earlier involved in the field of Urdu language such as literature and newspapers joined the Bombay Hindi film industry, and they established a distinct kind of cinema called 'Islamicate Cinema'; however, the participation of individuals from diverse cultures should not be ignored (Dwyer, 2006).

The main language used in northern India before Independence was Hindustani, which is a combination of Urdu and Hindi. Urdu was an extensively spoken language by the Muslims of Uttar Pradesh and Gujarat, and by a few non-Muslim groups such as Panjabis, Parsis, and Jews. Urdu was the communicative language to converse with each other in the Bombay film industry in the 1930s, before talkies were introduced (Dwyer, 2006). Urdu's origins as an Indian language are traced back by Haider Ali and also [mistakenly] a language attributed to only Muslims:

> Urdu was the maximum spoken language from North India to Central India right from Gwalior, Indore, Bhopal, and Lucknow. All the *nawabs* and Mughals were ruling in Delhi, so Persian got mixed with Sanskrit

and became Urdu which gradually became the national language and that spread to Calcutta. From Babar to Akbar, they all spoke in Turkish, Persian, and Arabic. They developed a mixed language because the army was from India and also from Persia, Arab, they had to communicate and to communicate they had to use each other's words. That's how Persian and Sanskrit got exchanged and Urdu was founded. It took centuries to develop the language. Then because of Hindi and Urdu mixing, Hindustani was formed. Hindi has purely come out from Sanskrit. (Personal interview, 5 April 2014)

Iqbal Masud stresses that from the late 1940s to the early 1960s, the Urdu language had huge influence over mainstream culture; even villains in films used to lure female protagonists, spouting the *shayaris* (Urdu poetry) of Ghalib. Iqbal Masud says, 'As late as the 60s, a film villain traps a heroine by using a disguise and quoting Ghalib: "*Badal kar faqiron ka hum bhes …*' Ghalib/'*Tamashai-I-abl-I-karam dekhte hain …*" ["We put on the garb of a beggar to test the generosity of the rich"]. The audience understood and applauded the quote' (Masud, 2005). In connection to this, when asked why so many Muslims were involved in Hindi cinema, Haider Ali explained that it was due to their mastery of the Urdu language, which was the key communicative language in the period between the 1930s and 1960s. He said:

After the introduction of Talkies, the industry needed the people who had good command of Urdu language. Generally, Muslims from Lucknow and the North Indian belt had expertise of the language and they joined the film industry. (Personal interview, 5 April 2014)

This entire phenomenon of shared culture mentioned earlier in this chapter was not an abrupt incident; it became a practice mainly because of two reasons: (1) renowned Urdu newspapers established in Bombay were *Karawan* and *Mussavar* and (2) Urdu writers started writing for films that were being made in the Bombay film world. Therefore, 'Writers like Saadat Hasan Manto, Krishan Chandar, Ismat Chughtai and Shahid Latif who were eminent writers were also a part of the film industry' (Bose, 2009: 62). Apart from people working in the film industry and Urdu newspapers, Parsi theatre also has an important role in integrating

Urdu as the language of Bombay films. Amit Khanna, a national award-winning lyricist, producer, and director, traces Urdu's influence in Muslim Historical films[5] of the 1940s to 1960s:

> When historical film started [getting produced], people like Kamal Amhori, Asgar Wajahat, all came from Lucknow and mostly from north India. Initially they started with the theatre and the theatre tradition goes back to Parsi theatre which had Urdu writers like Aga Kashmiri or other progressive writers. These writers wrote in Urdu which is a flowery language and Hindi writers could not write that; similarly in film songs, Urdu influence was much stronger than Hindi. (Personal interview, 24 March 2014)

From the 1940s onwards till the 1960s, Urdu writers were having much agency to set the priority and standard of Hindi film industry. Even now the majority of the Urdu poets still command the Bollywood film language and they disdain someone who is not competent with the grammar of Urdu. Amit Khanna has used the example of India's superstar lyricist, Javed Akhtar, to illustrate how Urdu writers are obsessed with maintaining the purity of Urdu language while writing in Urdu and they never mix Urdu with any other language.

> Javed still says to me that, 'yeh grammar wrong hain' ['The grammar is wrong']. I say, 'Aarey tera Urdu ke hisab se wrong ha but Hindi ke hisab se wrong nahi hain' ['This is wrong according to Urdu grammar but right on the basis of Hindi language']. (Personal interview, 24 March 2014)

In Bollywood, there is already a distinct demarcation of what is acceptable and what is not in representing people and cultures on screen. Different languages are used to communicate various emotions and signify social classes as well as cultural groups. Urdu is often used in connection with a Muslim protagonist or to convey romantic emotion through

---

[5] Like other Historicals, the Muslim Historical genre plays an imporant role to document the imagined past. The Muslim Historical genre started getting its cultural and political significance in the period after Independence.

songs and music; English is used to portray a refined elite class; and tapori Bombaiya is utilized to portray an underprivileged downtrodden class. In the 1970s, a number of films based on Hindu mythology were released and among them *Jai Santoshi Maa* (1975) achieved unprecedented success. Characters mostly speak in Sanskritized Hindi in all these Hindu mythological films. Following this trend, director B.R. Chopra used Sanskritized Hindi most distinctly to depict epics like the Ramayana and Mahabharata on the television screen. After the huge success of telecast of Ramayana and Mahabharata, usage of Sanskritized Hindi in mythological films of Bollywood cinema became a practice. Similarly, Urdu is still associated with Muslims and Pakistan and in the most recent film *Veer Zaara* (2004), Yash Chopra used Urdu for the Pakistani characters, while the Indian hero spoke in Hindi. Thus, Bollywood films have no common language and use language to create and convey a specific religious, regional, economic, and class status.

During the 1950s and 1960s, Bombay Hindi films fostered the idea of shared culture, which supports a sense of shared beliefs and customs between Muslims and Hindus. This shared culture is referred to as Ganga-Jamuna Tehzeeb in Urdu. Because of the hybrid culture of the Mughal Persians and the pre-existing culture of Varanasi, the Awadh region of Uttar Pradesh served as the primary centre for this culture. According to Asghar Ali Engineer:

> Immediately after Independence until right up to the 1980s, films were mainly based on north Indian Muslim culture: *nawab*, jagirdar, etc. Cultural ethos, secular ethos, Ganga–Jamuna Tehzeeb or composite culture: two religions developed a new culture to which both the communities contributed equally. Urdu was also the product of Ganga–Jamuna Tehzeeb. (Personal interview, 8 December 2012)

However, Amit Khanna strongly criticizes the idea of shared culture. He believes that the sense of shared culture contributes to the homogenized portrayal of many religious and ethnic groups in Hindi cinema. India is a culturally varied country, with distinct cultures in each state and every region. Because the majority of India's minorities converted from the Hindu religion, people there do not adhere to culture based on their religion. Therefore, they keep practising the same cultural practices and rites that they did before their conversion. Amit Khanna points out that the homogenized portrayal of various identities is the result of the notion of common culture. He claims:

What I disagree with most observers is [that] they put too much emphasis on Ganga–Jamuna Tahjeeb. This is an Uttar Pradesh phenomenon and Uttar Pradesh dominated our thought and created a process especially in Hindi cinema. Thus, there was a constant harping about a shared culture. It has actually backlashed because shared culture is a whitewash of an entire nation. I am not talking of community of Hindu and Muslim, the issue is not about minority and majority, the issue is you are taking away the identity of people, there is no such thing because a Muslim from Kerala has nothing to do with that. He lives a life completely like any other Hindu: he eats the same food, speaks the same language as Hindu or for that matter a Muslim in Assam. There was never a shared culture. It was always an elitist culture. I belong to a family which had shared culture but we were a minority. When we are discussing the world at large, in India, we have to understand the ground reality. Hyderabad had a shared culture, but Telangana no because that was not an issue. (Personal interview, 24 March 2014)

Few Muslims migrated to Pakistan in the post-Partition era, and many Hindus shifted to India. However, along with Hindus, also came many Muslims who later became film personalities. Ganti mentions, 'The post-Independence Bombay film industry was shaped by the histories of migration and displacement set in motion by Partition' (2013: 22). The most prominent names in the industry who shifted to India are Ramanand Sagar, B.R. Chopra, I.S. Johar, Omprakash, Jeevan, Gulshan Rai, A.K. Hangal (Avtar Kishan Hangal), O.P. Nayyar, Sunil Dutt, Rajendra Kumar, Dev Anand, Rajinder Singh Bedi, Surinder and Prakash Kaur Manorama, Naqsh Lyallpuri, Pushpa Huns, Dilip Kumar (Muhammad Yusuf Khan), Jaywant (Zakaria Khan), Pran (Pran Krishan Sikand), Yash Chopra, Prithviraj Kapoor, Vinod Khanna, Mohammed Rafi (though his parents shifted to Pakistan, he later migrated to Mumbai), Raaj Kumar, Gulzar, Manoj Kumar (Harikishan Giri Goswami), Majrooh Sultanpuri, Govind Nihalani, and Iftekhar.

The acceptability of Muslim actors became a significant problem in the post-Partition period. There were a number of riots across the nation in the pre-Partition era and across both the nations in the post-Partition period, which had a negative effect on ordinary human imagination of the social acceptance of Muslim actors and stars in India. The Muslim actors subsequently took non-Arabic names like Jaywant (Zakaria Khan), Dilip Kumar (Muhammad Yusuf Khan), Meena Kumari (Mahjabeen Bano), Johnny Walker (Badruddin Jamaluddin Kazi), and so on. Possibly they felt that it was a required change to hide their religious identity in order to be accepted by Hindus. Celebrated director Shyam Benegal had the following to say:

> when you had the whole business of Partition particularly, it was a problem for those who wanted be popular in film. That's why they changed their name from Muslim name to Hindu name because the majority audience was Hindu. It became a problem particularly at the time of the 1940s, and then these people came into the film business like Dilip Kumar (Yusuf khan) came into the film industry in 1944/45. It was a very crucial time. In that there were riots and the struggle between India and Pakistan and politics. Now, Dilip Kumar and similarly many of them changed their names. Gradually, it became a norm to do this. (Personal interview, 29 June 2013)

Hyder Ali on the other hand thinks that the decision of changing names is very situational. He provides many instances of people who were not compelled to change their names to hide their religious identity:

> See it's a very complex question and quite situational and we can't generalize. Even at that time, there were big Muslim stars even before Independence like Master Nisar, Al Naseem, S. Nazeem and they started in the silent era but stayed after Partition also. Big stars of the time like Yakoob Khan, Master Nazir, Nasir, Rehman did not change their names. I don't think Dilip Kumar changed his name to hide his [Muslim] identity. Probably, Yusuf Khan was not sounding good; that's why Debika Rani gave three options to him: Mahesh Kumar, Dilip Kumar, and something else. In films, changing name is very situational. Dilip Kumar probably felt his name was not attractive. Hamis

Ali changed his name to Ajit. Immediately after Partition, he was in a film called *Aapbiti* (1947) and the film was on Hindu–Muslim unity and as a result he had to change his name. The picture was not allowed to be released because Qurshid and Nurjahan left for Pakistan in 1947. Ajit stayed back, so he had to change his name from Hamid Ali to Ajit. In his second film which was *Bekasoor*, they changed his name as Ajit. (Personal interview, 5 April 2014)

Haider Ali shares a very interesting experience that his father (actor Kumar, who starred in the films *Mughal-e-Azam* and *Shri 420*) had experienced. It explains the circumstances surrounding his father's name change and the rise in popularity of the surname Kumar in the Bombay Hindi film industry. He states:

He was my father, Syed Hassan Ali Zaidi, and he was auditioned for a film, *Jinda Lash* (Shadows of Death) directed by Kumar Debaki Bose in New Theatre, Calcutta in 1932. It belonged to the silent era. Debaki Bose liked him and expressed his wish to make a talkie and decided to take him as hero in the film *Puran Bhagat* (1933). He was playing the role of Prince Puran. There was a tension between Hindus–Muslims at that time prior to the film's release, distributors and exhibitors grew worried, claiming that using the name Syed Hassan Ali Zaidi, who plays Puran Bhagat, would cause a lot of tension and result in riots. The role of a Bhagat cannot be played by a Muslim, Hassan Ali. Kumar Debaki Bose opted to play the character of a Prince, and Prince refers to Kumar, and Kumar Debaki Bose came from a royal family. Finally, he adopted his own name as Kumar and named my father's name as Kumar in the film. The next day, he saw his name is Kumar and asked Debaki Bose 'Dada ki holo?' ('What happened to my name brother?'). Bose narrated the story and said everybody would recognize you by this name. Later, the film became a box office hit. My father never changed his name again. Before people used Kumar to address Prince but now they indicate actor by the word Kumar. After to make yourself to be known as an actor, people use the name Kumar. Ashok Ganguly became Ashok Kumar. Yusuf Khan became Dilip Kumar, Rajendra Kumar, Manoj Kumar (Hari Krishna Gowasmi) right up until Akshay Kumar (Rajiv Bhatia). (Personal interview, 5 April 2014)

Because of the political turmoil and crisis, numerous film figures migrated from India to Pakistan. A group of successful Muslims who worked in the Bombay film industry migrated to Lahore. 'Some of the directors who migrated to Pakistan were Syed Shaukat Hussain Rizvi, S.M. Yousuf, Najam Naqvi, Munshi Dil, Nakshab Jarachavi, M. Sadiq, Zia Sarhadi, Sibtain Fazli (of Fazli Brothers), S.T. Zaidi, Zahoor Raja, Wali saheb, A.R. Kardar, Nazir, W.Z. Ahmed, Masood Pervez, Shareef Nayyar, Luqmaan, Dawood Chaand, Rakhan, Nusrat Mansoori, M.H. Qasim, Roop K. Shorey, Butt Kasher, and Barkat Mehra' (Deshmukh, 2014). Moreover, numerous actors who used to work in Bombay film production migrated as well such as 'Nazeer, Sadiq Ali, Masood, Sudhir, Santosh, Ratan Kumar, Najmul Hussain, Suresh and Nasir khan (both shifted back to India later), Sh. Mukhtar, M. Ismail, Ajmal, Gulam Mohd, Kumar, Ghori, Majeed, Shahnawaz, Himalayawala, Shyam Kumar, Allauddin, Shah Shikarpuri, Charlie, Nazar Faizi Noorjehan, Meena Shorey, Khursheed, Zeenat Begum, Asha Posley, Najma, Kalawati, Rehana, Swarnalata, Ragini, Bibbo, Renuka Devi, Geeta Nizami, Maya Devi' (Deshmukh, 2014). Apart from directors and actors, even some renowned musical artists also shifted their base to Lahore, some being 'Khursheed Anwar, Inayat Hussain, Rafiq gaznavi, G.A. Chisti, Ghulam Hyder, Firoz Nizami, Nissar Bazmi, Nashaad, Tufail Faruqi, Tanvir Naqvi, Faiyaz Hasmi, Iqbal Bano, Premlata, Khursheed, Zeenat Begum, Shevan Rizvi, Rasheed Atre, Fateh Ali khan, Babul etc.' (Deshmukh, 2014). In a meeting with the celebrated film correspondent B.D. Garga, Saadat Hossain Manto shared his disagreement with the action of sacking all the Muslim workers due to the establishment of the new Islamic republic Pakistan by the Bombay Talkies' management where Monto served. That incident forced a number of Muslim workers to relocate to Pakistan, including himself.

Soon after Independence, because of a significant number of people moving to Pakistan, there was a major absence of Muslim filmmakers in the industry. Just a few famous directors such as K. Asif (1922 to 1971), Kamal Amrohi (1918 to 1993), and Mehboob Khan (1906 to 1964) stayed back in India in spite of carrying the 'minority' identity tag. K. Asif was not only a director but also worked as a film producer and screenwriter. His noteworthy releases such as *Shehar Aur Sapna* (1963) and *Pardesi* (1957) received national and international appreciation. Kamal Amrohi was an Urdu author and worked extensively as a dialogue writer, later directing the masterpiece *Pakeezah* (1972). Mehboob Khan moved to Bombay to act as an extra in the films; however afterwards he developed his studio, which is still functioning and now owned by his family. With his film *Najma* (1943), he was the first director to establish the genre of Muslim Social dramas (I will discuss this film and the genre in the next chapter). Afterwards, he produced several remarkable social films including *Anmol Ghadi* (1946) and *Mother India* (1957).

Apart from K. Asif, Kamal Amrohi, and Mehboob Khan, in the post-colonial period we see the existence of a new group of filmmakers who started making their mark in the Bombay Hindi cinema. Saeed Akhtar Mirza was one of the most influential screenwriters and directors in the 1960s. He played an important role in bringing change in filmmaking practices and thus took part in the New Movement in Cinema.[6] *Salim Langde Pe Mat Ro* (1989) is regarded as the finest film by Saeed Mirza. It was also his first film in which he explored the issues that plague the Muslim community. Later he won the national award as best director for film *Naseem* (1995). Aziz Mirza, the elder brother of Saeed Mirza, is a famous director who directed films such as *Raju Ban Gaya Gentleman* (1992), *Yes Boss* (1997), *Phir Bhi Dil Hai Hindustani* (2000), *Chalte Chalte* (2003), and *Kismat Konnection* (2008). Moreover, there are Muslim filmmakers such as Farhan Akhtar, Zoya Akhtar, Farah Khan, Kabir Khan, Sabir Khan, and Imtiaz Ali.

Apart from film directors, the Bombay film industry has historically and gladly accommodated Muslim film stars. With the advent of talkies, the need for stars with accurate Urdu accents emerged. Urdu speakers—who were essentially Muslims or Urdu-educated Panjabis—from north India were often favoured. The female stars with the most potential and popularity were Meena Kumari, Madhubala, Nargis, and Waheeda Rehman. Afterwards, Saira Bano, Mumtaz, Parveen Babi, and Zeenat Aman ruled in the 1960s. Shabana Azmi, who is often associated with parallel cinema, was seen in the 1970s. Throughout the last twenty

[6] New Movement in Cinema in India belonged to a larger film movement in a number of filmmaking countries across the world; most popularly known as 'New Wave' in France or the 'Underground' in America. This new cinema tried to break free from the 'vulgarities of the established commercial cinema' and '[offer] the filmmaker, above all, the indispensable freedom to realize his vision, untrammelled by all considerations except creative and aesthetic. New Cinema looks upon a film as the personal expression of an individual artist'. Sen, M., Kaul, A. and Datt, G. (1968) New Cinema Movement: Extract from Manifesto. *Closeup*, 1(1).

years, there has been a dwindling number of Muslim female stars. The only names in contemporary Bollywood are Dia Mirza, Farhah Naaz Hashmi, Tabu (Tabassum Fatima Hashmi), Zareen Khan, Katrina Kaif, and Sara Ali Khan. One of the reasons of this development may be due to the absence of *tawaif* culture in India in the later years as well as the representation of *tawaifs* in Bollywood. Many of the Muslim actresses of the earlier age belonged to the lineage of *tawaifs*. Film historian Rachel Dwyer points out, 'the reasons for this shift are not clear but are perhaps to do with the changes in class and performative traditions' (2006: 102).

There were very few Muslim male stars even when there was a good percentage of female stars in the industry. One of the most prominent Muslim stars of that period was Dilip Kumar. Not only did some Muslim actors play a lead role, some became very successful as comedians such as Johnny Walker and Mehmood. Comedians like Johnny Walker and Mehmood are the celebrated film personalities of Bombay cinema. In films like *Pyaasa* (1957), Johnny Walker showed his mettle by not just mimicking a semi-inebriate, but was the master of verbal humour. There was substantial diversity in Mehmood's repertoire also. He was mainly known as a comedian, but he performed a number of other roles such as economically deprived person or a south Indian musician and so on. Until the 1990s, there were only a few Muslim actors in the industry. For his flamboyant style, with cowboyish swagger and cigar-toting persona that transformed the style quotient of mainstream film hero, Feroz Khan was very popular, his popularity peaking in the 1970s. Kader Khan gained repute as an actor, but he was also employed as a script and dialogue writer. He acted primarily as a villain, sidekick of the villain, and comedian in the films of the 1970s. Also in the 1970s, Farooq Sheikh and Naseeruddin Shah became very influential actors and their key contributions were to parallel cinema or to the 'New Wave' of Indian cinema. In many films, Iftekar was best remembered as a police officer. The three Khans (Shahrukh, Salman, and Amir) came into prominence in the 1990s. They are still considered the biggest stars of Bollywood cinema. Along with these three Khans, we see the emergence of a number of Muslim stars and actors after the 1990s. They are Arbaaz Khan, Sohail Khan, Zayed Khan, Arshad Warsi, Emran Hasmi, Farhan Akhtar, Saif Ali Khan, Irrfan Khan, Farhah Khan (also contemporary noteworthy choreographer), and many more.

Politicizing the Text of Post-Partition
Bombay Films

As discussed, Muslims have been an integral part of the Hindi film industry since its inception over a hundred years ago. We have also seen
how the involvement of Muslims was influenced by the political landscape of the nation. We must now examine how the Bombay film industry historically represented Muslims in films. Cultural texts play
the important role of being an active agent in the construction of historical narrative. In her *Trauma Culture* (2005), E. Ann Kaplan argues
that 'telling stories about trauma, even though the story can never actually repeat or represent what happened, may partly achieve a certain
"working through" for the victim. It may also ... permit a kind of em-
pathic "sharing" that moves us forward, if only by inches' (2005:37).
During the Second World War, the economic and political crisis had a de-
stabilizing effect on the Bombay film business. Only in the early 1950s did
the industry start to regain its footing, but the films made during this period completely ignored the trauma and suffering of the people due to the
Partition. Instead, films during that time were spectacles with intensified
romance, inter-religious romances, and friendship, with stories that celebrated communal harmony and the glamour of those texts offering some
relief from the misery and suffering of the recent past (Master, 2009).
Moreover, the government also became involved in the Bombay film industry and started monitoring it closely to ensure that ideological content
being disseminated was conducive to the notion of Nehruvian socialism
and nation-building concerns (Schulze, 2002). Films of the era upheld
Gandhian/Nehruvian ideals such as '*Naya zamana, naya roshni*', which
catered to the vision of the new nation's growth and prosperity through
India's rural and agrarian classes (Master, 2009). Nehruvian values were
articulated in the movies with their focus on labour struggle and the integrity of the labour class. Due to Nehruvian policies, Muslim culture was
propagated through film as a secular worldview after India became an
independent nation. Muslim culture was likely incorporated into secular
ideology as part of Nehruvian policy 'in the post-partition period to
counter negative attitudes towards Muslims in the country' (Bhaskar and
Allen, 2009: 6). Beginning in the silent era, the Islamicate culture carved
out a place for itself in Hindi film, but in the years following Partition,

the Muslim Historical and Courtesan genres provided it a significant new meaning (Bhaskar and Allen, 2009: 6). Much like representation in popular culture has the potential to bind a set of individuals and classify them without taking into account each member's separate identity in the group, while examining the representation of Muslims in Bollywood, one can easily identify the pattern which is followed to represent Muslims historically in films made in the industry. The portrayal of Muslims has over the years gone through a huge change reacting to the sociopolitical in India and across the world. Hence, depending on the altering image of Muslims, the representation can broadly be classified into four genres:[7] (a) the Muslim Historical genre; (b) the Muslim Social genre; (c) the Muslim Political genre; and (d) the Muslim Contemporary genre (since the 2000s). These categorizations will be explored in the following chapters of this book.

The Muslim Historical films form a separate genre primarily because of their accounts of magnificent past legends and renowned personalities. On the contrary, the recent genre of Historical films represent Muslim rulers through the prism of aggressive Hindu nationalist discourse. Most of the Muslim Historical films in the post-Independence period (the 1950s and 1960s)—the so-called Nehruvian era—were based on secular Mughal rulers and focused on the exoticism of those rulers. The films in this genre and the participants of my empirical study hint that Muslims were positively stereotyped at this time. On the other hand, contemporary Historical films are inspired by iconic Muslim historical figures, myths, and events to create 'enemy images' of 'outsiders' who have been marked with specific 'political signs'.

The next categorization is the Muslim Social genre, a subsection of the broader genre 'The Social', wherein films showcase everyday household narratives and romantic tales. The Muslim Social genre alludes to films that describe Islamicate culture. This genre flourished mostly in the 1950s and 1960s, and reflected an idealized Muslim world where *nawabs*, indulging in hedonistic pursuits, lived in grandeur with their aristocratic idiosyncrasies intact. The secular ideology of the state was additionally

---

[7] Genre is one of the major concepts in cultural studies and John Hartley refers to genre as 'the recognized paradigmatic sets into which the total output of a given medium (film, television, writing) is classified'. O'Sullivan, T., et al. (1994) *Key Concepts in Communication and Cultural Studies*, 2nd edition. London: Routledge.

reflected in the films of this genre, which enunciated the conflict between modern (refinement, learning, progress) and tradition (respect, pride, dedication). Muslim Social films typecasted Muslims in terms of multiple cultural elements such as language, culture, place, and socioeconomic status. During this time, Muslims were also portrayed extensively in parallel cinema. One of the most renowned filmmakers of this parallel form, Shyam Benegal says, 'while the films of the Nehruvian era reflected the "tolerant" secularism of the state (with all its attendant problems and anxieties), the 1970s and 1980s saw the emergence of an alternative politics of minority representation with the rise of the "new cinema" ' (Benegal, 2007: 225).

Next we will discuss the Muslim Political genre in which the films centred on Muslims released towards the end of the 1980s and the beginning of the 1990s. At this time India also witnessed the forceful rise of the Hindu right-wing movement. As the foremost schema was to formulate a national identity, Bollywood began showing a monolithic depiction of the nation undermining the diverse (gender-based, religious, and cultural) identities existing in that same nation. As a result, new changes could be noticed in the Bollywood cinematic space. To create a sense of national unity at the time of Hindutva nationalism, Bollywood filmmakers were inspired to formulate 'enemy images' of 'outsiders' who were set apart as 'others' using explicit 'political signs'. The 1990s likewise saw the ascent of movies which represented the category of terrorists. In the last two decades, Bollywood has also produced films that celebrate xenophobic rightwing ideology by representing an anti-Pakistan theme. In such films, the juxtaposition of Pakistani–terrorist–Muslim was loosely undertaken. This has been exacerbated by the fact that India and Pakistan have been engaged in many cross-border conflicts, such as in 1948, 1965, and 1971. The most violent of such conflicts was the Kargil War of 1999. Thus it is no coincidence that in the period between 1997 and 2007 Bollywood released a number of war films.

The Muslim Contemporary genre analyses Muslim characters in order to deconstruct them. The representation of Muslims in contemporary film narratives attempts to move away from formula-based stereotypical depictions of Muslims where the only two options to portray them were either as 'exotic' or as 'wicked' in relation to the nation-state. Interestingly, in this genre Muslims characters are not presented through the prism of religion. However, it has to be noted that although these Muslim characters are not shown as enemies of the state or as anti-nationals, they do have to prove their nationalism and demonstrate their patriotism, loyalty, and innocence in the course of the film. In these films, we find that Muslims are not presented through the prism of religion and they face day-to-day economic and social hurdles like other citizens. In most of these films, even the word 'Muslim' is not mentioned in relation to the characters.

Conclusion

In summary, Muslims have been an integral part of the Hindi film industry since its inception over a hundred years ago. The involvement of Muslims was also influenced by the political landscape of the nation. Though India has witnessed quite a few instances of political turmoil and those were reflected in the film text, the Bombay film industry has always adopted and sheltered people across all communities, especially Muslims. Hence, Muslims have been able to make an important contribution to the creation of many remarkable films. However, in the early history of Hindi cinema, Muslim culture was adopted more and the tradition of Muslim culture steadily slipped away from the cultural text of Bollywood cinema. In the Muslim Historic and Muslim Social genres, Muslim culture or Islamicate culture proved to be more predominant.

2

Muslim Historical Genre and Muslims in Historical Genre

From Diplomat Warriors to Barbarian Outsiders

Figure 2.1 From Diplomat Warrior (Hrithik in *Jodha Akbar*) to Barbarian (Ranveer in *Padmaavat*)

Source: Nadire Khatun; illustration by Sreeja Burman.

Postcolonial Bollywood and Muslim Identity. Nadira Khatun, Oxford University Press. © Oxford University Press 2024.
DOI: 10.1093/oso/9780198891017.003.0003

Muslim Historical films are a separate genre primarily because of their accounts of magnificent past legends and renowned personalities.[1] The recent genre of Historical films, on the contrary, represents Muslim rulers[2] through the prism of aggressive Hindu nationalist discourse. I shall examine the portrayal of Muslims in the Muslim Historical genre and shall map a sharp distinction between representations of Muslims in the earlier Muslim Historical genre and in the contemporary Historical films. Most of the Muslim Historical films in the post-Independence period (the 1950s and 1960s)—the so-called Nehruvian era—were based on secular Mughal rulers and focused on the exoticism of those rulers. The films in this genre and the participants in my empirical study hint that Muslims were positively stereotyped at this time. On the other hand, contemporary historical films, released after 2000, are inspired by iconic Muslim historical figures, myths, and events to create 'enemy images' of 'outsiders' who have been marked with specific 'radical signs'. Here I argue that by adopting an anti-Islamic stance, contemporary historical films in Bollywood have become a valuable tool for disseminating the idea of nationalism. The chapter shows how most recent Bollywood films such as *Bajirao Mastani* (2015), *Padmaavat* (2018), *Manikarnika: The Queen of Jhansi* (2019), *Panipat* (2019), *Kesari* (2019), and *Tanhaji* (2020) are suitably aligned with the saffronized version of historical narratives. These films adopt a right-wing political ideology to manufacture 'evil images' of Muslims as 'foreigners' and give currency to the idea of Hindu nationalism.

The recent Historical genre is considered to be the most significant one in terms of depiction of Muslims in Bollywood films. In film studies, period films are frequently debated because there is no particular

---

[1] This chapter draws on material previously published in Khatun, Nadira. (2018) 'Love-Jihad' and Bollywood: Constructing Muslims as 'Other'. *Journal of Religion and Film*, 22(3), pp. 1–36.

[2] Between the thirteenth to the seventeenth centuries, a number of Turko-Afghan invaders who happened to be Muslims largely conquered the Indian subcontinent. Delhi was the capital of several Turko-Afghan empires, including the Mamluk (1206–1290), Khalji (1290–1320), Tughlaq (1320–1414), Sayyid (1414–1451), and Lodhi (1451–1526). Turko-Mongol Muslim dynasties spread across the subcontinent, notably the Delhi Sultanate and Mughal India. Other Muslim states that governed the majority of South Asia from the middle of the fourteenth century until the end of the eighteenth centuries included the Bahmani Sultanate, Bengal Sultanate, Deccan Sultanates, Gujarat Sultanate, and Mysore Sultanate. Lane-Poole, S. (1896) *Aurangzib, and the Decay of the Mughal Empire (Vol. 5).* Clarendon Press.

iconography, context, and storyline typical to it, as is evident in genres such as thriller, comedy, drama, and mystery. Jonathan Stubbs writes, 'Simply being "in the past" cannot be regarded as a coherent textual characteristic in brief' (2013: 31). The Historical films are generally categorized as a genre mostly because of the narratives of the grandeur of historical legends, prominent figures, and myths. The films of this genre often celebrated nationalistic storylines in India. The Mauryan Empire[3] and the Maratha Empire[4] were the most commonly depicted in the initial years of Indian cinema. Shivaji Maharaj[5] (king) was glorified as a hero who battled against the Mughals invaders. *Poona Raided* (1924) represented the war between Marathas against Aurangzeb for trying to invade Poona (Dwyer, 2006). Afterwards, with the huge financial success of Sohrab Modi's *Pukar* (1939), Mughal kings and princes became the most admired and trendy figures in the Historical genre. Then we notably have the figure of Anarkali, who was glorified in a number of Hindi films in Bombay for sacrificing her life for the sake of her love for Prince Salim.[6] Jalal-Ud-Din Mohammad Akbar[7] was also frequently portrayed as a secular king and a great leader.

In this chapter I shall critically investigate the representation of Muslims in historical cinematic text in two categories: (1) Muslim Historical films from the 1950s to 2000s and (2) Muslims in Historical films from 2011 to 2019. I will also be connecting the narratives drawn from in-depth interviews with filmmakers, film critics, and audience

[3] The Mauryan Empire, based in Magadha, was founded by Chandragupta Maurya in 322 BCE, and it continued to function until 185 BCE. Dyson, Tim. (2018) *A Population History of India: From the First Modern People to the Present Day*, Oxford University Press, pp. 16–17.

[4] In the eighteenth century, the Maratha empire came to rule a large portion of the Indian subcontinent. When Shivaji was crowned Chhatrapati in 1674, Maratha rule formally began and because of the Maratha empire, Mughal rule over the Indian subcontinent was weakened. Duff, J.G., 1873. *A History of the Mahrattas. Published* at the Times of India Office.

[5] Shivaji Bhonsale, commonly known as Chhatrapati Shivaji Maharaj, was an Indian king and a descendant of the Bhonsle Maratha family (630–1680). Throughout his reign, Shivaji made alliances and fought in wars with the European colonial powers, the Sultanate of Bijapur, the Sultanate of Golkonda, and the Mughal Empire. Rajeshirke, A.B. (1981) Political and Economic Relations between the Portuguese and the Marathas (1630–1680). *In Proceedings of the Indian History Congress*, Indian History Congress, 42, pp. 233–240.

[6] The fourth Mughal Emperor, Nur-ud-Din Muhammad Salim (30 August 1569–28 October 1627), reigned from 1605 until his demise in 1627 and was known by his royal name Jahangir. Srivastava, S.P. (2001) *Jahangir, A Connoisseur of Mughal Art*. Abhinav Publications.

[7] The third Mughal emperor, Abu'l-Fath Jalal-ud-din Muhammad Akbar (1542–1605), usually known as Akbar the Great or just Akbar, ruled from 1556 until 1605. Smith, V.A. (1966) *Akbar the Great Mogul, 1542–1605*. Dalcassian Publishing Company.

members with those of the Muslim Historical film text to deconstruct the subliminal ideological message of those films. In this chapter the boundaries of analysis are limited to four major themes: (a) secular Mughal warriors and Islamicate culture; (b) enemy images as outsiders; (c) Bramhanical supremacy through historical films; and (d) gendering the politics of Hindu nationalism through historical films.

Secular Mughal Warriors and Islamicate Culture

During the 1940s, the films portrayed Muslim culture, sometimes known as 'Islamicate culture', which is essentially north Indian culture. The expression 'Islamicate culture' was articulated (in 1974) by Marshall Hodgson and Mukul Kesavan. According to them, the term 'Islamicate' does not refer to Islamic religion per se, 'but to the social and cultural complex historically associated with Islam and the Muslims, both among Muslims themselves and even when found among non-Muslims' (Hodgson and Kesavan, cited in Bhaskar and Allen, 2009: 3). The predominant cultural elements in films of the 1940s like language, sartorial choices, and music had a huge influence on Islamicate culture, with Hindus and Sikhs in north India following them as well. Apart from looking at this phenomenon, this section also focuses on the Historical films produced from the mid-1940s to 1990s such as *Humayun* (1945), *Shahjehan* (1946), *Baiju Bawra* (1952), *Anarkali* (1953), *Mirza Galib* (1954), *Mughal-e-Azam* (1960), *Taj Mahal* (1963), *Jahan Ara* (1964), *Noorjehan* (1967), *Taj Mahal: An Eternal Love Story* (2005), and *Jodha Akbar* (2008); the section will also interpret the trade and politics behind the production of such Muslim Historical films. I have explored the political and economic dimensions of filmmaking at that time, as most of the above-mentioned films were made shortly after Independence. It is crucial to understand the filmmakers' prevailing notions and how they were affected by state ideology. I interviewed filmmakers who belonged to the 1950s and 1960s and also filmmakers and film critics of the younger generation.

In India, Historical films became established as one of the oldest and most important film genres by the 1920s (Bhaskar and Allen, 2009). The genre started gaining popularity with the rise of the Indian freedom movement and the nationalist struggle. In the initial years, the Bombay film world mostly produced films based on the mythological kings of ancient India. *Raja Harishchandra* (1913), considered to be the first Indian feature film on the theme, was directed by Dhundiraj Govind Phalke, who later made films such as *Lanka Dahan* (1917), and *Sri Krishna Janam* (1918). Such films told the story of a 'glorious idealized past' that was culturally superior to counter the Western values represented by the British Raj in India.[8] In post-Independence India, during the Nehruvian era, 'Medieval history provided Hindi cinema with a perfect backdrop for nation-building narratives' (Merivirta, 2016: 5). During the Nehruvian era (1947–1964), 'most of these historical films always drew on the Congress Party's idea of history, and its heroes were those seen in Nehru's *Discovery of India* (1946), such as Akbar, rather than heroes of the Muslim community, such as Aurangzeb, Changhis Khan and Mahmud of Ghazni' (Dwyer, 2006: 116). That's how 'Islamic Empires', specifically the Mughal rulers, became the primary inspiration for the storylines and characterizations in the Muslim Historical genre. As most of the historical films of the period emphasized the Mughals as the heroes, the genre became a generalized imagination of Islamic culture, architecture, and so on and promoted the Nehruvian nation-building ideology of 'unity in diversity'. Muslim Historical films dwindled by the 1960s when the Nehruvian period came to an end.

As the narratives of the films focused more on inclusivity, it was reflected through the most syncretic among the medieval rulers. Further, most of these Muslim Historical films depicted the Mughal emperors as intellectual, secular, and revered for their effective governance. Until the 1950s and 1960s, secularism was one of the primary concerns in most films, and they demonstrated the unity of different religions primarily between Hindus and Muslims. Social activist and scholar Dr Ram Puniyani thinks filmmakers at that time were rooted in secular values:

In the earlier era, the scriptwriters were themselves deeply rooted in secular values. Films were trying to uphold the secular ethos and positive image of the communities. (Personal interview, 16 August 2012)

---

[8] See Sen, Titash. (N.D.) The Nationalism Gallery: An Interactive Timeline of Hindi Cinema, *Economic and Political Weekly: Engage.* Available at https://www.epw.in/engage/article/nationalism-gallery-interactive-timeline-hindi [Accessed 30 October 2022].

Much like Dr Ram Puniyani, other film scholars and intellectuals also think that filmmakers of that era were mostly influenced by the politics of the country in that period and the secular fabric of the state influenced them to write film narratives that expressed it. During a conversation, screenwriter Kamlesh Pandey conveyed his observation on the Historical film genre. He claimed that the secular orientation of filmmakers is more important than the politics of a country because the choice to propagate an ideology through films is ultimately taken by filmmakers. He says:

In the Nehruvian era, Muslim characters were portrayed as sane be-cause of the secular mindset of the common man. Above all, there were progressive movements, which included writers, artists, and employers who influenced filmmaking. Left ideology-inclined people were leaning towards progressive thoughts. That era was associated with progressive writers like Shahir, Akhtar, Kaifi Azmi, Majroo Sultanpuri, Aga Jani Kasmiri, Mojahed Moza, Ali Raza, Akhtar Ul Rehman, Aktar Mirza who were engaged in popular cinema. Thus, in popular cinema the Muslim character was portrayed as good. They were not coloured [by] any religious bias. (Personal interview, 29 March 2013)

Among all the Mughal rulers from the period of 1526 to 1757, the em-perors Akbar (reign 1556–1605), Jahangir (reign 1605–1627), and Shah Jahan (reign 1628–1658) are among the most celebrated protagon-ists of Muslim Historical films (Chakraborty, 1993). Filmmakers fre-quently 'presented the "Muslim period" as integral to Indian history, often presenting a composite religious culture as an ideal to be emu-lated' (Dwyer, 2006: 115). Ira Bhaskar and Richard Alan argue, 'In the post-Independence Nehruvian period, this rhetoric had a special signifi-cance in upholding the Mughal era and as a valuation of Muslim culture that marked the secular credentials of the new nation-state' (2009: 26). Nasreen Munni Kabir, a renowned television producer based in the UK and a renowned film historian, states;

There was culture, they were learned people and the *nawabs* and *shayers* or somebody who were able to speak so beautifully. They were charming people. They were integrated in this country. They were positively stereotyped. Because of their love stories of repression and grandeur, they were hugely appreciated by audiences. (Personal interview, 11 February 2013)

Most of these films can be placed into the category of historical fiction. K. Asif's 1960 classic *Mughal-E-Azam*, one of the all-time super hits with its latest reprint in 2004, featured Jodha Bai as the Hindu Rajput wife of Akbar. According to film scholar Sumita Chakravarty, Bollywood has never traditionally insisted on historical accuracies; neither did audiences of the post-Independence era question the historical accuracies of those historical film narratives (2011). History, Chakravarty further mentions, is 'an amalgam of mythical tales, legends, and folk knowledge rather than a search for the "truth" of past events and personages' (2011: 106). It is often argued that Indian films have not ever been particular about historical accuracy, as proved by several hit films of Bollywood. In continuation to this, Vir Sanghvi wrote in the *Hindustan Times*:

Nor have we insisted on historical accuracy in some of Hindi cinema's greatest hits. The late Prithviraj Kapoor made a terrific Alexander the Great in Sikander but the film had zero historical authenticity. Similarly, K. Asif's Mughal-e-Azam was more or less entirely made up (there's some doubt as to whether Anarkali even existed) but this was never an issue. So why are we insisting on historical authenticity now? Why should India be different from the rest of the world? And why should today's India have different standards from the India of a few decades ago? (Sanghvi, 2008)

As a result, a majority of the films of Muslim Historical genre represented fictional love affairs. This holds true even for later movies. Story-writer Haidar Ali of the epic film *Jodhaa Akbar* (2008) in a personal interview revealed his personal writing process for the story and script of the film and explained:

Akbar's love story is completely a fiction and the fact is that he [Akbar] married a princess called Jodha from Jaipur; she was Bharmal's daughter. This is the history. Akbar married a hundred queens, one of them was Jodha, but I wrote as if Jodha was his only wife. I just wanted to focus on the aspect that Akbar is marrying Jodha in spite of their religious and cultural differences. Actually, Jodha according to history was his third wife. (Personal interview, 5 April 2014)

The Nehruvian era was a time when the dominant philosophy of filmmakers was nation-building and encouraging secularism. There were also many filmmakers of leftist leanings and of a secular bent of mind. Kabir Khan, noted film director with films such as *New York* (2009), *Ek Tha Tiger* (2012) *Kabul Express* (2006), and *Bajrangi Bhaijaan* (2015), believes that mainstream cinema always stereotypes characters; but despite that fact producers of Muslim Historical films have attempted to portray Muslims characters as sensible and well-balanced. He points out:

> Mainstream cinema is always being stereotypical, cupboard character and the Muslim Historical is no exception. In the post-independence era, there was a conscious effort by filmmakers ... the social fabric of the country was torn apart by Partition and they attempted to show benevolent Muslims, the good Muslim. (Personal interview, 2 April 2013)

There are filmmakers and film critics who tackled the issue of Muslims being shown impartially in Muslim Historical films. In their imagination, Akbar portrays the picture of a secular ruler. We see a subtle shift from the earlier representation of Akbar when we consider the character in the last Muslim Historical film *Jodhaa Akbar* (2008). The Mughal emperor only becomes fully Indian by privileging the nation over faith within the narrative of the film. *Jodhaa Akbar* uses the strategy of the ideology of syncretism as 'Akbar is shorn of all oppositional elements: the proverbial Mughal bloodlust, the famed Muslim propensity for violence, and the forbidden pleasures of the flesh' (Mubarki, 2014: 262). He is subsumed into the nationalist order, and being nationalist, he indulges himself with the virtues of eating vegetarian food and practising monogamy and pacifism. Though, lest we forget, he is also represented as the 'Other' through his costume and language. But the focus, though he is portrayed as the Other, is on the fact that he is still assimilable; he does not carry an enemy image and his secular nature conforms to the Hindutva ideology which silently propagates that Muslims can stay in the country till the time they accept majoritarian practices.

In the Muslim Historical genre, through representing them as kings and *nawabs*, Muslims were portrayed from a single point of view and the characterization was often heavily romanticized. Therefore, Muslims became stereotyped in their portrayal. Noted film critic Nandini Ramnath observes:

> So, Islamicate culture, I think those movies gave space to a certain kind of Muslim expression. It is highly romanticized and poetic. My reading of it is—you are also trying to create an ideal Muslim citizen, the culture of Muslim, the one who is beautiful looking; who loves beauty; who loves beautiful houses and jewellery and clothes, all of which forms the image of Awadhi Muslims. But there are other kinds of Muslims in the country and I think very few movies are actually reflective of those other cultures. (Personal interview, 5 February 2013)

The highly romanticized and idealized world of Muslims was posturized through significant elements such as Muslim ethos, Islamic costume, and Ganga–Jamuna Tehzeeb. The Muslim ethos is a philosophy that goes back to the 1930s and is valid until the present day. It is a blend of Arabic, Turkish, and Persian influences. Iqbal Masud, a well-known film critic, points out, 'Classical or high culture [is] a mix of Arabic-Perso-Turkish elements in Historical work, fiction, music, and painting such as in the work of poets and novelists like Ghalib (or today Mr Qurratulain Hyder), artists like Abdur Rehman Chaudhtai, or ustads in the field of music' (Masud, 2005). Muslim ethos had huge influence on the Muslim Historical genre in terms of dictating its architecture, dress, language, and music.

The Urdu language, as mentioned in the previous chapter, is always associated to Muslims as an essential part of the Muslim ethos. It is often also employed to cater to the demand of the demarcation based on religion due to contemporary politics of the country. That's why we notice that Jodha Bai's character in classic film *Mughal-e-Azam* (1960) speaks a language which is a mixture of Hindi and Urdu but in the more recent *Jodhaa Akbar* she speaks pure Sanskritized Hindi. Noticing the contrast, I argue, here the cultural text is utilized to create the image of an outsider; Indian Hindus are not accommodative in that cultural milieu and to prove their superiority, they maintain a sharp cultural distinction from Muslims. The scriptwriter of *Jodhaa Akbar*, Haider Ali, points out:

> Akbar's family spoke in Urdu. They had to speak in Urdu because they came from Mongol and adapted a hybrid language of Persian, Arabic and Sanskrit to communicate with local people. Gradually, that mixed language was known as Urdu. (Personal interview, 5 April 2014)

While there is no distinct Muslim music genre in India, Sufi music is widely identified with Islamicate culture, much like the Urdu language. Hyder Ali explains why he chose the song 'Khwaja Mere Khwaja' (Noble Khwaja) for the wedding night scene in *Jodhaa Akbar*.

> I have the dilemma of Jodha on cultural differences throughout the films. Whenever Akbar had to take decisions, he used to go to Ajmer and used to do a lot of meditation. He was also yogi, very spiritual. He was not getting the comfort of making a decision. He went against the decision and came back to Agra. In every mazar, Sufi saints come and prey. At that time, a Turkish qawali group came to [the] mazar and they came to know of Akbar's dilemma. So to help the king to make a decision, they sang the song Khawja Mere Khawja. (Personal interview, 5 May 2014)

However, the purpose of making Muslim Historical films has been questioned numerous times. Despite the fact that the Muslim Historical was based on the love stories of emperors and *nawabs* who were not deliberately depicted as Muslims; the characters just turned out to be Muslims. Irfan Engineer, a well-known academic and social activist, says:

> Historical films mix history with imagined love affairs. Whether it happened that way, whether it happened at all or not, these are different things. But they were not actually portraying Muslims per se … they were portraying rulers … Indian rulers. Historical figures who happened to be Muslims. (Personal interview, 14 September 2012)

Moreover, on the one hand, some critics believe that Muslim Historical films were written for political or ideological purposes. On the other hand, there are others who believe that the films were made for solely commercial purposes—Muslim Historical films were more commercially viable than other genres at the time, so filmmakers made them. Rauf Ahmed, a well-known film critic and former editor of publications such as *Filmfare, Screen*, and *Zee Premiere*, said:

> All Anarkalis [films that portrayed Anarkali as an important protagonist] are big hits. *Anarkali* (1953) was a hit, later *Taj Mahal* (1963) was a hit, and most importantly *Mughal-e-Azam* was a blockbuster. (Personal interview, 28 August 2013)

Nasreen Munni Kabir echoed the sentiment:

> You can't say that in the Nehruvian era filmmakers wanted to represent Muslims as good and sensible persons. If a film makes money, Indian filmmakers copy the theme of the film any time and they will make four identical films. *Anarkali* (1953) did so well, so filmmakers started putting Ananrkali characters in many subsequent films like Taj Mahal (1963). I don't think it is wilful to represent Muslims as good in Muslim stories. (Personal interview, 11 February 2013)

Connecting to what Nasreen Munni Kabir pointed out, we need to look into the political economy of the genre apart from the ideological stand of the filmmakers. There are also commercial and political facets of such depictions, in addition to entertainment.

While there was a surge in demand for Muslim historical films in the 1950s and 1960s, demand for the genre started to steadily decline from the 1970s. It is important to look at the genre's demise objectively. I attempted to comprehend the filmmakers' point of view. In connection to that, when asked about the possible reasons of the fading away of the Muslim Historical, filmmaker Mahesh Bhatt ascribed the reason to Nehru losing power over the years. He says:

> Nehru lost his clout post [the] Chinese debacle in 1962. The fact was Congress had always had this problem of bigots within its own home rather than outside. So, when he was losing his own control, we saw slowly the death of Urdu and that kind of Muslim ethos. (Personal interview, 31 March 2014)

Haider Ali recounts a significant explanation for the collapse in depiction of the Muslim Historical genre. He believes one of the most significant reasons is commerce since any historical genre requires a large amount of finance to complete production. He used references to demonstrate how certain film production firms shut down following a single film's failure.

> Muslim Historical needs a big budget and needs a big canvas. So, the historical films demand a lot of economic investments to represent everything magnificent. Thus, if you are losing money, it's a lot of money. Companies began closing down not only because of Muslim Historical, but also because of the whole historical genre. *Jhashi ki Rani* (1953) flopped; Shorab Modi's company had to close down. Before that he made many historicals and they were big hits, for example *Pukar* (1939) and *Sikandar* (1941). For only one film he had to close down his production company. Vinod Kumar made a film called *Jahan Ara*, it flopped and the company closed. That's why after *Razia Sultan* (1983), nobody dares to make the historical film. Ashutosh Gowarikar did make *Jodhaa Akbar* (2008), not because of its history, rather to represent the unity between Hindus and Muslims. (Personal interview, 5 April 2014)

On the contrary, filmmaker Kamlesh Pandey disregarded the money aspect of filmmaking and mentioned that a potential cause might be a lack of talent. He claims:

> It is not easy to make a *Mughal-e-Azam*. It's not just the money, it's the kind of artists and actors. How can you get the same talented actors like Prithviraj Kapoor, Dilip Kumar, and Madhubala? (Personal interview, 29 March 2013)

Although the Muslim Historical genre has been almost unexplored in recent years, and the genre is mostly associated with the post-Independence era, some filmmakers remain intrigued by the historical subject. When asked why he makes historical films often, Ashutosh Gowrikar, the director of *Jodhaa Akbar* (2008), said:

> I don't know actually. Somehow, I am very fascinated with history. (Personal interview, 22 August 2013)

Apart from Mughal kings, a few Muslim Historical films exist where Arabian fantasy is a common theme. There are a number of films which were based on *The Arabian Nights* and were made during the silent period and before Independence, and many of them dealt with legendary tales such as *Laila–Majnu* (1922 and 1927), *Bulbul-e-Paristan* (1926), *Hatim Tai* (1927), *Alibaba and the Forty Thieves* (1927), and *Shirin–Farhad* (1931). *Alam Ara* (1931), India's first talkie, was based on an Arabian fantasy. Apart from the fact that these films were set in the Muslim world, they were not at all Islamic. Mahesh Bhatt recalls:

> My father Nanabhai Bhatt made more than a hundred films and he used to make so many Arabian Night fantasies. Muslims in those movies were dressed in very exotic attire. (Personal interview, 31 March 2014)

Over the last decades, representations of Muslims have changed in Bollywood films. When we analyse Historical films we find that Muslim protagonists have played important roles in them but this needs careful examination. Therefore, in the following section, I deliberate the mechanics of portrayals of Muslims in recent Historical films released in the last decade.

Enemy Images as Outsiders

Though with regards to the Muslim Historical genre, Ira Bhaskar and Richard Alan indicate that 'in the post-independence Nehruvian period, this rhetoric had a special significance in upholding the Mughal era and as a valuation of Muslim culture that marked the secular credentials of the new nation-state' (2009: 26), in the setting of the present-day political scenario, we find that contemporary Historical films present a different rhetoric than in the past. Cinema has always from its early history worked closely to align itself with state ideology; in this regard film scholar M. Madhava Prasad writes, 'The cinematic apparatus, i.e. the combination of image and spectator was, consciously or unconsciously, figured as a microcosm of the future nation-state' (1998: 123). In the last decade, Historical films of the Bombay film industry have become one of the most important platforms in projecting certain ideological dialogues such as communalism, nationalism, and secularism. Bollywood has made a concerted effort to reframe the Historical genre to include the re-interpretation and veneration of a glorious Hindu nationalist history. It is also worth noting that the Supreme Court of India's long-awaited Ayodhya Ram Janmabhumi verdict was followed by the government's repeal of Article 370 of the Constitution, which allowed special privileges and status to Kashmir, India's sole Muslim majority territory. The NDA (National Democratic Alliance) government has also introduced in Parliament the Citizenship Amendment Bill and Citizenship Amendment Act (CAA). As a consequence, there has been a long-running national outbreak of mass demonstrations, as well as a string of unfortunate assaults on residents, communal riots, and arrests of civil society members and student demonstrators who have been at the frontline of anti-CAA protests. The Citizenship Amendment Bill proposes to provide citizenship to marginalized religious minorities such as Hindus, Jains, Sikhs, Parsis, Buddhists, and Christians except Muslims from Bangladesh, Pakistan, and Afghanistan. While the debate of 'insider' and 'outsider' continues to be at its peak in the Indian political sphere, fuelling the discourse a number of Bollywood Historical films construct Muslim identity as 'Outsiders'.

The most well known of such films released in the last decade are *Bajiro Mastani* (2015), *Padmaavat* (2018), *Manikarnika: The Queen of Jhansi* (2019), *Paanipat* (2019), *Kesari* (2020), *and Tanhaji* (2020) (Sharma, 2020). These films construct an imaginary notion of the past in the light of the contemporary sociopolitical situation. As Islam plays an important role in contemporary Indian religious politics, it is also reflected in Indian Bollywood cinema. Most recently, in the Historical genre, these films are characterized by their exoticization of the 'Other', who are the 'invading barbarian' and 'enemy of the nation'. In this section, I shall examine the mechanisms of alienation and 'Otherization' embedded in contemporary Bollywood period drama. From the 1970s to the mid-2000s, there were a few films which could be classified under the Historical film genre; in the last decade Muslims have started reappearing in the Historical genre as barbaric outsiders. I argue that the sudden disappearance and reappearance of Muslims in the Historical genre—with the latter utilizing Muslim figures handpicked from medieval history of little similarity to the historical myths they seek to depict—are a reflection of public perception regarding Indian Muslims today using historical tropes. Therefore, I consider the Historical genre to be a well-established phenomenon that fuels the current political landscape of India itself. As history-making is always a retrospective fact-generation process, it is more often than not biased. In the process, one of the Mughal rulers, Aurangzeb, was always tagged as a bad orthodox ruler. Regarding this, Sitara Shabnam (name changed), a sociologist and academician mentions:

> Aurangzeb is created as an ideal picture of a villain who has all the negative traits, which are again a problematic construct. There are a number of scholarly works being done which says that Aurangzeb's image has been very distorted. Even if this distortion happened long back before the Hindutva thing came in, even if the standard history book we are following belongs to the so-called secular period, the portrayal of him is distorted. The distortion of history has been part of larger, longer lineage than the Hindutva regime. (Personal interview, 31 July 2020)

The films mentioned earlier are located in medieval India, which is commonly recognized by British colonial historians as 'an era of "Islamic despotism"' (Roy, 2018: 1). They depicted this period as a dark and depressing one, marked by the alleged tyranny of Delhi-based Islamic emperors. Underlying this depiction was Victorian England's anti-Islamic prejudice, which intensified in the course of the nineteenth century as British imperial powers clashed with Islamic regimes in parts of Asia (Beckerlegge, 1997). Historian Baijayanti Roy thinks such historians are likely to present Hindus as compassionate and peaceful, doomed to be subjected to persecution by 'Muslim despots' for decades until they were 'saved' by the British colonizers. These colonial historians narrate the conflicts of some regional groups such as the Rajputs and the Marathas against the centralized power of the Islamic (Mughal) emperors located in Delhi during the mediaeval era and tag them as incidents of Hindu nationalist opposition to Islamic rule, while ignoring the fact that such resistances were motivated predominantly by political and territorial aspirations (Roy, 2018). Unfortunately, in multiple cases, the consumers of these films start believing that the onscreen narratives of religious nationalism are based on fact. Connecting to that, when I asked an audience about her point of view on Alauddin Khalji in the film *Padmaavat*, without realizing that the film is entirely fictional, she connected the image of Khalji—what she has read in her history book—with the silver screen portrayal of him. Sunita Misra, an entrepreneur, says:

> I liked Khalji's character and I also find similarities [in] the way we read about him in our history book. I got resemblances in terms of his violent nature, barbarism. After watching the film, I immediately remember my childhood. (Personal interview, 28 July 2020)

Scholar and historian Urvi Mukhopadhyay mentions in her book *The 'Medieval' in Film: Representing a Contested Time on Indian Screen (1920s–1960s)* that during the nineteenth century, these perspectives of precolonial history were conveyed among the English-educated Indian elite. By the end of the nineteenth century, these elite classes were imbued with nationalist ideologies, consisting primarily of Hindu upper caste/class men. This nationalist explanation of India's medieval 'Islamic' history was echoed through mainstream popular culture, literature, and theatre for a non-elite, mainstream audience. Novels and dramas designed to instil widespread nationalism also portrayed acts of regional Hindu rebellion against centralized Muslim rule as stand-ins for anticolonial feelings as the colonial state clamped down on freedom of speech through the Vernacular Press Act of 1876. The Historical film in India was a continuation of these past literatures, cinematic and visual viewpoints. In post-Independence India, cinema, especially Bombay Hindi cinema, or Bollywood became the primary medium of popular culture mediator of the newly established nation's national consciousness (Mukhopadhyay, 2013) and the relation between politics and cinema has been implicit. That's the reason that after Independence, Bombay cinema has always tried to match up the ideologies of the state or ruling political parties. Therefore, to align with the contemporary saffronized political discourse, Bollywood has started representing extreme political stances by presenting some selective Islamic rulers from the medieval period. Historical genre supports filmmakers to bring up contemporary beliefs while eliciting the legends of the past. As a result, the stories of contemporary Historical films are based on Indian kings (mainly Hindu) struggling against some foreign ruler (mainly Muslims). Dr Kaifiya Fatehma (name changed), a doctor and blogger, points out:

These historical films are creating a narrative in the younger minds that Muslims are the invaders, outsiders who caused huge damage to our culture, heritage, they destroyed our temples, looted us, taxed us. The portrayal got changed, they are no more portrayed as someone who did something positive to the country, they contributed to the nation and nobody is questioning that. These cultural texts have become opium, people are just consuming it. (Personal interview, 30 January 2021)

The joint general secretary of the Rashtriya Swayamsevak Sangh,[9] Krishna Gopal, spoke with a group of Muslim professionals in Delhi's Nehru Memorial Museum and Library before the Supreme Court's decision on the Babri Masjid-Ram Janmabhoomi dispute. There he said: 'There came a phase in our history when outsiders destroyed this country's temples' (Tantray, 2019). When the present-day historical films represent Muslims as 'Historic outsiders', it reinforces the right-wing political narrative explicit in Gopal's comments. Therefore, even in the contemporary period, these arguably obsolete depictions of historical events are 'revived' and represented on screen to construct the saffronized version of history. These films promote a homogenized image of righteous Hindu rulers by juxtaposing them with fanatical, barbaric Muslim invaders, erasing the complexities of medieval politics. But audiences believe the Bollywood representation of the medieval past as the 'true' history of India. Let us look at the example of *Bajirao Mastani* (2015). The story was inspired by a Marathi novel *Raau* by Nagnath S. Inamdar, based on the life of the legendary warrior 'Peshwe Bajirao' and his second wife 'Mastani'. The film provides a disclaimer about the authenticity of facts depicted and mentions, 'This film, though made in consultation with eminent historians does not warrant represent or claim to be historically accurate' (quote from *Bajirao Mastani*, 2015). There are several novels which romanticize the relationship between the Marathi ruler and the Iranian prince, but very little authenticity can be vouched for regarding their marriage. When asked about his opinion on the negative image and representation

---

[9] The Rashtriya Swayamsevak Sangh (RSS), 'presents itself as a cultural, not a political, organization that nevertheless advocates a Hindu nationalistic agenda under the banner of Hindutva, or "Hinduness"'. The Editors of Encyclopaedia Britannica (2022), Rashtriya Swayamsevak Sangh. *Encyclopædia Britannica*. Available at https://www.britannica.com/topic/Rashtriya-Swayamsevak-Sangh [Accessed 29 October 2022].

of medieval Muslim invaders, one of my research participants, Sourabh Agarwal, who is an undergraduate student, seems to think that the filmmakers are correctly portraying Muslim characters as negative because that is how they were even historically:

> A lot of filmmakers stress upon some religious symbols but it's their job to portray historical events or characters correctly. Therefore, I am very much indifferent about the religious overtones attached to those texts. One can't portray, 'Akbar: The Great' as 'Raju: The Chayewala' right? (Personal interview, 3 October 2020)

Though Historical films claim that they create a space to reimagine the past, we must also admit that the makers of these films prop up their representations on today's perceptions while recreating past legends. They are creating a space within a space. In the broader spectrum of the Historical film genre, these films utilize the contemporary sociopolitical issues to gain acceptance in the current political climate. Here Michel Foucault's concept of 'heterotopia' can be utilized as a critical lens to argue how the film *Tanhaji* is proving heterotopia by valorizing the glorious Maratha history and demonizing medieval Muslim rulers. Therefore, these films are more about our contemporary times rather than about the past. That these films coincide heavily with current political narratives can be shown through the example of the film *Tanhaji* (2020). Ajay Devgn, who portrays the role of the protagonist of the film, started promoting the film by uploading the trailer on Twitter, writing '4th Feb 1670: The surgical strike that shook the Mughal Empire!' The expression 'surgical strike' gained special currency after the Indian military intervention against Pakistan in 2016 and has since then entered the public vocabulary. Though it is a very new term for a military tactic, audiences were led to believe, and accepted, that operations like surgical strikes shown in the film were actually conducted in the Mughal era. Schoolteacher Pushpanjali Rath, one of the participants, points out in a conversation:

> I liked the way they have strategized and planned the war. From the film, we get to know that such kind of planning was done even in those eras. We come to know so many things about the history as well. We

don't get that account of history from anywhere else. (Personal interview, 1 October 2020)

The trailer of Ashutosh Gowarikar's *Panipat: The Great Betrayal* was released on 4 November 2019 and the film came out on 6 December 2019, the day Babri Masjid was destroyed in 1992. It would be hard to believe that the film's release date is a coincidence. The prevailing political climate at that time also gives us pause. Lok Sabha elections were due in 2019, and Amit Shah, the present home minister of the country and president of the Bharatiya Janata Party (BJP), 'equated the upcoming general elections with the third battle of Panipat between the Marathas and Afghan King Ahmed Shah Abdali. The defeat of the Marathas led to India facing "slavery" for 200 years', Shah added. Until then, they had won 131 battles, he pointed out, but lost the decisive one' (HT Correspondent. 2019). Prior to the 2019 Lok Sabha elections, Amit Shah used the rhetoric of 'the great betrayal', which was also the subtext of Gowarikar's film; Shah likened the upcoming polls to the battle of Panipat, which this time could not be lost.

As these Historical films use legends of the past but represent them in the present-day sociopolitical context, I argue that the discourse of contemporary 'Hindu *rastra*' is propagated in these films through the ideology of 'Hindu Swaraj'. The entire trope of portraying Mughals as well as Islam as outsiders was invoked explicitly through the cultural politics evident in the opening credits of *Bajirao Mastani*. In it we see South Asian borders being delineated by the European imperial powers and their definitions of the territorial state being applied. In the opening credits, Bajirao (Ranveer Singh) is shown on horseback leading his troops, the voiceover narrating that the sword of the Peshwa was like lightning, his willpower was like the Himalayas, his presence embodied the strength of the Brahmins of Chitpavan (the caste group to which the Peshwas belonged) and his vision was to hoist the Maratha flag in Delhi. Later, Bajirao delivers an inspirational speech to his army to motivate them and says, '*Apni dharti apna raj, Chhatrapati Shivaji ka ek hi sapna–Hindu Swaraj*'. The accompanying graphics illustrate a map showing a map of the growing Maratha confederacy and labels the area as 'Hindustan', a Persian expression meaning 'Land of Indus' (Figure 2.2).

Figure 2.2 *Bajirao Mastani*: An imaginary territorial boundary
Source: Nadira Khatun; illustration by Saptarshi Kundu.

Several historians (Laine, 2003; Pansare, 2018), however, claim that Shivaji was never a religious extremist as represented in the Hindutva discourse; rather 'he was a secular king with several Muslims serving under him and never called for a Hindu Swaraj, but a "Hindavi Swaraj"—self-rule of Indian people' (Athavale, 2019). The erroneous religious undertone ascribed to Shivaji's rule is conspicuous when Bajirao[10] says: '*Ek Hindu raaja dusre Hindu raja ki madat karne jaa raha hai*' ('A Hindu ruler to support another Hindu king'), because he chooses to stand up for Maharaja Chhatrasal in the film. Bajirao led numerous conquests in the eighteenth century against the neighbouring kingdoms—particularly the Mughal kingdom; his decision to join the conflict on the side of Maharaja Chhatrasal was not a fight to protect the Hindu religion or for 'Hindu Swaraj' but for the Maratha kingdom's intention to take over every adjacent nation. It's crucial to remember that there was no such thing as defined geo-political territory of 'India' back then. During this time period the Marathas struggled for an all-inclusive Maratha kingdom. Here I argue that the fights, struggles, and battles in the medieval period were not for saving a religion or 'Indian' territory, rather it was for the acquisition of power through territorial domination.

---

[10] The Maratha Empire's seventh Peshwa, Baji Rao I (1700–1740), ruled from 1700 to 1740. During his 20-year reign as a Peshwa, he defeated the Mughals and their subordinate Nizam-ul-Mulk in numerous engagements, including the Battle of Delhi and the Battle of Bhopal. Chhabra, G.S., 2005. *Advance Study in the History of Modern India* (Volume 2: 1803–1920) (Vol. 2). Lotus Press.

Similarly in *Padmaavat* (2018), the binary of 'good' and 'evil' was established on the religious lines. The representation of Alauddin Khalji as the outsider is complete in Padmaavat as he is shown asserting his connection with and tracing his ancestry to Afghanistan. To drive home the point even further, the film begins with a shot of a fort in the middle of a desert and the *mise en scène* of the world inside the fort represents the lifestyle of Alauddin's paternal uncle and the founder of the Khalji dynasty, Sultan Jalaluddin Khalji. He is shown as nonchalantly relaxing in the midst of a huge heap of meat, and is being chastised by his fellow mates because of his excesses. The film pits against the outsiders the great, brave, and virtuous Hindus like Rawal Ratan Singh, a noble Indian Rajput king. The Rajput glory he is shown as upholding is reflected through the extravagance of his costumes. On the other hand, the ambitious and obsessive Alauddin Khalji is attributed a dark and ominous look because of his background as a nomadic Turkish tribal invader. Khalji's character became a perfect counterfoil to Rawal Ratan Singh through the use of dark-coloured clothes and by the depiction of a diametrically opposite lifestyle: the depraved and despotic Khalji is shown surrounded by women all the time and displayed an excessive appetite for meat (Figure 2.3).

The culture of showing the enemy in sexualized terms has been theorized by Joane Nagel. She writes, 'Accounts of many wars and nationalist

Figure 2.3 *Padmaavat*: Khilji's love for meat and his barbaric attitude
Source: Nadira Khatun; illustration by Sreeja Burman.

conflicts include portrayals of enemy men either as sexual demons, bent on raping nationalist women, or as sexual eunuchs, incapable of manly virility' (Nagel, 1998: 257). Moreover, in spite of claiming that the epic poem of Sufi poet Malik Muhammad Jayasi, penned in 1540, acted as the inspiration for the movie, we find that the narrative is changed to suit right-wing political ideology. According to the sixteenth-century poem, Ratan Singh was killed by Devpal, the ruler of Kumbhalner, and not by Khalji. Khalji's negative stereotyping in the film became a source of entertainment for the audience. He became one of the most recognized and appreciated villainous characters in recent times. Pushpanjali Rath points out:

> The entry of Ranveer Singh's (Allauddin Khalji) character with the ostrich was awesome. His character was completely overwhelming, the way he looked and depicted his character. I liked his dirty look. (Personal interview, 1 October 2020)

We learn from historical records that despite being an iconoclast and an expansionist, Khalji was a sophisticated speaker of Persian, who streamlined the economy of the Delhi Sultanate and is credited with having been the patron of the invention of two key instruments of Hindustani classical music, the tabla and the sitar. But the film never focuses on these positive aspects. Khalji is reduced to being the perfect example of a meat-eater, sexually depraved, and despotic Muslim invader. Kaifiya Fatehma points out:

> Now we have films which represent Khalji as a monster, even the way he looks, the way he talks, the way he eats, really very negative. Nobody felt bad about Khalji's portrayal, they just enjoyed it. At present, there are five to six such historical movies, all based on Muslim characters as villains. They are not just villains who are supposedly to be hated but a monstrous representation of the characters. And villains who are not targeting individual people rather are targeting the whole community or the whole country. (Personal interview, 30 January 2021)

On similar lines, *Panipat* portrays the third confrontation at Panipat as the battle to protect India from foreign aggression. In the film, both the major Muslim characters are introduced with some negative notes tagged. Najib ad-Dawlah[11] is a defaulter and owes the most tax revenue to the Maratha king, Shivaji. When he was asked to pay, the shrewd Najib is seen being adamant about teaching the Marathas a lesson. Najib establishes an alliance with Ahmad Shah Abdali (Sanjay Dutt), the founder of the Durrani Empire (considered the forefather of modern-day Afghanistan), and welcomes him to Delhi. In the very first scene where Abdali is introduced, he is shown crushing the head of a man who has tried to betray him. The cruel and violent nature of Abdali is thus introduced very deliberately to generate a specific reaction from the viewers. Muslims are seen in general in the film as grim, evil, and plotting takeovers—not only Ahmad Shah Abdali but also Najib ad-Dawlah as opposed to the uber-macho young Marathas who are desperate to save India. It bears repetition here that the Marathas went to war to acquire territories and political influence and not to keep their 'homeland' from the clutches of 'Muslim foreigners'. But in the film, to emphasize the fact that the war was mostly to defend the homeland, we find the mother of Sadashiv Rao Bhau[12] (played by Arjun Kapoor) inspiring her son saying, '*Iss baar Abdali ko aisa sabak sikhao ki woh Hindustan ki taraf dekhne ki himmat bhi na kare*' ('Teach Abdali a lesson that will prevent him from even daring to glance in the vicinity of India'). In response, in order to prove his patriotism, Sadashiv Rao utters the following dialogue: '*Mai iss dharti ki mitti ke ek kan ke liye bhi marne ko tayyar hun*' ('Even a single grain of the earth from my motherland is worth my life'). The narrative devices and tropes of the film are clearly aligned to contemporary political rhetoric. Northern Indian territories were not even the homeland of Marathas as they wanted to have their own nation through the establishment of the Maratha empire; they were primarily fighting for control over the fertile land of Punjab and not to drive away Afghan 'outsiders'. When I asked Sourabh

---

[11] Najib ad-Dawlah Najib ad-Dawlah was an Afghan named Rohilla Yousafzai who had previously served as a Mughal soldier but later left the Mughals and fought alongside Ahmed Shah Abdali in his attack on Delhi in 1757. He played a crucial role in the Third Battle of Panipat's success. Nag, A. (2020) Panipat. *Journal of Islamic and Muslim Studies*, 5(1), pp. 131–140.

[12] While Maratha Emperor Chhatrapati Rajaram II was in power, Sadashiv Rao Bhau served as minister of finance. The Maratha army was under his command during the Third Battle of Panipat.

Agarwal about his views on the Bollywood's depiction of the enemy in such Historical films, he says:

> They are mostly the looters from outside, basically the people who come to loot the country, create chaos from outside and tries to take advantage basically. (Personal interview, 3 October 2020)

The film *Tanhaji* is a true account of the victory of the Marathas against Udaybhan Rathod, the keeper of a Rajput fort under Maharaja Jai Singh (a senior general of the Mughal army). In 1665, Shivaji was mandated by the Treaty of Purandar to give up to the Mughals the highly defended and strategically situated Maratha fort of Kondhana. The notion of the Mughals possessing the fort infuriated Shivaji's mother, Jijabai, who pleaded with her son and his army to reclaim it. As a result, Shivaji assigned Tanhaji the task of reconquering Kondhana Fort. The storyline of the film produces a high-pitched nationalistic tone as Tanhaji is depicted as fighting to protect the Maratha kingdom as well as saving the country from the outsiders like Mughals. Some audience members liked the film only because of Tanhaji's character and his loyalty to his motherland and master. Pushpanjali Rath speaks emotionally on the topic:

> I liked the film *Tanhaji* because of Ajay Devgn's (who plays Tanhaji) loyalty towards Shivaji (the King). The way the film shows that how someone can sacrifice himself for his motherland and for his king, it shows his loyalty towards his emperor, everything was shown very nicely. (Personal interview, 1 October 2020)

The film portrays both the protagonist and antagonist as Hindus but the protagonist Tanhaji appears noticeably more Hindu with a *tilak* (a mark of different colours worn on the forehead mostly by the people who belong to Hindu religion), while Udaybhan, the antagonist, is made to carry a stereotypical image of a Muslim, with a beard and kohl in his eyes, attired in black clothes. Moreover, Udaybhan's character inhabits an ambience that is dark and shaded. The characterization and the ambience are very similar to those that we are accustomed to see for stereotypical Muslim characters on-screen. We can only assume that this association has been made because Udaybhan Rathod, Rajput general of Mughal emperor Aurangzeb, was fighting on the side of an Islamic ruler.

Like *Bajirao Mastani, Panipat,* and *Padmavaat,* the 2019 biopic *Manikarnika: The Queen of Jhansi* is about Rani Lakshmi Bai, an Indian queen who fought and was martyred in the First War of Indian Independence against the British colonial army in 1857. Much like other films mentioned earlier, this film too takes the stance of hyper-nationalism by reaffirming a geographical boundary of India. It upholds a civilization that inhabits a prosperous country with a rich culture and traditions; this film also marks clearly a superior Indian culture to align with discourse of Hindutva and the brand of nationalism perpetuated by it. The benevolent nature of the Hindus who are the natives of this country is well-established in the opening scene, which shows an Indian map and some clips of Indian landscape. An accompanying voiceover claims, 'India, a civilisation, rich in culture, and with an innate zest for life, a prosperous country, always welcoming visitors [outsiders] with open arms. But those visitors harboured cruel intentions.' The reference here is obviously to the British as invaders and outsiders who are cruel, inhuman, and whose only intention is to loot and hoard wealth. On the other hand, having internalized the benevolent Indian culture, Manikarnika has so much compassion that she doesn't even kill an animal, let alone other human beings. Though the main plot of the film does not directly align with the contemporary right-wing political discourse of religious nationalism, hyper-nationalism is well established through sub-plots. In the rise of Islamophobic politics disguised as cow protection and vegetarianism in contemporary India, these sentiments are echoed. Dr Kaifiya Fatehma echoed a similar opinion:

Even when the film has no Muslim character but still subtly it sends some message across when the protagonists are talking about non-veg food, it's been seen as something dirty, unclean, something that has not been encouraged rather looked down upon. Almost all the Muslims are non-vegetarians, so either it does openly or subtly in both the cases, these films try to vilify Muslims to a large extent. (Personal interview, 30 January 2021)

One of the most effective tactics of the Sangh Parivar is the use of the cow as a symbol of a holy and worshipped figure among Hindus. Thus, that the consumption of beef is an abhorrent act is a fact that has been ingrained in people's minds. People who eat beef are automatically labelled as 'outcasts' and 'misfits'. As the cow was associated with Lord Krishna it attained the status of a 'sacred' animal. Professor D.N. Jha (2002) wrote in his book *The Myth of a Holy Cow*:

> But the holiness of the cow is elusive. For there has never been a cow-goddess, nor any temple in her honour. Nevertheless the veneration of this animal has come to be viewed as a characteristic trait of modern-day non-existent monolithic 'Hinduism' bandied about by the Hindutva forces. (146)

Amidst the massive hue and cry and in the sociopolitical unrest relating to cow slaughter and beef-eating, there are a number of Muslim men who were lynched and killed because they were suspected of either carrying beef or consuming it. In the right-wing discourse, beef-eaters are tagged as 'Pakistanis', 'anti-nationals' and the term has turned into a slur. According to News of Hindustan Times, '86% killed in cow-related violence since 2010 are Muslim, 97% attacks after Modi govt came to power' (Abraham and Rao, 2017). These lynchings and attacks have been aimed at Muslims, who have been targeted because of rumours that they consume beef. Although several cases of mob lynching were reported from across the nation, there was initially no state intervention to tackle the matter (Khatun, 2020). At this critical time, the film included an intense scene where a calf is captured by British troops to slaughter for meat. Rani Lakshmi Bai rescues the calf and says: 'Respect the culture of the people and the values of the land you are standing on.' Moreover, the film's plot is rooted in Hindutva propaganda surrounding the holy worship and protection of the cow. In its effort to support the creation of a Hindu *rashtra* by using the story of Rani Lakshmi Bai, the film's plot totally disregards her alliance with the last Mughal emperor, Bahadur Shah Zafar II.[13]

---

[13] Bahadur Shah Zafar II was an Urdu poet in addition to being the twentieth and final Mughal Emperor. He was merely the nominal Emperor because the Mughal Empire only existed in name and his jurisdiction only extended to city of Old Delhi. The British deported him to Rangoon in British-controlled Burma in 1858 after convicting him of multiple charges stemming from

Actually, Indian freedom fighters fought in 1857 to reclaim the throne of the Mughal emperor;[14] rather than addressing this historical reality and upholding the vibrant sign of Hindu–Muslim unity, the film tries to instil Islamophobia in the minds of its viewers by instigating religious fervour. In another example, Manikarnika is seen risking the lives of her soldiers to rescue a temple in the midst of an exchange of fire. As one of her Muslim associates (Anil George) turns out to be a traitor, the commander of Lakshmi Bai's army, Ghulam Ghaus Khan (Danny Denzongpa), says: 'You have not just betrayed the country but also our religion'—an insignificant reference connecting nationalism with a particular religion, that is, Islam, but a Hindu mole's treachery is not equally assessed.

The main plot of Kesari centres around an actual historical event and it portrays the legendary last stand at Saragarhi in 1897 of 21 soldiers of the 36th Sikh battalion of the British Indian Army. To drive the British out of their homelands, the Pathans of the Orakzai and Afridi tribes came together to fight the battle. Here, the Afghan invaders metamorphose and are equated with the other Islamic ethnic groups such as Mughals, Arabs, Turks, and Pakistanis, who are mostly marked out for their wrong-doings in contemporary cultural politics. At the beginning of the film, Kesari introduces a fictitious scene where Havaldar Ishar Singh rescues an Afghan girl from an imam who wants to behead her for violating the alleged duty of a wife to her husband, reportedly mandated by *shariat*. The film reveals that the Pathan strike on Saragarhi was a reprisal against Ishar Singh's involvement in the internal relations of the Pathan tribe. Ignoring the tension over territorial politics between the British Indian Army and the Afghan tribes, the film uses the alleged barbarism of Islam as an enterprise for propagating religious nationalism.

Apart from geographical boundaries, the demarcation of insider and outsider was enacted through language. In Chapter 2 I have discussed scholar Asghar Ali Engineer who has articulated how Indian politics has systematically utilized and created linguistic identity. But there are some

his participation in the Indian Mutiny of 1857. Parvez, A. (2017) *The Life and Poetry of Bahadur Shah Zafar*. Hay House, Inc.

[14] See Kolhi, P. and Dhawan, P. (2020) Bollywood: 'Othering' the Muslim on screen. *Frontline*, 27 March. Available at https://frontline.thehindu.com/arts-and-culture/cinema/article31007 504.ece [Accessed 20 October 2022].

film genres that had to make use of a specific language, for example, the Muslim Historical films, which use the Urdu language extensively. As we have seen, Urdu was also an important language for the Historical films genre. But there is a striking difference of incorporating Urdu in the recent Muslim Historicals than in the earlier genres. I argue that contemporary Muslim Historical films utilize the Urdu language in a very deliberate way to create a distinct identity and demarcate 'Others'.

Mukul Kesavan (1994), a Hindi film scholar, believes Urdu was the primary communicative language of Bombay Hindi cinema. However, as already mentioned in Chapter 2, the Bombay film industry employs a mixed language made up of Hindi, Urdu, and Hindustani. Dwyer mentions, 'While historically the roots of Hindi cinema uses both Hindi and Urdu, as well as other forms of this lingua franca and a mixture of other Indian languages (Punjabi and English in particular), it is interested in creating a language that is suitable for its purposes, which can reach as wide an audience as possible' (2006: 105). Connecting to Dwyer, Haider Ali mentions:

> To make the language understood by larger audience, they [script-writers and lyricists] started writing dialogues in a mixed language of Urdu, Hindi, Sanskrit, and Persian. That fusion of languages was known as Hindustani. Still Hindustani is the communicative language in Hindi cinema unless they are making a mythology and pure Sanskrit is used for mythological films. Even in historical films like *Jodhaa Akbar*, whenever Jodha's family spoke, they spoke in Thet, Kathiyabadi Hindi. (Personal interview, 5 April 2014)

I posit that the trend is not only limited to *Jodhaa Akbar*, rather all recent Muslim Historical films followed the same pattern. In the recent Muslim Historical films where demarcation of 'Insider' and 'Outsider' is more prevalent, Urdu is specifically utilized as a spoken language for Muslim characters; on the other hand, Sanskritized Marathi or Sanskritized Hindi is the spoken language for the Hindu protagonists to mark out the insider and outsider identities. Other similar examples can be noted in *Panipat*, *Padmaavat, and Tanhaji* where Hindu characters are communicating in Sanskritized Hindi and Muslims are speaking in Urdu. Interestingly, Sanskritized Hindi-speaking characters are portrayed as Indian and fighting for the country; on the other hand, Urdu-speaking protagonists belong to Afghanistan or, if not, are somehow connected to Afghanistan lineage. The Urdu-speaking male protagonists of these films are mostly plunderers, invaders, and looters while the women are submissive and oppressed.

Bramhanical Supremacy through Historical Films

Right from the early history of Indian cinema, Bombay films have always aligned their political ideology with the state's political ideology of the time. In the last two sections we have discussed a very striking shift of the themes of the Historical films, from 'secular Mughal warriors' to 'Outsiders'. Apart from these themes, there are a few more narratives such as Bramhanical supremacy, glorification of masculine nationalism, and off-screen controversies which further propagate the state's ideology.

Many of these films try to establish Bramhanical hegemony along with a special emphasis on establishing a Hindu *rashtra*. In *Tanhaji*, ignoring the subaltern identity of her own, Savitribai Malusare, wife of 'Tanhaji' utters, *'Jab Shivaji Raje ki talwaar chalti hai, tab aurto ka ghoonghat aur Brahmano ka janeu salamat rehta hai'* ('When Shivaji raises his sword, it protects and endorses the dignity of women and the sacred threads of Brahmins remain intact'). Historically, it is completely an exaggerated narrative to glorify Brahmanical supremacy in the film. The egalitarian policies of Shivaji provided room in the administration of his empire for citizens of lower castes and various faiths, including Islam, and thus there is no such historical fact that he put special emphasis on protecting the honour of women and Brahmins. The film endorses the idea that Brahmins are more worthy of protection than others and therefore the film supports the idea that the Brahmins as a caste are superior than others. Similarly, there is a line in one of the initial scenes where Bajirao is being introduced in *Bajirao Mastani*. He is said to wield a sword as fast as lightning, has a determination as robust as the Himalayas and his appearance reflected the glory of Chitpavan Brahmins: *'Talwar mey bijli si harkat, iraado me Himalay ki adakta, chehre pe chitpavan kul ke brahmano ka tej ...'* By glorifying their Brahmin heritage, these films ignore the laws of the Peshwas that allowed them to commit the worst kind of caste atrocities. It completely overlooks the historical truth about the Peshwas as explained by Babasaheb Ambedkar in *Annihilation of Caste*. Ambedkar writes:

> Under the rule of the Peshwas in the Maratha country the untouchable was not allowed to use the public streets if a Hindu was coming along lest he should pollute the Hindu by his shadow. The Untouchable was required to have a black thread either on his wrist or on his neck as a sign or a mark to prevent the Hindus from getting themselves polluted by his touch through mistake. In Poona, the capital of the Peshwa, the Untouchable was required to carry, strung from his waist, a broom to sweep away from behind the dust he treaded on lest a Hindu walking on the same should be polluted. In Poona, the Untouchable was required to carry an earthen pot, hung on his neck wherever he went, for holding his spit lest his spit falling on the earth should pollute a Hindu who might unknowingly happen to tread on it. (1914)

The glorification of Bramhanism is not only limited to the Peshwas, and even Manikarnika does the same. The lead character of the film, Rani Laxmibai, utters an iconic dialogue of the film when she says, 'Rani Laxmibai was a Brahmin who fought like Kshatriyas.' One may argue that upholding the supremacy of the Brahmin caste has gained urgency in recent times as there has been a push to legitimize the rights of other caste groups as well. In this context, the caste-based reservation system in India comes under scrutiny time and again. Sandip Misra, a middle-aged manager in a Multinational Corporation (MNC) and a participant in my survey points out:

> When Br Ambedkar wrote the constitution, he said that ST (Schdule Tribe) and SC (Schedule Caste) privileges are to be given for ten years from 1951 to 1961 or reviewed but benefits are still there for the people belonging to those castes. How long? How long do you go on giving food on a golden spoon? (Personal interview, 28 July 2020)

It is perhaps not surprising then that in this sociopolitical situation, the upper castes perceive themselves to be the victims and filmmakers choose to re-establish their caste superiority through their films. From the above discussion of glorifying Brahmanism, I would like to argue that if Brahmins are threatened and therefore need to be protected from Muslim plunders from the past and from a caste-based reservation system in the present, it gets portrayed as other religions and other castes are either enemies or opportunists.

Gendering the Politics of Hindu Nationalism through Historical Films

In India, masculinity has been described by a self-assuredness that is forceful and propelled by liberalization, an economic framework through which India secured a place in the international political economy and also gave rise to the right-wing Hindutva politics. This particular section unfolds a specific gendered image of the nation-state of contemporary Indian sociopolitical context by sketching out the recent Historical films such as *Bajiro Mastani, Padmaavat, Manikarnika: The Queen of Jhansi, Panipat, Kesari,* and *Tanhaji*. Though gender has always been used as a crucial tool in Indian politics it has gained enormous importance in the last two decades. In this section, we will explore how women and Muslims are portrayed in diverse representational schemes and in films such as *Jodhaa Akbar, Bajirao Mastani, Padmaavat, Manikarnika: The Queen of Jhansi, Panipat, Kesari, and Tanhaji* and look at them as being products of multifaceted historical, cultural, and political nation-building projects in which gender plays a central role. Sikata Banerjee points out in her book *Gender, Nation and Popular Film in India: Globalizing Muscular Nationalism* (2016) that 'muscular nationalism' is the product of a colli-sion between a specific vision of masculinity and the nationalism political ideology. Masculinity is synonymous with physical prowess, muscular strength, and resilience, yet it is also linked with the image and construct of virtuous woman; thus, a gendered binary of a warrior man and a chaste woman is driven by the concept of nation (Banerjee, 2016). Banerjee coined the term 'muscular nationalism'—referring to a gender hierarchy in which a warrior man guards a chaste woman—which she claims is at the heart of all forms of nationalist ideology. First and foremost, we need to understand the connection between gender and the Hindu nationalist discourse.

From the colonial era onwards, gender became a critical component of nationalist discourse. Since the beginning of the anti-colonial movement, gender, especially that of women, has been used as a weapon to reinforce nationalist political rhetoric, depending on the nation's political situation. Women's images and plights are often used to awaken the nation's collective consciousness, and on some occasions they have been used purely for political gain. And this use of gender roles to construct a national imagery can be deduced from controversies associated with two very recent Historical films, *Padmaavat* (2018) and *Manikarnika: The Queen of Jhansi*, where women are the lead protagonists. According to the Karni Sena, a Rajput caste community, the film *Padmaavat* contains an intimate (and thus objectionable) scene in which the Muslim king Alauddin Khalji fantasizes about being intimate with the Hindu queen Padmavati. The Karni Sena vandalized cinemas and claimed that the nose of Deepika Padukone (the actress for the role of Padmavati) should be cut off, alluding to a tale in the epic Ramayana in which a woman is punished by having her nose cut off. A Bharatiya Janata Party (BJP) regional leader, Suraj Pal Amu, declared a $1.5 million (£1.3 million) reward for anyone who could behead Sanjay Leela Bhansali, the director, and Padukone (British Broadcasting Corporation [BBC], 2018). The Rajasthan-based Brahmin organization Sarv Brahmin Mahasabha objected to the film *Manikarnika: The Queen of Jhansi*, claiming that it contained a love scene between Rani Laxmi Bai and a British East India Company officer (Financial Express Online, 2018). All such outrage as was displayed in public forums was because these legendary/fictional/non-fictional historical characters were romantically intimate with foreigners in some dream sequences. Based on this I argue that the responsibility of safeguarding the cultural purity of a race is assigned to the chastity of its women.

Before discussing the term 'nationalism' we need to understand the concept of the 'nation'. A 'nation' is defined by political geographic boundaries. Kelly J. Bell opined that 'nationalism' is the belief that focuses on the ongoing support for that geographical boundary, and people visualize the boundary to be separated from the other nations of the world (2009). According to the Merriam-Webster dictionary, the definition of nationalism is 'loyalty and devotion to a nation; especially a sense of national consciousness ... exalting one nation above all others and placing primary emphasis on promotion of its culture and interests as opposed to those of other nations or supranational groups'.[15] Bell further mentioned, 'Nationalism is an ideology that focuses both on loyalty to and pride in one's nation ... Nationalism, at its core, instils a belief in citizens that their country is important and superior to other countries, and their individual identity is strongly tied to their homeland' (2009).

During colonial rule in India, nationalism became a dominant ideology for motivating and inciting people to fight for independence. Women played an important part in colonialist and imperialist discourses, either consciously or implicitly. The British were able to rationalize imperialism as a 'civilizing mission' in which they were rescuing Indian women from the reprehensible practices of a traditional Hindu patriarchal society because of the subaltern position of Indian women. We must also reflect upon the historical details of the manner in which the 'civilizing mission' came to be determined. The 'woman question' in the agenda of social reform in the early nineteenth century was not so much about the specific condition of women within a determinate set of social relations. Lata Mani rightly pointed out in her study of the abolition of *sati-daha*[16] that even later, the agenda of the 'woman question' was produced by postcolonialist discourses (Gilmartin, 1997). In connection to that, nationalism was not only a political struggle of power, rather, it related to the question of the political independence of a nation in virtually every aspect of the material and spiritual lives of its citizens. Partha Chatterjee, a prominent postcolonial theorist, provided a theoretical framework (1989) for analysing the contradictory pulls on nationalist ideology in its struggle against dominant colonialism and the resolution it offered to those contradictions. In brief, this resolution was built around a splitting of the domain of culture into two spheres—the material and the spiritual. Within the material sphere may be included the claims of Western civilization that its culture was superior and most powerful because of its reliance on science, technology, rational forms of economic organization,

---

[15] Definition of nationalism, Merriam-Webster, Available at https://www.merriam-webster.com/dictionary/nationalism [Accessed 7 May 2021].

[16] *Sati* (or Suttee) is mentioned as 'the Indian custom of a wife immolating herself either on the funeral pyre of her dead husband or in some other fashion soon after his death [Encyclopaedia Britannica, https://www.britannica.com/topic/suttee, accessed 6 May 2021].

and modern methods of statecraft. It was believed that these had given the European countries the strength to subjugate non-European people. To overcome this domination, the colonized people of India had to imitate the Western material aspect of life. However, it was assumed that Indians did not have to rely on the Western spiritual sphere as the spiritual domain of the East was superior to that of the West. Nationalists asserted that European powers failed to colonize the inner, that is, superior spiritual culture of the colonized. This in turn led to the ascribing of gender roles in our society. Material interest in the outer world was thought to be the masculine realm of society, and the inner world, that is, the spiritual, was considered to be the feminine domain. As women were thought to be situated in the sacred spiritual space, thus, during the anti-colonial period, it was easier to make people imagine that gender, especially womanhood, was of primary importance in the embodiment of the nation. Consequently, women have been used as a symbol of national identity from the time of India's freedom movement. The fact that national identity was constructed in gendered terms is apparent in the use of feminine nouns to address the nation, such as 'she' or 'motherland' to refer to the country. The most ideal image of the country was as Mother India, depicted as a goddess modestly dressed in a sari, seated on a lion, and holding a saffron flag (Soherwordi, 2013).

It has been argued by numerous scholars such as Tanika Sarkar (1999), Kelly J. Bell (2009), and Syed Hussain Shaheed Soherwordi (2013) that religious politics created a space for women to participate in the political discourse during the pre-Independence days. It can also be argued that Hindu women are represented as the 'repositories of the religious beliefs and the keepers of purity and integrity of the Hindu community' (Soherwordi, 2013: 39). If it is true that religious politics has created opportunities for women to become a part of the public space, it can equally be argued that it has simultaneously undermined women's autonomy (Basu, 2010); the identity of women has been reduced to 'mother', 'daughter', and 'sister', whose honour should be protected by the male members of the community. Also, it should be mentioned that only a small percentage of women got the opportunity to participate in the nation's political discourse. Thus, we see that in this way Hindu nationalist discourse legitimizes the dominance of men over women.

We must focus on another perspective to understand gender roles in the nationalist discourse. Initially, nationalism and its ideas gained popularity among the elite but it needed mass support for its wider propagation. Historically, ideals of nationalism were inclusive of various religions, races, and languages; later, however, nationalism drew on the idea of unification of diverse groups to form a new community of citizens. According to historian Romila Thapar, there were, and are, nationalist ideologies where an individual group identity is prioritized as opposed to a secular nationalist discourse. For example, there are concepts of nations based on a single exclusive identity: religious, linguistic, ethnic, and similar singular identities. Thapar has christened this phenomenon as 'pseudo-nationalism', which exaggerates the importance of a single history of one religious community as being the pre-eminent history of the nation and which denigrates and distorts the history of other communities. She went further to suggest that such ideals 'should be precluded from being called nationalism' (Thapar et al., 2016: 8). We can also argue that women only find a place as tools in the hands of men. In essence, women, as subjects, are excluded from the concept of nationalism except as being carriers of abstract notions of honour.

In the post-Independence period, India experienced Partition and many communal riots across the country. Those historical traumas, such as the violence of Partition, experiences of permanent exile, and sufferings due to communal violence, heightened the feeling for non-Muslims of being threatened by Muslims during the traumatic events of 1947. The identity of the Muslim 'Other' gained ground during British rule due to the colonial policy of divide and rule and later due to the partitioning of India and the creation of Pakistan. As already mentioned, the vilification of Muslim rulers in India originated during colonial times through the writings of British historians; but the notion of 'Otherness' has become more complicated in the last two decades after the demolition of the Babri Masjid in the country. In connection to this, Thapar has also pointed out that a version of history is currently being written by the RSS and Hindutva ideologues for whom the past has only to do with Hindu history of the early period and the victimization of Hindus under Muslim tyranny in the medieval period. During the 1990s, the narrative of communal violence began to be reframed in terms of allegations of the abductions of Hindu women by Muslim men during Partition. This approach was adopted and became the central theme because protecting the honour of Hindu women served as an important tool to mobilize citizens. 'At the end of the 1980s and the beginning of the 1990s, the Hindu right-wing groups effectively launched various campaigns to mobilize and gain popular support; a support that was primarily garnered through anti-Muslim propaganda' (Khatun, 2016: 46). At that time, the most successful of these campaigns was the Ayodhya movement (Tully, 2017).[17] Along with communal mobilization, the new emerging political discourse, that is, Hindutva, also justified the inferior situation of women in the patriarchal system. As a result, Hindutva politics tried to justify the sati of Roop Kanwar (Sharma, 2007) in 1987 by seeking justification for the act of sati in religious Hindu scriptures and by idealizing a woman's role as a dutiful wife.[18] Women are taught to embrace the values of established gender hierarchy in Hindu nationalist discourse. It is assumed that 'if women do not perform their cultural role in a proper manner, then the family suffers and then the nation' (Soherwordi, 2013: 43). As a result, defying patriarchal representations of women is interpreted as disrespectful for Hindu women, and the individual is seen as a threat to the family and, by extension, the government. Thus, Hindutva philosophy inspires Hindu women to think in terms of common interest rather than individual rights in order to build the ideal society and a nation. 'The gender ideology of Hindutva, a factor that touches the very essence of Hindu nationalism, reinforces the "supremacy of the family over the individual" with the implication that "family considerations should reign supreme," not only in marriage, but in "career"' (Basu cited in Soherwordi, 2013: 44). This entire concept was reinforced by deploying the image of Hindu goddesses to promote the ideal of the Indian female

---

[17] '[On 6 December 1992] right-wing Hindu mobs razed to the ground the sixteenth-century Babri mosque, claiming that it was built on the site of a temple destroyed by Muslim rulers ... It was the culmination of a six-year campaign [mentioned as Ayodhya Movement] spearheaded by the BJP to destroy the mosque and replace it with a temple.' Tully, Mark. (2017) 'How the Babri Mosque Destruction Shaped India. *The BBC News*, 6 December. Available at https://www.bbc.com/news/world-asia-india-42219773 [Accessed 22 October 2022].

[18] 'On September 4 1987 ... a young girl of 18 in the village of Deorala in Rajasthan was murdered. She was burnt alive on the funeral pyre of her husband. Yet, according to local tradition, Roop Kanwar had become a 'sati' and had 'voluntarily' immolated herself.' Sharma, Kalpana. (2007) Remembering Roop Kanwar. *The Hindu*, 23 September. Available at https://www.thehindu.com/todays-paper/tp-features/tp-sundaymagazine/remembering-roopkanwar/article2275587.ece [Accessed 6 May 2021].

by appealing to the religious sentimentality of Sita's chastity[19] and was one of the most popular stories which was referenced multiple times by the RSS.

Because nationalism refers to the feeling of oneness or unity, there can be different kinds of threats which try to break the feeling of oneness or being united. This threat can be in the form of physical violence against national borders, as already discussed in the last section, where we saw how the medieval Islamic ruler became a threat in the form of physical violence against national borders. In this section I am going to discuss the threat to nationalism in the form of psychological violence perpetrated by challenging the normative values or the gender status quo of the nation state. Just as the threats can break down the feeling of oneness, they can also help in creating a bond within the community to counter the enemy. Following this point, I argue that the fear of psychological violence is instilled in people to strengthen the feeling of oneness, and the female body is utilized as a component to generate that threat. One of the most controversial campaigns that creates such fear is 'love-jihad'. As we have seen, women become active agents in propagating the feeling of nationalism; thus, we need to discuss the concept of how in the nationalist discourse the divine feminine should be protected by the male members of our society from being threatened by the Historical 'Others'.

The female body as a social construct has been shaped by the colonial discourse of strategic retreats, resistances, and collusions between the colonizer and the colonized. The imagination of the nation symbolized by the Hindu female body can be traced back to colonial discourses. Scholars such as Asish Nandy (1980), Partha Chatterjee (1989), Sumathi Ramaswamy (2008), and Charu Gupta (2009) have referred to the centrality of the symbolic feminine in the imagination of the Indian nation. Women became the only inspiration to maintain ethnic identities, 'demarcating the distinction between the alien and the autochthonal through what their wombs brought forth' (Mubarki, 2014: 258). This discourse imposed 'the Hindu woman was allotted a unique responsibility as the site of past freedom and future nationhood', (Sarkar,

---

[19] *Sita* is the central character in the Hindu epic the Ramayana and 'the consort of the god Rama … Sita worshipped as the incarnation of Lakshmi … Though often regarded as the embodiment of wifely devotion and self-sacrifice.' (https://www.britannica.com/topic/Sita).

1999: 136). Righteous Hindu women started to symbolize the nation and the community from the colonial period. During the anti-colonial movement, the nascent nation state was considered a physical entity, that is, Bharat Mata (Bhardwaj, 2016) as mother, woman, and goddess (Ramaswamy, 2001). Mythological characters and goddesses such as Sati,[20] Savitri,[21] and Sita became the inspiration for the ideal devotional wife committed to virtue and conformity. To emphasize Indian values and ethos during the colonial period, a non-sexual image of women was presented. Depicted mostly as the 'virtuous, chaste, submissive, self-sacrificing Hindu woman', she was 'the manager of this hearth [and] came to symbolize the incorruptible abode of the nascent nation, "who had to preserve the Hindu family because the [Hindu] male had already succumbed to Western colonial power in the material realm"' (Gupta cited in Mubarki, 2014: 259). According to Charu Gupta, 'In a large part of canonized high Hindi literature there was a gradual shift in emphasis from the erotic and sexually active nayika and Radha of medieval poetry to the chaste and virtuous Hindu wife and mother' (Gupta, 2001: 40).

As the woman's body came to be used symbolically as the nation, it was supposed to be protected from outsiders or the 'Other' by the male members of the community. M.A. Mubarki writes, 'When the woman's body came to represent the nation it became out of bounds for the "Other"' (Mubarki, 2014: 259). He further argues, 'women's [were] bodies deemed the repositories of men's honour, the community's morality, and the nation's territorial integrity, which were subjected to brutal violence both sexual and otherwise, since as a symbol of lineage and purity, women's bodies once violated sexually would purportedly designate the entire collectivity as dishonoured and shamed' (Mubarki, 2014: 259). Though the identification of Hindu women with the nation's honour is an early nationalist concept, it achieved unprecedented significance only after the rise of Hindu nationalist politics. As Hindutva ideology supposes that women have to be protected by the male members of society, the

---

[20] Sati is the goddess of marital felicity and longevity in Hinduism.
[21] Savitri is a goddess according to Hindu mythology. 'The Mahabharata recounts how Savitri used the power of her dedication to her husband Satyavan to prevent Yama, the god of the dead, from taking him when he was fated to die. She became the epitome of the faithful wife' [Encyclopaedia Britannica, https://www.britannica.com/topic/Savitri, Accessed 6 May 2021].

'love-jihad' campaign became an important tool to propagate that line of thought.

In this section, I will discuss the portrayal of historical female characters as the nation in the films mentioned earlier and their fictitious portrayal of history in Bollywood to support the larger political discourse in present times, as many Indian filmgoers tend to get their knowledge of history from such films. Sourabh Agarwal points out in a personal interview:

> I was so surprised to watch *Tanhaji*. You can say, it was my favourite war movie because I got to know about a great warrior like Tanhaji after watching the film. After watching the film, I researched more about him and I was shocked to know that the film was based on a real historical character. I learned a new thing about which I didn't have any idea. I was just wondering why it was missing from our history books. I think people should take pride in the people like Tanhaji, an unsung hero, who really tried for the good of the people of the country. People like him should be glorified, recognized, and acknowledged. (Personal interview, 3 October 2020)

On the one hand, we have female characters such as Jodhaa, Mastani, Rani Laxmi Bai, Savitri Bai Malusare—all quasi-historical characters about whom very few historical facts are available—who are shown as trying to retain their Hindu religious beliefs and values; in the case of Jodhaa this even after her marriage to Akbar, a Muslim ruler. On the other hand, we see Padmavati, a fictitious character (also known as Rani Padmini), sacrificing her life in fear of losing her honour at the hands of the Muslim ruler Alauddin Khalji. Most interestingly, the nineteenth century saw Rani Padmini's existence in poetry being transformed into a 'fact'. Colonial writer Colonel James Tod, political agent of the English East India Company in Rajputana, 'manufactured the enduring impression of Indian history as a confrontation between Muslims and Hindus—which justified British rule to keep the peace in a land of competing antagonisms' (Pillai, 2017). Later on, the legend of Rani Padmini or Padmavati was used for anti-colonial mobilization in the early twentieth century.

In *Jodhaa Akbar*, the Muslim emperor was projected as an ideal example due to his tolerant ways as he willingly accepted Jodhaa's cultural superiority. A period drama, the film can claim to have a pioneering role in the context of portraying communal harmony. It narrates the story of the romance between Mughal Emperor Jalal-ud-din Muhammad Akbar and the Rajput princess Jodhaa Bai, daughter of King Bharmal of Amer. When Akbar plans to attack Amer, King Bharmal reluctantly offers his daughter's hand in marriage to the emperor himself to avoid war and strengthen relations between their kingdoms. Akbar agrees to the marriage, as such a union would forge a truly strong alliance and long-lasting peace between the Mughal Empire and the Rajputs. Jodhaa holds on to her duty and honour in adverse circumstances as the proud embodiment of the nation when she is banished from Akbar's kingdom on charges of being disloyal towards her husband. She faces grave humiliation and shame when she has to leave her husband's home; however, she willingly returns to the emperor's palace after Akbar renounces the *jaziya* tax[22] (Mubarki, 2014). Here, love is an overarching concept because Jhodhaa compromises her dignity and self-esteem for the general interest of the larger society and nation. Film scholar Anustup Basu points out that 'human (heterosexual) love is a unifying middle term which sets up an organic bridge between spirit and substance, between the particular and the general interest' (2010: 166). The film portrays Jodhaa as a character imbued with zeal and self-assertion and makes her an active counter of Akbar. It is through her agency that the Oriental despot Akbar turns pacifist at the end and seeks peace even with the evil and rebellious Sharifuddin.

Bajirao Mastani, based on a fictional work, also represents a complex and nuanced narrative—a mixture of secular ideology and rising right-wing majoritarianism. On the one hand, the film sympathizes with Mastani's character who is a brave warrior who goes through betrayal and pain; on the other hand, Kashibai, who is characterized as an imaginary Hindu Goddess who is a representative of the nation through positioning her in the Brahmanical patriarchy, which was supposedly *Peshwa* rule. In one of the scenes, Kashibai is shown wearing headgear and dancing holding a saffron flag much like an image of Bharat Mata. To create her image as pure, chaste and as an embodiment of the idealized Hindu

---

[22] *Jizya* was a per capita yearly tax imposed on non-Muslims. Narain, H. (1990) *Jizyah and the Spread of Islam*. Voice of India.

woman, the film does not sexualize her except in one erotic scene between her and Bajirao. She is undoubtedly faithful to the Peshwa family's Brahmanical principles in spite of knowing her husband's relation with Mastani, the other woman. Because of her projection as a symbolic Bharat Mata, Kashibai's character sheds all her feelings such as pain, insecurity, and jealousy; moreover, she accepts Mastani in her life.

On the contrary, in the same film, Mastani is represented as a woman with agency, a warrior, and with overt sexuality. These are supposedly not the characteristics of 'docile submission [to] Hindu patriarchy' (Roy, 2018); therefore, those traits make her a subject of exclusion. When I asked Sandip Misra his opinion of Mastani, he says:

> I look at Mastani more as a warrior princess than Bajirao's wife. (Personal interview, 28 July 2020)

Because of her aggressive sexuality, in one of the scenes she is shown as seducing the Peshwa by expressing her feelings publicly. On the other hand, Bajirao displays an initial restraint that supposedly fits with a code of conduct of the Hindu warrior monk (Banerjee, 2016). Mastani is humiliated several times either by Bajirao's mother or the society itself for her religious identity and sexuality. Mastani was not accepted by Bajirao's mother (Radhabai) because of her mixed parentage; Radhabai even offered her the position of dancing girl due to her characterization as a courtesan. Bajirao never revolted against his mother for doing such things. The film in these ways reinforces the idea of an ideal Hindu Bramhanical society. Sandip Misra further points out in an interview with me:

> I like the way he is falling in love with Mastani who has a Hindu father and a Muslim mother like she was different. It shows how powerful Bajirao is. He couldn't revolt against his mother who didn't want Mastani to be queen. (Personal interview, 28 July 2020)

Mastani holds a secondary position in terms of self-respect and her physical safety is always in question. It becomes more evident at the time when Bajirao's family members conspire to disregard her with the help of local Brahmins. In the whole film, we see that due to Mastani's choice to be with Bajirao, she leads an isolated, Islamicate subaltern existence which is only briefly interrupted when Kashibai invites her to participate in a Hindu festival. Kashibai offers her a sari, which is predominantly the dress of Hindu women. Mastani accepts the symbolic Hindu gesture and participates in a dance along with Kashibai to celebrate. Thus, it becomes clear that the position of Mastani symbolizes the peripheral, insecure status of minorities in India.

In *Panipat*, women play important roles in film right from the beginning. It starts with Parvati Bai's account as she had witnessed the third battle of Panipat. The entire narrative of the film was presented through the voiceover of Parvati Bai unlike most other films in the Historical genre, which usually has a masculine orientation. In the last decade, India has witnessed resilient and influential women expressing their religious, political, and ideological positions. Inspired by the agency of women and their position in the country's political space, director Ashutosh Gowarikar adopts a modern approach and portrays Parvati Bai, alongside her husband, as participating in war politics and framing political strategy. We even find her delivering an intense and passionate nationalistic speech in order to further encourage a more modern approach to state governance. Unlike Jodhaa and Mastani, Parvati's character is much more straightforward and less layered. She simply tries to protect Shadashiv, who fights to protect the country and at the end sacrifices his life to save the nation. Parvati Bai metaphorically safeguards the nation and the same is enacted in multiple scenes. In some scenes, she is arranging food for soldiers; at other times she manages to procure more soldiers from other kingdoms. Throughout the film, she is symbolized as a dedicated, trustworthy, and dutiful spouse who performs all her wifely responsibilities—she even she makes the journey to join her husband in the military expedition. The film shows that after Shadashiv's death she is devastated and silenced for the rest of her life, thus proving her love and faithfulness.

Keeping in mind the contemporary popular connection, we see how historical facts are camouflaged with contemporary politics through Manikarnika's character, even Parvati's personality in *Panipat*. *Manikarnika: The Queen of Jhansi* alters the popular idea of male legends of historical films with a female heroic character. Though the film replaces the predominant image of a historical character, it still endorses the masculine hyper-nationalism through the transgressive nature of Rani Laxmi

Bai. Her masculinity is established in the opening scene of the film, where a tiger is about to attack villagers and it roars and leaps; Manikarnika shoots an arrow at the animal and she only sedates it. When the injured tiger collapses at her feet, an innocent villager asks, 'Why didn't you kill it?' In reply she says, 'I never meant to kill him, just wanted to save the village.' This heroic act of Manikarnika resonates well with her masculine avatar. Though the film adopts a feminist approach to paint the character of Laxmi Bai who is shown as being equally brave, strong, courageous, valorous like any other warrior king, she is also shown as possessing feminine traits such as kindness, motherly instinct, dutiful wifeliness.

Padmaavat was inspired by the eponymous epic poem by Malik Muhammad Jayasi. Rani Padmavati, a Rajput queen known for her beauty, was the wife of Maharawal Ratan Singh. Sultan Alauddin Khalji hears of her legendary beauty and attacks Ratan Singh's kingdom to claim her. Here, the enemy is not only trying to invade or harm the nation but also running after its women. Connecting to the phenomenon of representing the enemy as sexual demons and repressive to their own women, Dr Kaifiya Fatehma points out:

> These days Muslim villains are extremely violent and monstrous who are not only looting but also behind women. If you look at Khalji's character in *Padmaavat*, his perversion is portrayed very clearly on his wedding night when he unites with other women and [does] not [care] about his wife. Even his wife is subjugated and assaulted multiple times. These representations do have an effect on people. I have heard people are talking you know that's how Muslim women are treated, that's how these people treat women and 'these people' are very common words, they are violent and that sets the tone for 'love jihad'. (Personal interview, 31 January 2021)

While the *Padmaavat* not only portrays the Rajput queen as symbolically representing the nation, the eruption of controversies associated with the film before its release also shows how the female body is constructed as a site of a community's honour in the nationalist discourse. The film narrates the transactions between Rajput kings and the Khaljis of the Delhi Sultanate. Several Rajput-caste organizations, including Shri Rajput Karni Sena, protested the making of the film. The film's sets were also vandalized as the miscreants claimed that the film portrays Padmavati, a Rajput queen, in bad light. It was assumed that there was a song during which Khalji is shown fantasizing about the queen as an object of his sexual desire. Even the film's director, Sanjay Leela Bhansali, was assaulted on the film set. The protests were not limited to Rajasthan, where the Karni Sena and Rajuts were protesting; there were multiple protests that were organized across the country. Bhansali and Deepika Padukone received death threats. The beliefs and psyche of the common people are evident from such protests. For them, the honour of a Rajput queen and the nation's honour are one and the same, representing something that an outsider such as Khalji cannot be allowed to claim.

In *Padmaavat*, the cultural superiority of the Rajput queen is obvious in almost every scene. There are many sequences such as greeting an enemy such as Khalji, culinary choices, and sartorial choices that portray the rich cultural heritage of Hindu Rajputs and which symbolize the entire nation's culture. In this imaginary world of the Rajput kingdom, Ratan Singh gets the chance to kill Khalji but refuses to do so because of his ethics and values of life as he believes that a guest should be treated like a god and that is the practice of a true Rajput. Sartorial choices are also highlighted multiple times through the elaborate costumes of the whole Rajput clan, especially through the characters of Padmavati and Ratan Singh. One can even argue that the lotus motif, which is omnipresent in the entire film from being in costumes to wall paintings, symbolizes the current ruling political party of India. Vegetarian food is also treated as a source of pride and this is evident when Khalji is offered such a meal.

That the nation's pride lies in the hands of women is most evident through the glorification of the ritual of mass suicide, which is termed jauhar. Though Khalji's army succeeds in defeating the Rajputs and capturing Chittor, it is unable to capture the Rajput women, who commit jauhar with Rani Padmavati. It fundamentally propagates the message that the honour of the community or clan rests with women. If the woman cohabits with an outsider, the community's and thus the nation's integrity and pride are lost. It also inspires women to sacrifice their lives if they face similar situations to save the nation's pride, encouraging them to see things from the perspective of the community's larger interest rather than their own individualistic interest. Padmavati emerges within the narrative as a protector of Hindu values. She inspires other women to commit jauhar and in her speech she says, 'In every age, a war for right-eousness is fought between good and evil. Like the one between Lord Ram and Raavan, between the Pandavas and Kauravas and now between the Rajputs and Khiljis.' To encourage other women to sacrifice their lives, Padmavati further says in her concluding speech, 'Those who lust for our body, would not even get their hands on our shadows, our bodies will be reduced to ashes, but our pride and honour will remain immortal, and that will be the biggest defeat of Alauddin's life.'

In the films we have discussed, we find that the Hindu queens have been represented as embodying the nation in one way or another. Thus, as already discussed in the earlier sections, one of the important features of the new-found Hindu nationalism is the construction of the image of ideal women as virtuous, chaste, without sexual desire, self-sacrificing. To make the image of women pure, almost all the queens were shown trying to save their husbands from enemies; they can be compared with mythological characters such as Savitri and her journey to bring back her husband from Yamaraj.[23]

Conclusion

To summarize, I have tried to deconstruct the portrayal of Muslims ei-ther in the Muslim Historical genre or in the Historical genre through the lens of the sociopolitical context of the country. To strengthen the argument, I have used primary data and critical sociological theories. The chapter paints a chronological shift in terms of Muslim representa-tion from king or *nawab* to despotic invaders—from making them an in-tegral part of the country to intruders. Most interestingly, in the initial period after Independence, the Muslim Historical genre was one of the most celebrated genres, even though the Partition and subsequent riots had scarred the people's minds. The Muslim Historical genre is not com-monplace now and several reasons have been put forward for its fading away. But it is difficult to accept completely the reasoning that such fac-tors as commerce and less currency of the Urdu language are behind the decreasing popularity of the Muslim Historical genre from the end

---

[23] Yama or Yamaraj is a god of death as per Hindu mythology.

of the 1960s. These justifications are simplistic because after India's economic reform in the early 1990s, a large number of big budget films have been made. To survive and to be distributed in the overseas market, the same films have made use of huge publicity budgets. Western film studios with heavy financial backing, such as Warner Bros Pictures, Fox Star Studios, Sony, and Viacom18, have begun to produce films in India. Consequently, the argument of a lack of knowledge of Urdu that surfaced during the interviews can only be treated as an uncertain explanation. The most important and justified reason may be that texts suitable for the Muslim Historical genre are not too acceptable to the audience. As some of the participants in my survey have pointed out, they really enjoy watching Indian (Hindu) warriors fight against the trespassers (Muslim invaders); it then seems obvious that according to the contemporary filmgoer Muslims cannot secure a space in Indian history as anything but 'outsiders'.

Another important point to note is that very important roles are being reserved for Hindu women in recent Historical films. Although most of the women characters in those films are not directly involved in any clash or conflict, they are used as agents to fuel the political narrative inspired by the current sociopolitical situation of the country. As we have seen in the preceding discussion, one of the most commonly used tropes in the recent Historical films is that the masculine Hindu heroes not only try to save the country from Muslim foreign invaders but try to protect their women from them. With women's bodies becoming the repository of the country's 'honour' safeguarding them is shown to be of primary importance. This notion has also gained wide currency in the contemporary political space with leaders of the political party currently in power at the centre propagating similar ideologies and treating women as precious objects that symbolize purity and chastity. For example, during the state assembly election of West Bengal in 2021, we saw the ex-BJP Member of Parliament (MP)[24] Babul Supriyo glorifying and sharing a meme featuring an image of Union Home Minister Amit Shah along with a quote which states 'Beti paraya dhan hoti hai, iss baar vida kar denge' ('A daughter is someone else's property, will send her off this time'). This was

---

[24] During state assembly election of West Bengal in 2021, Babul Supriyo was MP of BJP, later he changed his political affiliation and joined All India Trinomul Congress.

an obvious reference to Mamata Banerjee, the incumbent chief minister of the state whom the BJP was trying to overthrow. The meme pandered to the traditional idea that women have value only in their marital homes and do not belong to their paternal families. My argument gets further strengthened when we find the Uttar Pradesh chief minister posting an article on his website saying the following: 'Considering the importance and honour of women ... our scriptures have always spoken about giving her protection ... As energy can go waste and cause damage if left free and uncontrolled, women['s] power also does not require freedom, but protection.'

3

The Muslim Social Genre

From Exotic Exclusive to Ordinary Inclusive

Figure 3.1 From Exotic (Rekha in *Umrao Jaan*) to Ordinary (Farhan in *Zindegi Milegi Nahi Dobara*)
Source: Nadira Khatun; illustration by Sreeja Burman.

Postcolonial Bollywood and Muslim Identity. Nadira Khatun, Oxford University Press. © Oxford University Press 2024.
DOI: 10.1093/oso/9780198891017.003.0004

We have already discussed in the last section of the previous chapter that the decline of the Muslim Historical genre started in the mid-1960s.[1] An interesting development that took place during that time was the noticeable emergence of the Muslim Social genre; though the genre can be said to have begun in the late 1940s and lasted through the 2010s, it was most evident in the 1960s and 1970s. The Muslim Social is a subset of the wider genre known as 'the Social', which depicts family conflict, marriages, and romantic stories. As the name signifies, the Muslim Social genre encompasses films that depict the 'Islamicate world'. This chapter argues that through this genre a separate identity for Muslims was constructed by very specific use of language, region, socioeconomic status, and culture. In the article 'Secularism and Popular Indian Cinema' (2007), Shyam Benegal sketches the genre and mentions the following:

> While the Social is a loosely defined term for melodramas with the modern setting, the term 'Muslim Social' is broadly used to describe a sub-genre of narrative films that focused on social issues distinctive to Muslim culture and lives. Often imbued with a sense of nostalgia for an older traditional culture even when set in a contemporary framework, these films tended to constitute Muslims as an isolated and archaic community faced with a singular problem. (2007: 238)

This chapter explores the representational pattern of the Muslim Social and political economy of filmmaking in the genre. Based on reading the film texts and reviewing in-depth interviews I conducted, the chapter is divided into four sub-themes: (i) Ideology and political economy of the Muslim Social genre; (ii) Courtesans: objects of 'male gaze'; (iii) Sociopolitical aspects of portraying Muslims as antagonists and side character in social films; and (iv) New Wave: the Muslim Social. The first section focuses on the film texts of traditional Muslim Social films, as well as their portrayal and the ideology espoused in them. The second segment discusses the role of courtesans and how they are viewed as objects of the 'male gaze'. The third segment reflects the political economy of the

---

[1] Parts of this chapter draw on material previously published in Khatun, Nadira (2020) Courtesans and Male Gaze: Imagining Muslim Women's Identity. In *Social and Cultural Dynamics of Indian Cinema*, edited by Santosh Kumar Biswal. Pennsylvania: IGI Global Press.

films where Muslims are represented as sidekicks to the protagonists. The last part of the chapter locates the films that are mostly termed parallel cinema or middle cinema where ordinary Muslims are represented in their everyday lives.

Ideology and the Political Economy of the Muslim Social Genre

Hindu customs and practices are considered to be the predominant norms of Indian culture; as a result, there is no need to create a separate genre called The Hindu Social genre. On the other hand, Muslim rituals and practices are identified as a distinct form, which is tagged with and gets its identity from religion. Film historians such as Rachel Dwyer (2006), Ira Bhaskar and Richard Alan (2009), and Ravi Vasudevan (2015) have identified and classified the films that are centred around the Islamicate culture (discussed in detail in Chapter 3) of Muslims as the Muslim Social genre. When we consider the themes of a number films in this genre—*Najma* (1943), *Elaan* (1947), *Chandni Chowk* (1953/1954), *Mirza Ghalib* (1954), *Mere Mehboob* (1963), *Chaudhvin Ka Chand* (1963), *Benazir* (1964), *Gazal* (1964), *Bahu Begum* (1967), *Mere Huzoor* (1968), *Mehboob ki Mehndi* (1971), *Pakeezah* (1972), *Garam Hawa* (1974), *Junoon* (1978), *Umrao Jaan* (1981), *Nikaah* (1982), *Bazaar* (1982), *Tawaif* (1985), *Salim Langde Pe Mat Ro* (1989), *Mammo* (1994), *Naseem* (1995) *Sardari Begum* (1996), *Dedh Ishqiya* (2014), and *Fitoor* (2016)—we find that they focus primarily only on aristocratic Muslim life, mostly belonging to the north Indian area of Awadh, disregarding the significant majority of the Muslim population in the nation. The dissolute feudal nobility, on the one hand, and the magnificence of architecture and lavish décor of aristocratic daily lives, on the other hand, defined this genre. The identity construction was marked only on the basis of cultural elements; therefore, Ravi S. Vasudevan points out that it was 'one not based on ethnicity, but on a broader sense of cultural habitation through the familiarities of linguistic and musical idiom, narrative convention, and architectural and sartorial engagement' (2015: 27). While promoting *Najma* (1943), Mehboob Khan mentioned the 'grand Majestic yet serene Domestic life of the U.P. *nawabs*' (cited in Bhaskar, 2009: 70). Rarsa Venkateshwar Rao remarks:

> The Muslim characters in these films spoke a strange and stilted Urdu which a majority of non-Urdu speakers took for a sophisticated and delicate language and recited verse at every turn, spent an enormous time in saying their hellos and goodbyes, elaborate aadaabs, and the khuda hafizs. They were mostly from *nawabi* families, and they almost always came from Lucknow. All they ever seemed to do was move in and out of their havelis, visiting the *tawaif's* kotha as one would perhaps a movie hall, fall in and out of love, and all that, and all that. (1997)

Shyam Benegal points out that in the post-Independence era, there was a deliberate effort to make Muslim characters as secular as possible, owing to controversial issues such as Partition and subsequent riots at that time. They were repeatedly depicted in films as *nawabs* in order to depict them as secular and benevolent people who only indulged themselves in cultural affairs and indirectly endorsed culture and cultural practices rather than religion. All these films show an Islamicate culture and *nawabs* are supporting the same in those films (Figure 3.2).

Figure 3.2 *Chaudhvin Ka Chand*: Islamicate culture of bourgeoise *nawabs*
Source: Nadira Khatun; illustration by Sreeja Burman.

These films serve two purposes of portraying them as *nawabs*: first, the films emphasize aristocratic class identity of Muslims; second, most interestingly these films glorify Islamicate culture which has nothing to do with Islam, therefore primary protagonists of those appear to be the secular *nawabs* who don't have any religious baggage. As a consequence, they have been the victims of typecast images. Benegal further says the following about his personal experience of the characterization of a Muslim character:

> You became self-consciously secular; if I have created a Muslim character, [he/she] always had to be very good and that is another reason of representing Muslims as *nawab* all the time. (Personal Interview, 29 June 2013)

Adding to Shyam Benegal's point, there are a few more reasons and because of that we see a specific type of Muslim characterization in the Muslim Social genre. Since the inception of the Bombay film industry, Hindu characters have ruled Hindi cinema. One can argue that the Muslim Social was developed as a reaction to the lack of depiction of the Muslim community in Bombay Hindi films. It provided a platform for the portrayal of Islamicate culture, brotherhood, and values on screen. Therefore, while examining the production part of the Muslim Social genre (predominantly belonging to the 1960s and 1970s), I locate that the writers and makers of those film texts were mostly Muslim men— Mehboob Khan (director of *Pukar* and *Elan*), Mohammad Sadiq (director of *Bahu Begam* and *Chaudhvin Ka Chand*), Aghajani Kashmeri (writer of *Najma*), Muzaffar Ali (director of *Umrao Jaan*), Kamal Amrohi (director, producer, and writer of *Pakeezah*), and Jan Nissar Akhtar (producer of *Bahu Begam*). Ghulam Mohammad, Naushad, Rafiq Ghaznavi, Mohammed Rafi, Shakeel Badayuni, and Shahir Ludhianvi were the most prominent singers, music composers, and lyricists of that period. In spite of having a visible group of Muslim filmmakers who tried to uphold Islamicate culture and tradition to some extent, they did not address the mundane issues faced by ordinary Muslims in their everyday lives.

The exaggerated expression of the Muslim elite as seen in the Muslim Social genre created controversies multiple times. It is mentioned in Ravi S. Vasudevan's seminal article (2015) that films of Muslim subjects often elicited media outrage due to misleading portrayals of Muslim practices and religious beliefs. Producer Hasnain acknowledged that making such films against the political backdrop was difficult, but one had to deliberately choose to take on the task notwithstanding the complications:

> Muslim Social and cultural life must be portrayed on the screen as it has numerous facets worthy of emulation by the masses in general and unless the Mahomedans see them as presented through the artistic emotions of a motion picture producer, how will they ever come to love their way of living? I am a Mahomedan, and if I don't risk it [a violent response], who would? (Filmindia cited in Vasudevan, 2015: 40)

As Lucknowi culture through the depiction of *nawabs* was the primary focus in classical Muslim Social films, legendary film writer and lyricist Javed Akhtar is critical about the genre. He is of the opinion that the stereotyped representation in such films had a striking reaction on audience psychology.

> We created an image of a good Muslim. Good Muslim who is either a *nawab* or a poet, and every girl is a beauty queen, and the houses are full of chiks and chandelier, shamadan, and so on. This is a total imaginary culture which cinema had created. Indian cinema created an alternate Muslim culture where everybody is a poet—talking quotes of poetry and so on so forth. So now we had two Muslims in our lives. One was the screen *nawab*, Shikandar Shah, and the other, the man who was my neighbour who was a small shop owner who was selling bicycles, and had more difficulty in understanding Urdu in spite of the fact that he was a Muslim but this was an ordinary Muslim. On the other, the poet and *nawab* was the Muslim. Now this cycle-wallah also started fantasizing, this was our background, this was our past, and they connected with that. Like this a delusion within the community itself was born. And on the other side, people felt that yes, that Muslim who has chiks and chandelier, and candlestand, poetry, *daru* [liquor], that's a good Muslim and I have great respect for him. But this small shop owner needs to progress, modernize, and so on. (Personal interview, 16 March 2021)

That Muslim filmmakers tried to glorify Muslim cultures through these Muslim Social films, can be seen as a business strategy rather than a benevolent attempt at upholding Muslim values on screen. Filmmakers also explored how a film could appeal to a specific audience segment. According to Ravi Vasudevan, audience segmentation means categorization of films by genre and target demographic, with the suggestion that different genres charmed the viewers with diverse cultural and social backgrounds. Simply stating the fact, Indian Hindi film viewers were diverse, and cinema as an institution did not guarantee a homogenized identity of audiences united by cultural and intellectual interests. 'The most commonplace discursive segmentation of audiences lay across the rural–urban divide, but audiences were in certain trade circles conceived of in terms of gender and generational difference (women, children, and college-going youth), religious persuasion (orthodox and devout audiences, usually meaning Hindus, Muslim audiences being separately referred to) and class configured audiences (intellectuals, middle class, and "masses")' (Vasudevan, 2015: 29). Because of the audience segmentation, we see the rise and demand of films belonging to different genres such as mythology, nationalistic melodrama, historical epic dramas, social melodrama, and so on. Moreover, due to the sociopolitical crisis from the late 1930s, we see the rise of a more homogenized collection of demands for how societies could be portrayed in Bombay Hindi cinema. Therefore, it can be argued that the Muslim Social genre was actually fulfilling the demands from a particular kind of audience. Though there are multiple criticisms of the Muslim Social genre for not being realistic and for being outdated, archaic, and homogenized, many Muslim filmmakers were involved in the entire filmmaking process for this particular genre, be it as producer, director, or music composer. To understand the reasons behind it we need to understand the critical cultural context of the time. The period when the Muslim Social genre witnessed the greatest popularity was that of decolonization and partition in the subcontinent; this was a critical time for the institutionalization of ideas about the ties of the so-called Hindu majority to Muslims, the most significant minority (Vasudevan, 2015). Cinema acted as an important platform for discussing cultural diversity. Here we can deduce that Muslim Social films were particularly made to cater to Muslim audiences. Nandhini Ramnath, a film journalist and critic, believes that

Muslim Socials were portrayals of the Muslim community, targeted specifically at a Muslim audience.

> Muslim Social is fantasy based genre … fantasy is a too strong a word, but even escapist is a too strong a word … but a genre that is part real and part romantic fantasy. I usually see Muslim characters in those contexts as you know [in] films of the 1960s, 1970s, like *Tawaif*, *Chaudhvin ka Chand*, later *Nikaah* were essentially set in a Muslim world or feature Muslims' world; they are often not necessarily made by Muslims but I think were aimed at treating Muslims as a separate audience and catering to their needs and desires and fantasies and their … moral values and moral ecosystem. (Personal interview, 5 February 2013)

As per Ramnath's conceptualization, when I spoke to an audience member, Dr Kaifiya Fatehma, she expressed the nostalgia of watching films of that genre. From the conversation, it was very evident that Muslims consumed such film texts quite eagerly and appreciated them. She mentions:

> Earlier we used to have Muslim Socials where the main protagonist used to revolve around Muslim households, Muslim stories. Male characters would be dressing in sherwani; female [characters] would be dressing in ghararas. In those films, Muslims are portrayed as very *tehjeebwale*, well cultured. The overall ambience was over the top. During my childhood, I used to go with my aunt to enjoy the grand setting of that portrayal. (Personal interview, 30 January 2021)

Though there was a claim that the films of this genre were made to glorify Muslim culture and were appreciated by a section of audience, the genre was also criticized for a number of reasons such as depicting old-fashioned and archaic ways of representing the everyday lives of Muslims, misrepresentation of the Muslim community, and lack of inclusivity. For example, we find the exaggerated way of representing Islamicate culture in the earliest Muslim Social film *Yaad* (1942, directed by Mazhar Khan). The film was also not well received by critics at the time. One negative review read as follows:

Was it necessary that because 'Yad' happened to be a story of Muslim family life, one of its legal situations should also be decided in a multi-bearded court? This was rather too much of a Muslim colour to a Muslim subject. The court scene should not have had Pakistan paint on it. (*Filmindia* cited in Bhaskar and Allen, 1943: 66)

Mehboob Khan's *Najma* (1943) was the Muslim Social film that firmly established the genre, and it was followed by another film of the same genre, *Elaan* (1947). Both films were critical of the *nawabi* class and emphasized the importance of Western education (Masud, 2005). The narratives of these two films showcased a conflict between Western modernism and Islamicate culture. While reviewing *Elaan* (1947), *Filmindia* 'stated that the film "misrepresents Muslim life", and, that "as a good Muslim himself", it was Mehboob's "sacred duty to present his community in the best light possible", because the "crude and vulgar behaviour [of Raziya] towards her husband" cannot be taken as an accurate portrayal of the "relationship between a middle-class Muslim husband and his wife"' (cited in Bhaskar and Allenn, 2009: 70).

However, in spite of widespread criticism of the Muslim Social's lack of representation of ordinary working-class Muslims, we find that there were some films, such as *Yaad* and *Naukar*, that depicted protagonists who were working-class individuals. *Yaad* was the love story of a *tanga-walla* and the daughter of a horseshoe artisan. *Naukar* (1943, directed by Shaukat Hussain Rizvi) is based on the life of Fazlu, who works as a servant. The New Wave films too depicted everyday Muslim life.

Another significant trend during the 1940s and 1950s saw Muslims being depicted in non-Islamic social genres. One reason for this could be that before Independence, the Bombay film industry consciously tried depicting cultural ties in order to combat simmering communal tensions. Whatever the cause, at that time, there was a rise in the number of Muslim characters in films. Despite the fact that they were depicted as secondary characters, they played a major part in the storyline. For example, films like *Padosi* (1941, directed by V. Shantaram), *Bhai Chara* (1943, directed by G.K. Mehta), *Bhalai* (1943, directed by Nazir Ahmen Khan), and *Dhool Ka Phool* (1959, directed by Yash Raj Chopra) promoted narratives like national integration through communal harmony, brotherhood, and bond between communities.

Muslim Social films have covered a wide range of subjects. Most interestingly, we see a number of films from the 1970s and early 1980s that emphasize a religious message rather than propagating a note of communal harmony. Films such as *Mere Gharib Nawaz* (1973), *Dayar-E-Madina* (1975), *Niyaz Aur Namaz* (1977), *Aulia-E-Islam* (1979), and *Bismillah Ki Barkat* explicitly focused on religious messages for Muslims. In particular, Mastan Haider Mirza—alias Haji Mastan—the infamous Mumbai smuggler and underworld don, financed a variety of such Muslim Social films with an explicit Islamic appeal (Zaidi, 2012).

Women characters in traditional Muslim Socials are those mostly shown as oppressed owing to the genre's mystification of the female body, which was furthered by the depiction of the practice of *purdah* (veil/curtain) 'which confines women to the interior spaces of the home and physically segregates them through walls, curtains and screens as well as restricts their activities outside the home' (Bhaskar and Allen, 2009: 81). In Muslim Social films, Muslim women are doubly marginalized: first because of their Muslim identity and second because of their gender identity. We also notice that there are two dominant portrayals of Muslim women in such films: as *tehzeebwale* (cultured) women and as *tawaifs*. A senior journalist Abhinash Dey (name changed) expressed the same opinion in a conversation with me.

Nadira: If you are asked to recall the image of Muslim women in Bollywood cinema, what is the first thing that you remember?

Abhinash: Firstly, the image that comes is, you know, old Hindi movies, where, you know, [there is this] very cultured *shayari* and so on. Right now, I remember the very famous song 'Mere meheboob tujhe mari muhabbat ki kasham'; he's on a stage and singing, and remembering his *burqa*-clad lady love who's fluent in *shayaris*. Next obviously is the *tawaif*; even [when] the portrayals of *tawaifs* were shown to be intellectually very strong like Umrao Jaan. (Personal interview, 14 March 2021)

According to Irfan Engineer, Muslim women have been stereotyped in Hindi cinema since its inception:

They were very much stereotypical. Muslim women [in] *burqa* ... or at least that salwar kameez dress ... It's typical Muslim salwar kameez dress ... not the one that all women wear and with head covered and all that ... so mostly, you will rarely find a normal secular character ... as Muslim. (Personal interview, 14 September 2012)

The narratives of these films showcase the practice of *purdah* as something that endorses the pride of a woman, yet sometimes leads her to misery. But *purdah* also 'dramatizes' the romance between the hero and the heroine, since it conceals and mystifies a woman's presence. Filmmakers of Muslim Socials have conveniently utilized the custom of *purdah* to suit the needs of storylines. Critics criticized the *purdah* system in films like *Najma*, because of the repressive nature of the practice; on the other hand, in *Mere Mehboob*, the *purdah* was utilized to act as a spark for 'mystifying' romance. The *purdah* system is also used by Muslim Socials to express tragedy. One of the most celebrated filmmakers, Shyam Benegal, has utilized the *burqa* (a dress covering the entire body) in multiple films to express the subjugation of women or to mock the societal practices. When he was asked about this during an interview, he said:

If you take my opinion, I think the custom of wearing *burqa* I find is not very interesting. [But] it also has a sense of security and safety for a lot of women. You are much more secure when you have *burqa*. They feel that they can't be attacked. It's like armour, precaution. I asked many women; they say it's not because of belief but I feel safer when I go out alone on the street. If you are going in a bus and a lady is wearing *burqa*, people will leave her alone and [there] will not be any sexual gesture. (Personal interview, 29 June 2013)

In the 1970s we find that a change occurred in the portrayals of Muslims. They were depicted as 'lower-class Muslims rather than aristocrats synonymous with a glorious history' (Dwyer, 2006: 126). *Coolie* (1983) was the first Bollywood film to cast Amitabh Bachchan, the superstar, as an oppressed Muslim man who stood up to upper-class citizens and advocated for his basic rights. Fareed Kazmi explains the sociopolitical reasons behind the production of *Coolie* by pointing to the political situation of the time. In 1980, Indira Gandhi was re-elected as prime minister of India. By then she did not have much left in her electoral arsenal to ensure her survival, utilizing both populist (*Garibi Hatao*, abolish poverty) and coercive measures (the Emergency[2]). So she chose to play the 'number game' by 'emphasizing the numerical power of the majorities versus the minorities' (Kazmi, 1999: 116). Afterwards, following army exploits in Punjab,[3] 'Mrs Indira Gandhi openly and directly said in Garhwal[4] that the Hindu *dharma* was under attack. And she made an impassioned appeal to save the Hindu *sanskriti* (culture) from the attack that was coming from the Sikhs, the Muslims and the others' (Kazmi, 1999: 116). Kazmi goes on to say that the popularity of *Coolie* among Muslims was one of the reasons for its massive success: '*Coolie* was released at a time when the Muslims were generally sulking, feeling insecure, cornered and on the defensive ... thus its timing was such that it was bound to go down very well with Muslim audience' (Kazmi, 1999: 117). Even the film's co-writer, Javed Akhtar, acknowledged that *Coolie* was especially apt for that time due to the country's sociopolitical scenario.

Nadira: In the films of the 1970s or early 1980s, suddenly there was a shift and we have seen the emergence of a new kind of hero who belonged to a marginalized or downtrodden section of the society. Superstar Amitabh Bachchan became the face of those films. Did you write the films of the period keeping in mind the political scenario of that time?

Javed Akhtar: When I look back, I can see that; but at that point of time we were not aware at all. Now I can see the process ... And, yes, it's true. That was a time [for films] like *Vijay*, *Zanzeer*, or *Sholay*, which was not possible in 1955, it was only possible in 1975. Because that was the time when we believed that now things will become all right. Pandit

---

[2] Prime Minister Indira Gandhi imposed a nationwide state of emergency which lasted for 21 months from 1975 to 1977 in India. The Emergency, which was formally declared by President Fakhruddin Ali Ahmed under Article 352 of the Constitution in response to the then-current 'internal disturbance', was in place from 25 June 1975, until 21 March 1977, when it was officially lifted.Nanda, V.P. (1974) *The Constitutional Framework and the Current Political Crisis in India.* Hastings Const. LQ, 2, p.859; and Williams, R.J. (2014) Storming the Citadels of Poverty: Family Planning under the Emergency in India, 1975–1977. *Journal of Asian Studies*, 73(2), pp.471–92.

[3] During 1981 and 1982, Sikh militants were seeking to establish Khalistan as an independent Sikh state. Indira Gandhi rejected the Anandpur Resolution on 1 June 1984, and 'the Indian state responded with military force, launching Operation Blue Star on the night of 4 June 1984. After an intense overnight battle employing tanks, the army secured the Golden Temple, damaging it seriously in the process and suffering over three hundred casualties. Many Sikh insurgents and some pilgrims perished in the attack. The state was traumatized.' Wolpert, Stanley. (2006) *Encyclopedia of India.* Scribner, p.728.

[4] One of the two administrative regions of the Indian state of Uttarakhand is named Garhwal.

Jawaharlal Nehru was the prime minister, there was a belief in a social-istic pattern of society. And we were convinced that good days are the next page of the calendar, and so on. So it's a matter of days or weeks, when everything will be all right. By the time we reach [the] 70s, dis-illusionment entered in Indian psyche. And for the first time you saw extra-constitutional forces raising their head, for the first time you saw the Supreme Court being poorly ruled by the parliament to change laws and that brought some kinds of different economic and political and social [changes?] and unhappiness, frustration. And that brought the Emergency in 75 [1975]. The Angry Young Man was possible, only that time when people were losing faith in the institution. Because this was a vigilante; he was not depending on any other institution to get justice. That is why he was the Angry Young Man and the vigilante. This vigilante would have been a misfit in 1955. (Personal interview, 16 March 2021)

Furthermore, Amitabh Bachchan's association with films such as *Mukaddar Ka Sikandar* (1978, directed by Prakash Mehra) and *Coolie* may have increased the prominence of middle-class Muslims. Film scholar Madhav Prasad argues about the new development and points out that in such films 'the hero acquired the mandate of workers or ghettoized subalterns' (Prasad, 1998: 143). *Coolie* is also notable for its symbolic use of the number '786', which Muslims consider to be an auspicious number as it propagates the meaning as *Bismillah al-Rahmaan al-Raheem* (In the name of the Most Merciful and Compassionate God). This is in spite of the fact that this number has no particular significance in Islam, but is construed as sacred in India and Pakistan. The number became well-known because of the following dialogue from *Coolie*: '*Apni taarif jara lambi hai. Bachpan se hain sar pe Allah ka haath aur Allahrakha hai apne sath. Baju pe 786 ka hain billa, 20 number ki bidi pita hu. Kam karta hun coolie ka aur naam hai Iqbal.*' ('My introduction is a little longer. From my childhood, I have the blessings of Allah and Allarakha is with me. There is a badge of 786 on my arm; I smoke *beedi* number 20; I am a porter by pro-fession and my name is Iqbal.') In a conversation, Rauf Ahmed points out how meaninglessly '786' has been symbolically used in *Coolie*:

I mean even using constantly, 786, which Amitabh used in his film *Coolie*, is a kind of stereotyping. These are all symbolic uses of things;

there is no such thing as a representation of a Muslim character with all the complexities involved in being a Muslim character. (Personal interview, 28 August 2013)

By the mid-1980s, the Muslim Social genre had lost its appeal and had all but vanished from Indian film culture with the exception of a few occasional appearances. Rauf Ahmed recounts the initial flop of the genre:

By the time they came to *Deedar-E-Yaar* (1982), it collapsed badly. Nobody went to the theatre ... [it was] one of the biggest failures in spite of a huge star cast—Rishi Kapoor, Jeetendra, Rekha, all big-time actors at that time; it flopped because by then the glamorization of Muslim lifestyle and *parde-ke-peeche* (behind the veil) kind of a thing was nostalgia which they used in *Mere Mehboob*. (Personal interview, 28 August 2013)

Shvetal Vyas (2001) observes that if a Muslim Social were to be produced presently, it would appear outdated; not because Muslim culture does not exist anymore but because of a constant demand for new cinematic representation. He cites two explanations for this. To begin with, Indian cultural identity has been fused with that of north and West Indian cultures in the country's popular cinema. Second, 'religious identity in a non-issue based film seems anachronistic because what we understand and see as "natural" or "real" is a depoliticized, non-religious space' (Vyas, 2001: 2). Ramnath believes that the depiction of Lucknowi identity has faded away as a result of a vast number of young people who are more interested in travel, international content of popular culture, and international locations.

We have a very large number of young populations watching the movies, it will be interesting to see movies which fulfil their desires. It's about consumerism. The movies are about travel such as *Zindagi Na Milegi Dobara* (2011) that drives them. Who wants to go back to some Lucknowi era, when we are already in 2013? So nobody wants to go back to that. (Personal interview, 5 February 2013)

In the previous decade, we have seen the emergence of Muslim Social films in a different format; these have some conventional elements of the genre such as *nawabs*, *begums*, *shayari*, and *ghazals* on the one hand, and modern characters on the other hand. Some of these films are set in small towns or somewhere abroad, showcasing inter-country or interreligious relationships, and most importantly, show the characters as facing more mundane problems of day-to-day life. *Ishqiya* (2010), *Dedh Ishqiya* (2014), or the Kashmir-set *Fitoor* (2016) are not Muslim Socials in the traditional sense, but they are the stories about contemporary India. These films did not do very well at the box office, but the audience got a glimpse of small-town stories and relished the refreshing vocabulary in these films. Moreover, they try to tell stories that are different from the conventional narratives we are accustomed to encountering in Bollywood films. Most noticeably, ignoring the recent debate on the issue of 'love jihad', the film *Ishqiya* narrates a love triangle between a Hindu widow and two Muslim men. Instead of representing the central protagonist as an aristocrat like in a conventional Muslim Social film, *Ishqiya* portrays the Muslim men as cons and crooks. *Fitoor*, in spite of showing a glimpse of terrorism in Kashmir, focuses mainly on class conflict. In an interview Abhinash Dey expressed that:

Ishqiya was one of those movies where the Muslim characters were not there as Muslims; they were there as characters of the movie and the plot had nothing to do with their being Muslim. It could well have been [that] the *mama-bhanja* duo [was] Hindu, or Sikh, or so on. As far as I recall, Nasiruddin Shah's love interest in that movie was a widowed Brahmin; which was kind of bold for Bollywood and, surprisingly, it did not generate any controversy possibly because the movie failed at the box office or it was subtle. So, a movie like that is certainly welcome to break the stereotype of portrayal of Muslims in Hindi cinema. (Personal interview, 14 March 2021)

As I have already discussed the image and representation of the Muslim Social genre and the mystifying image of women, we now come to one of the most iconic character types in Muslim Social films, the courtesan. In the subsequent section, I am going to discuss in detail the construction of courtesan figures in Muslim Social films.

Courtesans: Objects of the 'Male Gaze'

This section locates the multilayered status of courtesans in Muslim Social films and traces how that creates an imaginary notion of Muslim women. Looking at the representational pattern, the section also will explore three specific arguments: first, Muslim courtesan films focus on the art of seduction. Second, to make the representation seductive, they are positioned in a particular *mise en scène*. Last, the chapter points out how the makers of these films tried to fit the courtesan characters into the normative majoritarian gender discourse, in which women are represented as subservient by ignoring the liberated identity of *tawaifs*.[5] While courtesans are visible in numerous literary and cultural texts, perhaps nowhere is the portrayal of courtesans as prevalent as in films, in several of which courtesans are the central characters. Films with courtesans as protagonists gained much popularity among audiences and have proved to be a favoured plot device of noted filmmakers until recent times. Such films include *Mamta* (1966), *Mandi* (1983), *Chetna* (1970), *Dastak* (1970), *Khilona* (1970), *Amar Prem* (1971), *Pakeezah* (1971), *Bhumika* (1977), *Utsav* (1985), and *Ram Teri Ganga Maili* (1987).

The Indian courtesan films can be characterized into two broad classifications: first, courtesan films based on religion such as Hindu courtesan films and Muslim courtesan films; second, modern-day and historical courtesan films. I shall focus on Muslim courtesan films—it is worthwhile to note here that such films stand out as an independent genre named the Muslim courtesan genre. In this section, I will be discussing courtesan films under the sub-genre of Muslim Socials because *tawaif* characters are frequently found in Muslim Historical and Muslim Social films (Khatun, 2016). Historically, courtesans evoked the attraction of their audience, generally heterosexual men, by facilitating the production of a variety of pleasures. In the case of courtesan films, it is the film viewer who occupies the position of the audience, that is, the heterosexual men. Thus, courtesan characters are portrayed as the objects of 'male gaze'. Such representation is universal and visible not only in cinema but in all cultural texts. Christine Gledhill writes: 'Women as women are not represented in the

---

[5] The word '*tawaif*' is defined in different ways such as a dancing–singing girl, a prostitute, and courtesan. In this chapter, *tawaif* and courtesan are used interchangeably.

cinema, that they do not have a voice, that the female point of view is not heard. Recognition of this fact unites all attempts at a Feminist critique of cinema' (1999: 251). I seek to examine the representation of courtesans in Muslim courtesan films individually. Here, I argue that Muslim courtesan films communicate the notion of seduction as a form of art by their use of exotic Islamicate culture, which is represented through extravagant costumes, among others.

Muslim courtesan films locate *tawaifs* in a dizzyingly rich past where they are represented as exotic beings dolled up in their glittery jewellery and dazzling clothing, practising their art of seduction and alluring dance steps. Therefore, the portrayals of courtesans are so eccentric that they seem antiquated and old-fashioned in contemporary times. In this section, I will be documenting and analysing films such as *Mere Mehboob* (1963, courtesan as the sister of the hero), *Mehboob Ki Mehendi* (1971, courtesan as the mother of the heroine), *Pakeezh* (1972), *Umrao Jaan* (1981, 2006), *Tawaif* (1985), and *Rajjo* (2013). In these films, courtesans are shown either as central characters or the 'Other Woman' who acts as a foil to the heroine.

The representational pattern of these films can be deconstructed through the lens of Laura Mulvey's (1975) theoretical paradigm of 'to-be-looked-at-ness'. Mulvey (1975) introduced the notion of the male gaze. It helps to distinguish between 'other women' as *tawaifs* and normative heroines as 'sanskari' (a strict follower of Indian culture). Mulvey argued that the nature of female representation in cinema is of three gazes: first, through the male characters of the film; second, through the film's audience; and third, through camera movements. In most films, women mostly get objectified by camera movements and the viewer but not through the male characters within the narrative frame. Muslim courtesan films objectify women in all the three categories because those films objectify *tawaifs* through the eyes of the heroes who are the patrons of those courtesans. In addition, courtesan-genre spectators were put in the role of a male heterosexual audience.

Lucknow was the cultural centre of India until the early twentieth century and *tawaifs* played a vital role in establishing a syncretic cultural tradition during that time. The courtesan culture attained extreme popularity and turned into a highly erudite and admired institution that was patronized by the *nawabs*. Veena Talwar Oldenburg, in her seminal work *Lifestyle as Resistance: The Case of the Courtesans of Lucknow, India* (1990), writes a detailed account of the courtesan's life and profession. According to her, courtesans belonged to a larger, complex, and hierarchical system that was run by a *Choudhurayan* (chief courtesan). After a successful career as *tawaifs*, courtesans set up their own houses and were able to recruit young women. Sometimes, they hired their daughters and nieces or daughters from wealthy households. The real-life stories of courtesans closely resemble Umrao Jaan's biography narrated by Ruswa in the novel *Umrao Jaan Ada* (Dwyer, 2006), where Umrao was sadly kidnapped and sold. There are also narratives of famous courtesans who were born into the profession in the *kotha*.[6]

According to Oldenburg, 'the British usurpation of the kingdom of Awadh in 1856 and the forced exile of the king and many of his courtiers had abruptly put an end to royal patronage for the courtesans' (1990: 260). In later years, although there were a few landowners who maintained a courtly culture, it could never achieve the refinement of the earlier days. Moreover, during British rule, the provisions of Britain's Contagious Diseases Act of 1864 required a periodic medical examination of all prostitutes and courtesans living in cantonment cities all over India, which also harmed the lives of courtesans. Later, courtesans had to pay huge fines and penalties due to the protest over the contagious diseases regulations. Women who once enjoyed an esteemed position in society and affluent living conditions had to opt for prostitution.

In Indian cinema, the depiction of courtesan culture has been prevalent from the initial period of the Hindi film industry where they were portrayed as character actors and mostly portrayed as Hindus. Later on, courtesans became the central characters in films, and they were represented as Muslims. Religion played an essential role in acquiring a special status for a courtesan. Rachel Dwyer says, 'Many of the courtesans in north India took Muslim, often Shi'ite, names even if they were Hindus to associate themselves with Lucknowi culture' (Dwyer, 2006: 117). *Umrao Jaan* (1981, directed by Muzaffar Ali) and *Pakeezah* (1971, directed by Kamal Amrohi) are some of the relevant films.

---

[6] *Kotha* is an institution where several *tawaifs* reside and perform their art form and these women are cut off from the wider community and outside world.

Figure 3.3 *Pakeezah*: Voyeuristic pleasure of *tawaifs'* performance
Source: Nadira Khatun; illustration by Sreeja Burman.

On viewing mainstream Bollywood films such as *Umrao Jaan* (1981 and 2006), *Pakeezah* (1971), *Mere Mehboob* (1963), and *Mehboob Ki Mehendi* (1971), we observe that Muslim courtesan cinema heightened the power of seduction as an art, which had a few peculiar characteristics. The courtesan always dressed fully covered while performing a mujra.[7] Rather than exposing the body, their facial expressions, dialogues, and lyrics served as the tools of seduction. '*Tawaif*, the women who combined feminine graces and sensual charms with courtly etiquette and the arts of singing and dancing, had become, before the arrival of European colonizers, valued embodiments of the nazakat and nafasat, the delicacy and finesse, of Lucknow *tehzeeb*' (Singh, 2014). Further, filmmakers employed many tricks to portray the *tawaif* as desirable and seductive: they make her wear bright and richly coloured clothes, make her alluring by using transparent veils, deck her in heavy jewellery, and cover her in unnecessary accessories. The overall effect is turning her identity into an exotic one (Figure 3.3). In these films, the elaborate costumes worn by the courtesan were an amalgamation of eroticism, sexuality, and the immoral.

---

[7] Dancing and singing by *tawaif* in the mehfil (gathering) in front of male or mixed audience.

Her femininity is sexualized through the dazzling and extravagant display of the external self; 'the courtesan [is] made to embody exotic femininity for Indian audiences, the exotic being an amalgam of hyper-erotic and the sinful or taboo' (Hubel, 2012: 227). It was clear that the Muslim courtesan films adored women's bodies even though they covered them with glittery clothes and heavy jewellery. In such films, elaborate items of clothing acted as a means to objectify the female body, and the costumes became an essential component of eroticism and sexuality (Khatun, 2016: 67). While carrying out an empirical enquiry on courtesan films, I spoke to Diviya Kodoth, who is a research scholar doing her PhD on gender studies. She primarily recalled the elaborate costume of the *tawaif* characters and said:

> There are films which had all these dance sequences and the characters dressed with all gold, [big] chains much like Aishwarya Rai wore in *Umrao Jaan Ada*. (Personal interview, 14 January 2013)

While performing the *mujra*, the courtesan's body is fetishized, especially the feet, which are the only exposed part of the body. In the film *Pakeezah*, we notice that the courtesan Shahibjaan's feet are used as a metaphor to represent love and anguish. The feet are painted in red and adorned with heavy jewellery. There is a sequence in that film where the lover leaves a note for the Shahibjaan in the train: '*Aapke paon bahut haseen hain. Inhen zameen par mat utariyega, maile ho jaayenge!*' (Your feet are gorgeous. Do not let them touch the ground, they will get dirty). Moreover, on the wedding day of Salim (Shahibjaan's beloved), Shahibjaan gashes her feet on broken glass, thereby conveying the pain and anguish of being separated from her beloved. Shahibjaan exhibits her exemplary talents in Urdu poetry, song, and Kathak dance. She demurely lifts her veil over her eyes, waves her arm, wrist, and fingers to the delight of her male spectators, and raises her skirt above her ankles to highlight the rhythmic beating of her bell-adorned feet. Shahibjaan masterfully fulfils her role as a courtesan.

One of the most important legacies of courtesan culture is the development of Kathak as a dance form. 'Kathak owes its origins and sophisticated elaboration largely to the *tawaifs* of India's medieval period' (Ward, 2008: 5). Red-coloured palms, manicured and bejewelled fingers, her masked face and dark black-painted eyes are the only uncovered parts of a *tawaif's* body as well as essential components to expresses her sexuality. Thus, considering all aspects of the *mise en scène*, the representation of sexuality becomes an art, and the courtesan becomes an object of desire for men in the *mehfil* (gathering) as well as for those in the audience.

Beauty is another critical component in achieving the art of seduction. That is why courtesan films always represented *tawaifs* as especially attractive, and the most gorgeous and glamorous actresses were chosen for these roles. The most well-known Muslim courtesan films are *Pakeezah* (1972) and *Umrao Jaan* (1981 and 2006) and in these films, Meena Kumari, Rekha, and Aishwarya Rai respectively acted in the protagonist's role. These three actresses have been the most desirable and beautiful of their time. Shiladitya Sen mentions how *Umrao Jaan* was well appreciated by audience as he compares it with *36 Chowringhee*, a film released in the same year:

> *Umrao Jaan* and *36 Chowringhee Lane* were released in the year 1981. Although both the directors, Muzaffar Ali and Aparna Sen, were non-mainstream directors, *Umrao Jaan* did better in the sense that it was more appreciated by the audience. Even actor Rekha got the National Award for the best actress. The public appreciated the film more because it was about Umrao Jaan and she was [very] beautiful and glamorous. All these romanticisms are important factors to attract audiences and especially Hindus. (Personal interview, 13 April 2013)

Music and lyrics play an enormously important role in Muslim courtesan films. The best courtesan houses boasted of the services of skilled male musicians who were also masters of Urdu poetry. Thus, we see Umrao Jaan discussing poetry with Maulvi Sahib. Lyrics also had the role of enhancing the art of seduction. It becomes evident in the following words of a song Umrao Jaan sings, '*In aakhon ki masti ke mastaane hazaaron hain*' (Thousands are intoxicated by these eyes). It shows a 'level of intimacy between the protagonists' and articulated a level of yearning that visuals alone could not achieve (Somaaya, 2012: 11).

The courtesans are portrayed as 'Others' who attain a distinct social situation and economic position, which is very different from that of the other female protagonists in Hindi films. This difference in depiction is only because of their profession, which is linked to sexuality and the *tawaifs* are displayed as a sexualized object most of the time and they are looked at through the lens of value structures about seduction and morality of the bourgeois patriarchy. Thus, courtesans could be the object of desire or even the affection of men. However, they could never be married to these men. It is what we see in *Umrao Jaan* when a *nawab* Sultan marries another woman to please his family. A similar fate befell Sahibjaan in *Pakeezah*. Salim Ahmed Khan could not marry her as she was a *tawaif*. Sahibjaan makes the ultimate sacrifice and leaves Salim Ahmed Khan so that he could be free from any kind of societal burden and live a respectable life in a normative ideal society. However, during the closure of the film, everyone comes to know that Sahibjaan's father belonged to the same respectable family as her beloved. It is only this new-found social acceptance that allows her to marry Salim Ahmed Khan. Therefore, it can be argued that sexual identity and respectability have a close association in Indian culture. In the films that are discussed here, we notice that even other family members of the courtesans are not accepted and cannot marry into a reputed family. In *Mere Mehboob*, the central character, Anwar Hossain, is the brother of a *tawaif*. So he has to prove his ethical nature and high moral values during the film before he can be accepted as a suitable groom for Husna, the female lead of the film.

In both the films *Umaro Jaan* (1981 and 2006) and *Pakeezah* (1972), young women are forced into prostitution because of unfortunate or impecunious circumstances. The constrained conditions of these women already mark them out as individuals outside respectable society for whom there is no other option but to turn to prostitution. Thereby, these films position the courtesan outside of decent society. Because courtesans, as represented in these films, do not occupy a respectable status in society, to gain any sort of respectability the only hope that the *tawaif* had was to get married to a man from a well-regarded family. A courtesan could not achieve any acceptable social standing on her own. Even though both the characters Shahibjaan and Umrao Jaan from the films *Pakeezah* and *Umrao Jaan* respectively are very successful in their profession, they could not hope for a noble identity for themselves (Khatun, 2016: 69). Shahibjaan yearned to escape her *tawaif* life in *Pakeezah* and be with her beloved, who, incidentally, drops a letter flattering her feet. Her cousin tries to convince her that the letter was not intended for a *tawaif* like her. In this case, the cousin acts as a social moral force. In his essay 'Ways of

Seeing', John Berger points out that a man's social existence differs from that of a woman. He mentions, 'While men act, women appear, while men survey, women are surveyed. Men look at women, women watch themselves being looked at. Thus a woman becomes an object, an object of vision, a sight to be seen' (1985: 112). When Shahibjaan is deceived by the entire world and forced to abandon her beloved towards the end of the film, she returns to the *kotha*, which is the only choice left for a courtesan. She compares her body to a carcass in a metaphorical sense. She laments her situation to her cousin, who is also a *tawaif*, and says:

> My vagabond dead body has returned to be buried in this colourful tomb ... every courtesan is a dead body. I am a dead body and you too. And this marketplace is a graveyard of women whose souls are dead but bodies remain alive. These mansions are our tombs in which the living coffins of we dead women are kept after being decorated. Our coffins are left open ... I am a restless dead body of one such open coffin which is lured by life again and again.

Sumita S. Chakravarty points out, 'In this way Indian mass culture links the taint of money with the taint of women' (2011: 276). Therefore, there is a conflict between the reel and real life of a courtesan: though in real life courtesans were very independent, they were represented on screen as hapless creatures who needed to be rescued from a life of dishonour. In this regard, Oldenburg mentions:

> Most women [*tawaifs*] told their stories with enthusiasm. They had wanted to escape 'hell' (the word jahannum, the Islamic hell, was frequently used to describe their earlier homes) at any cost. Learning professional skills and earning their own money helped them develop self-esteem and value the relative independence they encountered in Rahat Jan's[8] kotha. (1990: 267)

Courtesans are portrayed as tragic heroines but because of their financial independence, they embody a dichotomy between women's autonomy

---

[8] One of the courtesans whom Veena Talwar Oldenburg interviewed for her empirical work *Lifestyle as Resistance: The Case of the Courtesans of Lucknow* (1990).

and their aspirations of being a wife or a prospective wife. In this regard, Abhinash Dey says:

> There is a mismatch between the representation and with reality. Because [in] Bollywood movies, you know, the portrayal of the *tawaifs* was actually based on nautch girls who used to sing in the court of kings and *nawabs*. So they were poets and writers in their own right. It is said that they were not married and, you know, didn't live the social life. That's why they were shunned. But they were also admired. I wouldn't call those representations negative, in the sense that those portraits, even if they show them as *tawaifs*, as organic characters, were themselves very strong portraits. (Personal interview, 14 March 2021)

Here I argue that the masculine view of Indian Hindi cinema from its early history has been trying to project society in a particular way; it is an attempt to showcase mainstream Indian culture and stereotyped gender roles in it. Courtesans' portrayals in films show them as self-sufficient as well as economically independent. On the contrary, traditionally men are the ones who acquire status and position in a society. This has the effect of endowing courtesans with a defeminized identity in popular culture. However, economic independence gave them the identity of an immoral person. Almost all the courtesan films culminated in a distressing loss experienced by the *tawaifs*. The primary conflict in the courtesan films centred around the dichotomy between their treatment as either *devis* (goddesses) or loose women. They highlighted a 'woman's quest for *Devi* status and domesticity, not a man's physical battle for control of her destiny' (Booth, 2007). I argue that the desire to portray women as normative middle-class wives started during the colonial period because of the nationalist struggle when women were ascribed the responsibility of protecting the spiritual space and spiritually belonged to the home. It means women were primarily supposed to take care of the home and men's responsibility rested on fulfilling the material needs of the family.

I would like to argue that in films about *tawaifs*, even though the *purdah* is perceived to uphold the dignity of a woman, it still imbues her body with a sense of confusion. On the other hand, we find that the *purdah* also 'dramatizes the romance' (as in *Mere Mehboob*) by mystifying women's bodies by concealing their sexuality. Thus, Muslim courtesan films expressed both tragedy and romance by their depiction of the *purdah* system. Repetitive usage and association of the *burqa* with the Muslim community builds a typical image of Muslim women in courtesan films and makes the representation of the city of Lucknow a stereotypical one. Like other Muslim Social films, all the protagonists in this genre are also represented as the Other. Muslim courtesan films always represent courtesans as exotic and the Other. Muslim ethos or 'Islamicate culture' is the primary element used to make the representation appear to be an exotic one. As Muslim Social films represented Muslims from a single perspective, the characterizations of Muslim protagonists were also highly idealized. As a result, Muslim courtesan films fall into the trap of stereotyping. They depict the courtesan with shimmering jewellery, glittering sartorial choices, and captivating dance steps. In this genre of cinema, filmmakers used lavish sets, detailed song-and-dance numbers, dialogue in flowery Urdu language, and overtly Islamic architecture. The focus was mostly on upper-class and noble Muslim life in the northern Indian state of Awadh and its association with courtesans, ignoring the vast majority Muslim community across the rest of India. 'All depicted an idealized Muslim world where *nawabs* lived with all their grandeur and idiosyncrasies intact. *Shairi* (Urdu poetry), *qawwli* (form of singing) and the *tawaif* (courtesan) were their leitmotifs. This was the cinematic equivalent of a golden past' (Farooqui, cited in Kavoori and Awin, 2008: 137). As Indian popular culture continues to identify Muslims as the 'Other', Muslim women continue to be the object of the male gaze in particular. It is perhaps only natural then that Muslim women are often represented as courtesans/ *tawaifs*. Activist and politician Al Nasir Jakaria says that Hindi cinema has always represented Muslims as one-dimensional characters in a stereotyped way, which leads to the distrustful interpretation that most men are *nawabs* and women *tawaifs*.

Even if you see Muslim women, usually you see them in what they call in Hindi like sitting in a *kotha* [as *tawaif*] or you know there is a *mehfil* arranged and rich people [*nawabs*] come to that place ... The boss over there is arranging mistresses for them. The lady is ... given some fancy Muslim name. I think by and large the representation is negative. (Personal interview, 27 August 2012)

Moreover, the entire ambience of those films—the use of flowery Urdu language by the characters, life in opulent palaces, wearing outdated clothes like Aligadh-cut sherwanis and ghararas, men keeping beards, and wearing skull caps, women donning the *burqa*—are also old-fashioned. The overall effect is to represent Muslims as the exotic Other in these films.

From the overall analysis as presented in this section, I argue that the stereotypical portrayal of women in general and Muslim women in particular is a political act. In this regard, sociologist and academician Paola Bacchetta explained that right-wing politics, specifically the politics of the Rashtriya Swayamsevak Sangh, projects sexuality onto Others. She goes on to point out that 'the counterpart to the chaste Hindu male is the Muslim male polygamist or rapist, and to the chaste motherly Hindu woman is the Muslim Woman as a prostitute or potential wife' (Bacchetta, 2004: 101). Courtesans in film became the subject of the 'male gaze' and were represented as the goddesses of seduction. There were multiple instances where the dichotomy of morality and temptation arose. The woman who redefined seduction as a fine art at the same time claimed to be pure and real. In *Pakeezah* and *Umrao Jaan*, filmmakers were compelled to represent the courtesan characters as both absolute and virginal heroines who are trapped in the system. Though courtesans held a prestigious position in society because of their economic and cultural superiority, directors chose to ignore the fact, and these films placed the courtesan in a normative societal gender structure. Therefore, they were represented as a marginalized group without any agency to express their suffering. Above all, in these films associating Islamicate culture with the identity of *tawaifs* makes them seem more exotic. It is necessary to establish a counter-hegemonic feminist as well as Islamic discourse to locate the realities within women's world with greater sensibility, which is perhaps lacking to date.

Social and Political Aspects of Portraying Muslims as Marginal Characters in Social Films

In the 1970s, there was a euphoria of secularism. We have addressed the romanticized portrayals of Muslim *nawabi* culture until the 1970s in the previous sections. The social unity depicted in *Amar Akbar Anthony* (1977) within the 'family theme' is nothing short of a potential metaphorical link between the secular family and the country—with the nation treated as an extension of the family (Elison et al., 2016). As Chidananda Das Gupta points out, '*Amar Akbar Anthony*, an improbable tale of a Hindu, a Muslim, and a Christian who turn out to be brothers; the overcoming of communal prejudices and emergence of a deep camaraderie among the three, had tremendous appeal, and the film was a landmark in the growth of the "family" theme' (Chidananda, 1980: 35). To mention the transition of Muslim characters, Teesta Setalvad narrates:

> You have a certain kind of image in cinema in the early [days]; it was a very benevolent image but it was a very stereotypical image. There was a period in cinema in the 1970s and 1980s, [in] films like *Amar Akbar Antony*, [where] the formula of unity was used in many films though [the] Hindu was a big brother or the main protagonist. (Personal interview, 4 September 2012)

At this time, remarkable changes in the representation of Muslims also occurred. Muslims had acted as sidekicks in non-Muslim Social genres in Hindi cinema's early years, but these were minor roles. However, it was during this period that certain characters grew in popularity. Prasad rightly points out, 'Interestingly, these were often Muslim figures, who stood not only for the minority community, but by extension for the entire subaltern population. Sher Khan in *Zanjeer* and Rahim Chacha in *Deewar* are figures of this type, as is, with slight differences, the blind Muslim in *Sholay*' (Prasad, 1998: 143). In three-hour films, their roles were squeezed into ten- to fifteen-minute slots. Similarly, it has been argued by Sohini Ghosh Sen about the village of the Rangarh in *Sholay* (1975), 'It's almost a microcosm of the "secular India" of the 1970s'. She continues:

> Here, a mosque and a temple nestle comfortably on opposite hillocks and the blind Imam is respected, admired and even helped down the steps by the village folk, irrespective of religion or caste. When the blind Imam's son, Ahmad, departing for his new job in the city, is waylaid and murdered by Gabbar's men, his dead body carries a letter from

Gabbar, threatening worse retaliation if Veeru (Dharmendra) and Jai (Amitabh Bachchan) are not handed over to the dacoits. As the old man weeps over his dead son, the villagers angrily tell the Thakur that they cannot take any more: he must hand over his two-man army to Gabbar. But the Imam shames the villagers by asking Allah why He didn't give him more sons to sacrifice as 'martyrs' for the village. He reinforces the popular sentiment of communal harmony, where the village becomes a symbol of the nation, and the young boy becomes a Muslim soldier who died serving his country. (Sen, 2007)

Regarding the same analysis, when I asked the co-writer Javed Akhtar about his thoughts behind Imam Sahab's characterization, he said:

We were blissfully unaware of any sociopolitical relevance of these films or the scripts, blissfully unaware. We were trying to write an interesting script that's about it; [which] will be appreciated by the audience, which will interest the audience, that was the only consideration, they will not [have] the slightest idea that this is actually mini India. Not at all. Not at all [emphasizing]. We were just writing a film and enjoying it, and creating different kinds of character. Even in *Deewaar* [Rahim *chacha's* character], people see how it related to the contemporary sociopolitical theme and so on and so forth; we were not aware of that, and good that we weren't aware. (Personal interview, 16 March 2021)

During the 1970s, character actors who played the role of the hero's most faithful friend or an ethical individual rose to prominence. Side characters such as Sher Khan (*Zanzeer*, 1973), Imam Saheb *Sholay*, 1975), Rahim *chacha* (*Deewar*, 1975), Zohra Bai (*Muqaddar Ka Shikandar*, 1978), Rahim Chacha (*Khud Daar*, 1982), and Bighu Chacha (*Dacait*, 1987) were prominent in popular cinema as filmmakers attempted to appeal to the lowest common denominator. That is why, when I asked Javed Akhtar, the co-writer of the side characters Sher Khan, Imam Saheb/ Rahim *Chacha*, Rahim *chacha*, he mentioned two specific inspirations behind creating those characters:

Showing some character of some ethnic minority and showing him a nice person, or her a nice person, it gets you some extra audience also,

and some people who are not in the film or their culture, their community is not represent[ed], this token representation gives them a certain
kind of happiness or satisfaction, and as a matter of fact, by and large it
brings some goodwill in society. So, that is what we were doing, because
we had also seen that it had worked in the film where most of the characters are from community A, but you bring one character from community B, who is a good person and who helped the protagonist and
so on. So, there are some dividends, box office dividends, there were at
least at that time, so we used that; not so cold-bloodedly as I am looking
back and looking at it with 20–20 vision, but instinctively we knew that
it will be appreciated. (Personal interview, 16 March 2021)

Despite the fact that the side characters were used on a regular basis
in day-to-day situations, Islamic religious symbols were always used
for them and these tagged Muslims as 'Others'. 'We thought of Rahim
Chachas and Ruksana *behens* as Muslim and not much else ... we thought
of these north-Indian upper-caste Hindu heroes and heroines as Indian'
(Cine Blitz, 2012). Regarding this new development, when I spoke to
film-writer Shibani Bhatija, she said that she believed it was purely a
strategy to manipulate audience reception and consumption. Film critic
Rauf Ahmed further said:

Filmmakers use the word 'chacha' frequently with some name attached
to it such as Rahim Chacha. The side character does not play an important role in the whole film. He is just there to give Islamicate flavour
in the film. Sometimes Muslim audiences find some identification with
those Muslim characters as well. Rahim chacha becomes a father figure
to them. And he [A.K. Hangal] himself told me once, 'In five films, I am
Rahim chacha'. (Personal interview, 28 August 2013)

As it was pointed out that Muslim audiences would like to see the
onscreen representation of their community, I would like to raise a question: Do all the Muslims enjoy watching such stereotyped representations
or is it a mechanism to construct a separate identity of the community?
Ramnath believes that film-goers' consumption and filmmakers' production are the two most important influencers in the film industry, both
of which are regulated by the majoritarian community. By including a

Muslim protagonist, they avoid offending the minority population. With a lot of scepticism, she said:

> The film business is run by majority and the majority happens to be Hindu in India. As it is a business, it is always a mixture of philosophy, art, and commerce. So, filmmakers do not offend Muslim viewers beyond a point. But because of their minority identity, filmmakers do not make entire movies about them as it is a common belief that the public doesn't want to watch them [minorities]. (Personal interview, 5 February 2013)

Echoing the same argument, filmmaker Mahesh Bhatt points out that when a Muslim character takes centre stage in a film, it fails to find an audience. He quoted a study to back up his argument:

> Recently a very responsible person, who works for one of the major television networks, came and said to me in private about research which was conducted on audience consumption and reception all over India. The research indicates that the majority of viewers don't want to see the serials which are overtly Islamic, even in remote villages. Muslim stories and Muslim characters do not find viewers. He also said to me that once they changed the story to Hindu names, they found the response was stunningly high. It is sad but it is true. Despite [there] being all the talk of secular fabric, there is deep divide inside. People's choice becomes clear from the pattern of audience consumption because they try to follow similar things in what they watch in the entertainment world in their real life. (Personal interview, 31 March 2014)

Despite the fact that this explanation has obvious indirect commercial ramifications, film director Shyam Benegal suggested a political explanation for the existence of prominent Muslim character actors in Hindi films, particularly during this era.

Nadira: Why are Muslim side characters visible mostly in the 1970s and 1980s?

Benegal: That's because there was a fear in the film industry, if you have dominant Muslim characters in a film, it may not run because of the war between Pakistan and Bangladesh. Also, there was always a little fear particularly because of Partition. (Personal interview, 29 June 2013)

One more important development that took place around the 1970s and 1980s was the rise of alternative cinema or New Wave Muslim Social films. In the following segment, I shall be discussing the genre in detail.

New Wave: Muslim Social

In the first two sections, we saw how Muslim Social films emphasized *nawabi* and *tehzeeb* (high) culture while ignoring the 'economic struggles and social discrimination of common folk' (Bhaskar and Allen, 2009: 91). Most interestingly, Muslims were never central characters in these Bollywood films. In a conversation, Nasreen Munni Kabir, a noted documentary filmmaker and film critic, lamented this fact and said:

> There were not many films on Partition. Somehow, Hindi cinema really [shies] away from the realistic portrayal of Muslims and even [when] so many of the filmmakers were Muslims, so many of the *shayars*, lyricists, writers were Muslims. Even in a film like *Mother India* (produced, written, directed by Mehboob Khan), which is a symbol of Indian cinema, there is no Muslim character. (Personal interview, 11 February 2013)

After the 1970s, traditional Muslim Social films started to disappear, as they no longer served the pressing sociopolitical needs of the times. Then came a tough post-Partition period of introspection through the New Wave Muslim Socials where filmmakers for the first time started depicting Muslims as everyday people with everyday issues in a realistic set-up. The films depicted ordinary working-class or middle-class Muslims and the difficulties they faced on a daily basis. These films highlighted the issues of 'social discrimination, the economic deprivation and communal violence that ordinary Muslims faced on an everyday level' (Bhaskar and Allen, 2009: 91).

'New Wave Muslim Social' is a broad genre that represents diverse filmmaking techniques such as cinematic realism, removal of the melodramatic form of narration, using realistic settings, and ushered the rise of a new set of filmmakers. The New Wave movement was initiated in France in the early 1950s and 1960s, but in India the rise of the New Wave movement could be noticed only around the late 1960s and early 1970s. There was certainly a development in Indian realist cinema inspired by Italian neo-realism and by critically acclaimed Bengali filmmakers, mostly auteurs, such as Satyajit Ray, Mrinal Sen, and Ritwick Ghatak in the 1950s and early 1960s, who came to prominence long before the New Wave movement.

As already mentioned in the previous chapter, Hindi film made a significant contribution to the development of a national consciousness through its visible public representation and its dialogic association with the mission of nation building. It is true, as Bhaskar Sarkar mentions in *Mourning the Nation: Indian Cinema in the Wake of Partition* (2010), that the Indian film industry had a shaky relationship with the emerging nation-state's policy during this period. Filmmakers had the option of representing the India–Pakistan partition which was arguably the most remarkable event in the postcolonial era. But, we find that there is hardly any film that foregrounds the Partition narrative—except *Chhalia*, which partly shows a link with the Partition through one of the protagonists in the film. Sarkar further argues that Raj Kapoor's directorial debut *Aag* (1948) and later *Awara* (1951) renewed the pain of Partition through indirect and metaphorical gestures and points to how allegory can be a powerful instrument for constructive remembrance mobilization. M.S. Sathyu's film *Garam Hawa* is the first Hindi film on Partition, where we see the protagonist Salim Mirza is an Agra-based Muslim shoemaker who is denied citizenship in his own nation. It became an important film because it was the first to showcase the hardships of ordinary Muslims against the backdrop of communal hatred. Pointing out the issue, Javed Akhtar said:

The first film which had an important Muslim character, and our contemporary issue, was *Chhalia*. *Chhalia* was the first film made by Manmohan Desai with Raj Kapoor, Nutan, and Pran; Pran had played a very important role in that film as a Muslim pathan, and the film has a strong background of the Partition; [it shows] how people were displaced ... perhaps Partition is such a dramatic happening, perhaps even more dramatic than the Second World War. You ever heard of any film on it? There is no film ... we have not made any film on the Partition; on that mayhem, with huge, humongous, grand part of Indian history.

Perhaps Indian cinema did not have the language; we don't have the syntax to deal with [it]; so we just pretended it has never happened. And there was total silence in Hindi cinema vis-à-vis this chapter of Indian history. (Personal interview, 16 March 2021)

In the article 'Secularism and Popular Indian Cinema' (2007), Shyam Benegal states that there was a specific reason for producing Garam Hawa—the partition of Bangladesh and Pakistan in 1971. Prior to that, there was a glimmer of faith for Indian Muslims migrating to Pakistan, but after the formation of Bangladesh people realized that language could be an additional source of anxiety. For Indian Muslims, the option of migration became irrelevant, and Muslim nationalism was no longer a topic of discussion. Therefore, Benegal says, 'A film of this kind would have been impossible to make before 1971' (2007: 235). Partition and citizenship have again become a topic of discussion in contemporary political debate, especially after the passing of the Citizenship (Amendment) Act, 2019. Apart from Garam Hawa, Mammo (1994) is one of the most relevant films for us today because of the perilous path we've taken in recent months with our citizenship laws. Mammo tells the story of Riyaz, a young boy who lives in Bombay with his Naani and Fayyazi. The film, written by Khalid Mohamed, is based on the life of Mehmooda Beghum, also known as 'Mammo Nani'. It tells the story of a woman in India who is both 'seeking' and asking for a place to call 'home'. But her Muslim origin and status as a 'Pakistani immigrant' complicate her quest for a home in India. The film is about the lingering consequences of the trauma of the 1947 Partition on ordinary people's lives. Mammo's characters not only paint a vivid image of Muslim families, but the portrayals are also realistic, presenting the characters to the audience as individuals.

Returning to the discussion on Garam Hawa, let us consider what Benegal further points out: 'Until Garam Hawa was made, Muslim characters in popular Hindi films were routinely depicted in token roles, and often without blemish. In this way they were separated from the community, effectively making them the Other' (2007: 234). He echoed the same during a personal interview:

If you ask my opinion, they are not representative at all because those movies dealt with the subject like nawab, sarab, kabab. Muslim Social means it's a *nawab* … very important films in early 1970s, after the war between Pakistan and Bangladesh, were emerging. The film called *Garam Hawa* … broke away from this stereotype, say, Rahim chacha's stereotype. (Personal interview, 29 June 2013)

According to Benegal (2007), there were two reasons for producing New Wave films during that time. First, initially, studio culture suffered and to fight for survival after Independence a new entrepreneur class emerged to finance filmmaking. As a result, since filming was a high-risk industry at the time, mostly formula films were made to ensure returns on invest-ment. Famous cinema at the time portrayed religious and ethnic groups, with Muslims appearing as a token. Only classic Muslim Socials featured Muslims as core characters. Second, at the beginning of the 1970s gradu-ates of film institutes such as the Film and Television Institute of India and the National School of Drama began producing films that were fi-nanced by the Film Finance Corporation. Because of the government grants, films could be made for reasons apart from purely profit; but even then these films struggled 'to provide a more realistic depiction of con-temporary Indian life' (2007: 234).

Due to the lack of commercial risk that may have arisen if Muslims were depicted in films due to the security provided by government funding, filmmakers began to make offbeat films including *Salim Langde Pe Mat Ro* (dir. Saeed Akhtar Mirza, 1986) and *Naseem* (dir. by Saeed Akhtar Mirza, 1995), which were produced by National Film Development Corporation of India (NFDC). *Salim Langde Pe Mat Ro* was set against the backdrop of the Hindutva movement in the 1980s, the subsequent violent communal landscape, and its effect on the lives of Muslim youth in central Mumbai. Iqbal Masud writes:

Saeed Akhtar Mirza was part of the New Movement in cinema which rose to prominence from the late 60s onwards. His work has always been marked by an 'adversary element', meaning a critique of the status from a radical point of view … In his *Salim Langde Pe Mat Ro* he exam-ines the problems of Muslim lumpens in central Bombay. The film won the best Hindi film National Award for 1990. What is impressive about the film is the multi-layered approach to the subject. It rises be-yond its specific city and class and becomes a probing into the condition of Indian Muslims. The gradual economic and educational decline of urban Muslims is portrayed. Also the shift of the young to crime, a flight from a society which they feel rejects them. The problems of communalism, ghetto mentality, and search for an ethnic identity which does not clash with a national identity are also explored ... Salim is a complex and reflective work which in itself is a search for identity. Indian Muslims have found a place in the increasingly metropolitan culture of India. Salim is an extremely sensitive and intelligent attempt to depict this cultural process. It says there are no easy answers but it also opens up ways of resolving the crisis. (Masud, 2005)

Both *Garam Hawa* and *Salim Langde Pe Mat Ro* represented the struggle of ordinary Muslims due to the lack of livelihood opportunities in a system filled with communal prejudice. 'Apart from the identity and security questions, both these films tried to raise the essential questions regarding class dimensions and equity by highlighting how Indian Muslims face the problems of poverty and unemployment' (Islam, 2019: 140).

According to Madhav Prasad (1998), the New Wave films gave rise to new heights of Hindi cinema. Directors such as Baladev Raj Chopra, Hrisikesh Mukherjee, Sagar Sarhadi, and Basu Chatterjee made films with realistic plots and deglamourized stars (such as Smita Patil, Naseeruddin Shah, Farooq Sheikh, Supriya Pathak, and others), but with mainstream-style song sequences. Due to mixing of the elements of commercial and art-house films, and because of its popularity, Madhav Prasad refers to this particular category of films as 'middle-class' cinema (Prasad, 1998). Moreover, this so-called middle cinema or middle-class cinema had an influence on Muslim representation. Films such as Sagar Sarhadi's *Bazaar* (1982) and Baladev Raj Chopra's *Nikaah* (1982) dealt with the Muslim world and depicted numerous topics related to Muslims, like patriarchy, economic deprivation, and marginalization of women. These films starred Muslim protagonists. *Bazaar* (1982), set in Hyderabad, depicted parents who were forced to sell their daughters to wealthy sheiks from the Gulf countries due to economic constraints. The film also highlights the practice of polygamy as the most serious issue plaguing the Muslim community. Stars of parallel film, such as Naseeruddin Shah, Smita Patil, Supriya Pathak, and Farooq Sheikh, are among its cast members. When reviewing the film Asgar Ali Engineer lamented:

> Even just two years ago, a 70-year-old Arab came and married two girls at a time; one after the other Nikah was performed. Both were about 19–20 years old and obtained a fatwa that such nikah is valid. And later they ran away. The Quran does not allow that. That is not the intention of the Quran. The Quran does not encourage marrying any women you like. You can marry a woman who is a widow and orphan and that also to take care of their property. (Personal interview, 8 December 2012)

Continuing Engineer's criticism, here I would like to mention another film, *Nikaah* (1982), which dealt specifically with the issue of *talaq*. This film was also noteworthy for its depiction of patriarchy and the plight of Muslim women in the institution of marriage. Though the film sought to depict the serious issue of triple *talaq* within the Muslim community, it did so in a simplistic way and as a result lacked a nuanced portrayal of the severity of the problem. Rauf Ahmed points out:

> *Nikaah* was done by B.R. Chopra, one of the biggest filmmakers at that time and again, it was based on, time to use that thing about talaq-talaq-talaq... that's how easily you can free yourself from a marriage. It's not actual representation; most of them are simplistic actually. (Personal interview, 28 August 2013)

Mammo, which we have discussed earlier, is the first in a trilogy by Bengal that includes *Sardari Begum* (1996) and *Zubeidaa* (2001), and is followed by *Well Done Abba* (2010). This trilogy broke the stereotypes of the traditional way of Muslim representation either as the nice, kind-hearted Rahim chacha or as a faithful friend of the Hindu hero. Also these above-mentioned films broke the stereotypical usage of language and songs such as Abbujaan, Amma Huzoor, Ammijaan, and Abba Huzoor are the names given to their parents by their children in these films. The words 'Allah', 'Mashallah', 'Bismillah', and 'Subhan Allah' are thrown around a lot in conversations. And then, out of nowhere, a *qawwali* starts. These films have a theatrical release and initiated a shift by recapitulating and restoring the very heart of cinema, emphasizing the role of women in films.

From the enquiry and discussion in different sections of this chapter, it is obvious that in spite of onscreen representation of a rich culture and tradition of Muslim life, Muslims are represented as the exotic Other. Muslim Socials mostly illustrated an 'idealized Muslim world where *nawabs* lived with all their grandeur and idiosyncrasies' (Chada and Kavoori, 2008: 136). The stories were situated in the *havelis* of Lucknow and featured grand architecture such as tombs and minarets, which are often associated with Islamicate culture. Muslim women in the films of the Muslim Social genre either had a mystifying image or were shown as living in ill-reputed *kothas* as *tawaifs*. Some of the films of the genre explored the struggle between the modern (education, reform, and progress) and traditional (dignity, honour, and devotion). While there are plenty of criticisms of the genre, we must agree that it preserved Muslim art, music, literature, and identity at a stage when Muslim culture was in decline after Independence. Classic Muslim Social films are no longer made frequently. The demise of the Muslim Social genre is due to sociopolitical causes. The main reason, among many others, is low interest among viewers; a substantial portion of the film-growing crowd is now made up of young people who are unfamiliar with Lucknowi culture. We see a new group of filmmakers dealing with various issues pertaining to the Muslim community from the end of the 1980s and the beginning of the 1990s, owing to globalization and liberalization, as well as the emergence of multiple political scenarios during the time. A new genre—dubbed 'The Muslim Political'—has now emerged, which we will be discussing in the next chapter.

4

The Muslim Political Genre

From Anti-Pakistani Jingoism to Islamophobia

Figure 4.1 From Anti-Pakistan (Naseeruddin in *Sarfarosh*) to Islamophobia
(Nawazuddin in *Gangs of Wasseypur*)
Source: Nadira Khatun; illustration by Sreeja Burman.

Postcolonial Bollywood and Muslim Identity. Nadira Khatun, Oxford University Press. © Oxford University Press 2024.
DOI: 10.1093/oso/9780198891017.003.0005

While the films of the 1950s and 1960s, the so-called Nehruvian era, re-flected the 'tolerant' secularism of the state and also depicted an ideal-ized Muslim world, where *nawabs* and the upper class lived with their grandeur and idiosyncrasies intact, the 1970s and 1980s saw the emer-gence of an alternative politics of minority representation.[1] During this period, while the aristocrats were pushed out of the frame, the portrayal of Mumbai's underworld characters, mostly as Muslims, came into vogue. At the end of the 1980s and the beginning of the 1990s, the Hindu right-wing movement emerged as a robust presence in India. The Babri Masjid (Babri Mosque) demolition (6 December 1992) and the concomitant hardening of communal identities was a major turning point in Indian contemporary history. It was followed by communal riots in many parts of India. The demolition of the Babri Masjid and the riots that followed became the theme of many memorable films. The genre of the Muslim Political,[2] which intertwines religion and politics, was born at this time. These films grew in number and visibility following the attacks on the World Trade Centre and the Pentagon by members of Al-Qaeda, a mili-tant group affiliated with Islamic extremism, in 2001. These Bollywood films portrayed the moral struggle between the nationalist victim and the *jihadi* militant, and they were instrumental in the creation of a fictitious Muslim identity [see Figure 4.1]. Throughout the 1990s and afterwards, Bollywood created an imagined Hindu country by portraying Muslims as the 'Other' and an enemy of the community. This hegemonic con-struct is referred to as a 'techno-cultural transmitter'[3] by Sanjeev Kumar (2013: 459).

The current research examines the construction of communalism and Hindu nationalism by examining the portrayal of Muslims and Hindus

---

[1] Parts of this chapter draw on material previously published in Khatun, Nadira (2016) Imagining Muslims as the 'Other' in Muslim Political Films. *Journal of Arab and Muslim Media Research*, 9(1), pp. 41–60.

[2] I have borrowed the term 'Muslim Political' from an article, *Ghararas to Guns–From the Muslim Social to the Muslim Political*, published in Cine Blitz (Issue December 2012).

[3] Techno-cultural transmitter refers to the synergy between technology and culture where the former is used as a pedagogical tool. In this article, Sanjeev Kumar pointed out, 'The Bollywood film industry has acted as a techno-cultural transmitter in this regard, with its engagement in the production of nationalist cinema that projects in its setting the definition of this Hindu nation.' Kumar, Sanjeev (2013) Constructing the Nation's Enemy: Hindutva, Popular Culture and the Muslim 'Other' in Bollywood Cinema. *Third World Quarterly*, 34(3), p. 459.

in popular Hindi films[4] released after the 1990s and afterwards. In this chapter, apart from studying the position of Muslims in the complex representational scheme in the above-mentioned Muslim political film texts using a sociopolitical lens, I shall also examine the perceptions of film critics and filmmakers and audiences regarding these films. The chapter is split into five sections: (a) 'Nationalism vs Patriotism and Secularism vs Communalism' deals with the ideologies of nationalism and communalism; moreover, I try to locate how they have recently become relevant in Indian politics as well as Bollywood; (b) 'Ideal Image of an Indian Family and "Hindu-ized Nation"' exemplifies how Hindutva philosophy portrays India as a nation of Hindus, with adherents dedicated to preserving the Hindu Rashtra's ethnic and geopolitical boundaries. In films, stereotypical depictions of Muslims, such as clothing and rigid adherence to Islamic religious codes, have been used to create a sharp contrast with Hindus' modern and secular portrayal; (c) 'Politics of Portraying Muslim Gangsters and Mafias' demonstrates social and political aspects of portraying Muslims as antagonists, who were depicted as smugglers, underworld dons, gangsters, and so on; (d) 'Nationalism, Communal Conflicts, Terrorism, and Geopolitics' examines 'terroristic films' inspired by the terrorist attacks across the country and around the world. These films have given Bollywood a new face of the 'enemy' as jihadists, villains, and anti-nationals; (e) 'Pakistan as Enemy' illustrates Pakistan as India's everlasting foe; Pakistan and Muslims became conflated, and both became a threat to the nation, as depicted in multiple Bollywood films.

---

[4] *Maine Pyar Kiya* (1989), *Roja* (1992), *Angaar* (1992), *Hum Aapke Hain Koun ... !* (1994), *Bombay* (1995), *Dilwale Dulhania Le Jayenge* (1995), *Pardes* (1997), *Border* (1997), *Ghulam-e-Mustafa* (1998), *Zakhm* (1998), *Kuch Kuch Hota Hai* (1998), *Hum Saath Saath Hain* (1999), *Sarfarosh* (1999), *Fiza* (2000), *Pukar* (2000), *Mission Kashmir* (2000), *Kabhi Khushi Kabhie Gham* (2001), *Gadar: Ek Pre Katha* (2001), *Maine Dil Tujhko Diya* (2002), *Anarth* (2002), *Main Prem Ki Diwani Hoon* (2003), *Maqbool* (2003), *Once Upon a Time in Mumbai* (2003), *LOC Kargil* (2003), *Lakshya* (2004), *Black Friday* (2004), *Dev* (2004), *Veer Zara* (2004), *Black Friday* (2004), *Mumbai Meri Jaan* (2008), *Mission Istanbul* (2008), *A Wednesday* (2008), *Kurbaan* (2009), *Shikandar* (2009), *New York* (2009), *My Name is Khan* (2010), *Parzania* (2005), *Fanaa* (2006), *Vivah* (2006), *New York* (2009), *Road to Sangam* (2010), *Gangs of Wasseypur* (2012), *Ishaqzaade* (2012), *Shahid* (2012), *Ek Tha Tiger* (2012), *The Attacks of 26/11* (2013), *Shootout at Wadala* (2013), *D-Day* (2013), *Baby* (2015), *Haider* (2015), *Bajrangi Bhaijaan* (2015), *Phantom* (2015), *Neerja* (2016), *Haseena Parkar* (2017), *Secret Superstar* (2017), *One Less God* (2017), *Lipstick Under My Burkha* (2017), *Naam Shabana* (2017), *Raees* (2017), *Tiger Zinda Hai* (2017), *Raazi* (2018), *India's Most Wanted* (2019), *Uri: The Surgical Strike* (2019), *Hotel Mumbai* (2019), and *Shikara* (2020).

Nationalism vs Patriotism and
Secularism vs Communalism

To comprehend the Muslim political genre, we must first look into the postcolonial Indian political landscape. From the time of the independence struggle in the early twentieth century, the discursive notions of 'nationalism', 'patriotism', 'secularism', and 'communalism' have been prominent tools of Indian politics; but in the last 30 years, and especially in the last decade, India has experienced a great political churning and is undergoing a transition, which has given rise to a growing concern that these philosophies would be utilized for electoral gains. Considering India as a secular country as defined by the Indian constitution, we need to revisit the above-mentioned concepts from the lens of the kind of majoritarian politics seen in recent times. Though we have discussed in Chapter 3 some aspects of how nationalism is weaved into Bollywood films, here I want to contextualize the same concept with the contemporary political scenario prevailing in the country.

Today, nationalism and patriotism are used as synonyms in India as well as across the world, but these concepts are distinctly different. 'Patriotism' is perceived as an emotion whereas 'nationalism' is an ideology. Social theorist Ashish Nandy in his seminal article 'Nationalism, Genuine and Spurious: Mourning Two Early Post-Nationalist Strains' illustrated a clear distinction between the two. According to Nandy, 'Nationalism is an ideology and is configured in human personality the way other ideologies are. It rode piggyback into the Afro-Asian world in colonial times as an adjunct of the concept of nation state. Patriotism is a non-specific sentiment centring on a form of territoriality that humans share with a number of other species' (2006: 3500). As per his definition, patriotism is a feeling, a bonding or an investment; it is a sentiment. Therefore, patriotism can be a non-ideological territoriality. On the other hand, nationalism is a more specialized, ideologically defined, and passionate form of 'love of one's own kind' (2006: 3502). Consequently, nationalism demands uniform allegiance to the state and patriotism allows different 'levels of loyalty, affiliation and allegiance to the state' (2006: 3502). Nationalism emphasizes the primacy of national identity over subnational ideologies such as religions, castes, parties, racial affiliations, and ethnicities. It supports decontextualized formulae or slogans such as 'first and foremost, we are Indians, then Hindus, Tamils, and Dalits' (2006: 3502). Nationalism, on the whole, recognizes such identities as possible enemies and subversive forces. Thus, simply put, patriotism is an inclusive emotion whereas nationalism is an exclusivist ideology. Therefore, in the contemporary political space, we notice a harsh criticism of a pluralistic society, which is considered a threat for the nation. This theorization of nationalism had become a source of propaganda in post-Independence India and has again become intensely visible in contemporary right-wing politics whose main aim is to override the pluralistic nature of Indian society and impose a homogenous culture. As a consequence, when a section of activists, scholars, students, and academicians counters or criticizes the ideologies and activities of right-wing parties as well as the state's and proposes to have a more inclusive society, they are called a part of 'tukde tukre gang'[5] by right-wing supporters who claim that these people conspire to divide the country into fragments and the right-wingers propagate to create a monotheistic society ignoring the crux of India as 'unity in diversity'. As historian Gyanendra Pandey writes, 'Nationalism that stood above (or outside) the different religious communities and took as its unit the individual Indian citizen, a "pure" nationalism unsullied, in theory by the "primordial" pulls of caste, religious community, etc.—was I suggest, rigorously conceptualized only in opposition to this notion of communalism' (1990: 234–5). He reminds us that 'Hindu' and 'Muslim' political mobilization—the Khilafat/Non-Cooperation Movement and the Hindu Mahasabha—have played a major role in the Indian nationalist movement since its beginning. Pandey goes on to conclude that political mobilization was inevitable in the early days of Indian nationalism due to the colonial policy of divide and rule. It turned out to be the 'birthplace of the nationalist version of the concept of "communalism"' (1990: 234–5). In India, the word communalism has a somewhat different meaning than

---

[5] After 2016, the phrase 'tukde tukre gang' was used to label JNU (Jawaharlal Nehru University) students, but right-wing leaders have lately used it to refer to political opponents. Tripathi, Rahul (2020) Who Are Members of 'Tukde Tukde Gang': RTI. *The Economic Times*, 15 January. Available at https://economictimes.indiatimes.com/news/politics-and-nation/who-are-members-of-tukde-tukde-gang-rti/articleshow/73263876.cms?from=mdr [Accessed 15 January 2021].

it does elsewhere in the world. The word generally refers to a sense of inclusiveness, but 'in its common Indian usage the word "communalism" refers to a condition of suspicion, fear and hostility between members of different religious communities' (Pandey 1990: 6). Asghar Ali Engineer's words resonated with similar thoughts in a personal interview:

> Communalism in English is a positive word but in the Indian context it is a very negative one because of the two major communities, Hindus and Muslims, who take part in the whole process of power control. Those who fought for power and said 'my community should be most powerful', they would be communalist; and those who stood by secular democracy and agreed to follow a parliamentary system where people from all communities should be represented, they are called secular or nationalist. For example, the Muslim League, the Hindu Mahasabha are the communalist organizations. (Personal interview, 8 December 2012)

When India attained freedom from her colonial masters the word secularism was enshrined in our constitution. And unlike the West where there is a domination of the Church upon the state and its citizens, in India all religions are constitutionally treated as equal and individuals from every religious community enjoy the fundamental right to practise, propagate, and preach their faith. Ram Puniyani mentions, 'The values of secularism are deeply ingrained all through and particularly in Articles 14, 19, 22, and 25 [of the constitution]' (Puniyani, 2021). Hence, the notion of secularism is assumed extensively to be 'equal respect for all religions' that offers the possibility of the respectful coexistence of various communities, faiths, and traditions. Indian historian Romila Thapar writes, 'Secularism assumes the right to follow the religion of one's choice, a right that is given in the Indian constitution' (2007: 192). Echoing the classic definition of secularism, Shyam Benegal mentions:

> Suppose you are a Muslim and you have certain customs that you celebrate, that is your business, I won't interfere. I will not tell you that you should do this and you should do that. That's why despite the fact that we have many religions in our country, we have many sects in our country,

apart from religious, we have different kinds of lifestyle even clothing styles as everything was perfectly all right for everybody ... Which is why, Nehru said, 'unity in diversity' because we are very diverse people. That was the definition to work for the nationalist movement of the country and the largest number of people followed that principle led by Gandhi, Nehru, Maulana Azad, [and] there were Christian and tribal leaders also ... This is our natural ethos, ethos of South Asians, I would say. You see, we have had this but we had a lot of communal strife. (Personal interview, 29 June 2013)

India had witnessed the worst forms of communal violence in the post-Independence era, but at the same time there was a sense of state-sponsored secular euphoria. The crisis of secularism became progressively prominent because of the increasing dominance of Hindutva in the last three decades. The discontent with the Congress after declaration of Emergency in 1975 and the judgment in the Shah Bano case (1986),[6] provided an 'opportunity to the political parties and organizations associated with the Sangh Parivar[7] to consolidate their positions and political ambitions by gathering Hindu support for their mass mobilization campaigns of the 80s' (Bhaskar, 2005: 50). In the Shah Bano case, the Congress government appeased the Muslim fundamentalist section of society while 'at the same time putting the needs of Muslim masses on the backburner [sic]' (Puniyani, 2010: 21). At the end of the 1980s and towards the beginning of the 1990s, the Hindu right-wing groups launched various campaigns to effectively mobilize and gain popular support, which was primarily garnered through igniting Hindu religious

[6] In 1986, the government under Rajiv Gandhi overturned the Supreme Court judgment in the Shah Bano case by enacting the Muslim Women (Protection of Rights on Divorce) Acts. Because of the election in the same year, the Congress government tried to appease a certain section of society through this means. In 1986, a new law called the Muslim Women (Protection of Rights on Divorce) Act went into effect. According to the Muslim Women's Act, the husband must pay the mehr amount, provide one-time provision for her as prescribed in the Quran, and offer three months' maintenance at the time of divorce. As a result, the woman was to get a lump sum amount at the time of divorce. Engineer, Asghar Ali (2000) Maintenance for Muslim Women. The Hindu, 7 August. Available at https://archive.ph/20150902123704/http://www.thehindu.com/2000/08/07/stories/05072524.htm#selection-219.1-219.301 [Accessed 22 February 2021].

[7] Right-wing Hindu organizations such as the Rashtriya Swayamsevak Sangh (RSS), the Hindu Mahasabha, Bajrang Dal, the BJP, and Shiv Sena are part of a larger group called the Sangh Parivar (Sangh family).

sentiment among the majoritarian population. The most successful of these campaigns was the Ayodhya movement. Popularizing the notion of Ayodhya as the birthplace of the Hindu God Rama, the Hindu right wing achieved their first major victory with the demolition of the Babri Masjid on 6 December 1992 when the volunteers and cadres of the Sangh Parivar brought down the historical structure. In the subsequent years, the Bharatiya Janata Party (BJP) won a massive electoral mandate and formed the central government of the country. Ira Bhaskar writes, 'The Ayodhya movement catapulted the BJP to power in the 1990s thereby justifying and legitimizing Hindu–Muslim opposition, antagonism, and the politics of violence that has made communal riots an accepted means for the realization of the Hindu rashtra' (Bhaskar, 2005: 51). Afterwards, fomenting communal tensions and profiteering from it became a part of the Indian body politic. Paul Brass points out, '[…] the maintenance of communal tensions, accompanied from time to time by lethal rioting at specific sites, is essential for the maintenance of militant Hindu nationalism' (Brass, 2005: 9). While giving a historical account of contemporary communal violence, social activist Ram Puniyani mentions:

Things have changed a lot after the 1960s; at that time we were worried that secularism is not coming fully, how the blind religious beliefs will not be there … They [the government and political leaders] were [lobbying] for rationalism, scientific temper, secular values. Now in the last three decades, we are swimming against the tide. There are some global factors also. One thing that happens is a demonization of the Muslim minority and Christian minority and this has become a sort of social common sense … and social common sense started picking up in the 1980s and it was unchallenged; then through media, through word of mouth, through textbook and through different bureaucratic policies, people's mindsets have got formed. So today I think that is one of the major problems. I even say that communal violence does not take place in a vacuum. Communal violence is only possible because social common sense which gets converted into hate for the other community. Only because of the prominence of hate, violence can start. Paul Brass has written a very interesting thing that in India, communal riots mechanism is commonplace. Communal mechanism is a social common sense, hatred for others. (Personal interview, 16 august 2012)

As pointed out by Dr Puniyani, in the last three decades we find that there has been a rise in communal violence as government policies have exclusively targeted marginalized communities, especially Muslims; this also justifies Brass's claim mentioned earlier. We have noticed a substantial shift away from the secular fabric of India and towards a more Hinduized polity. Major incidents of communal violence were witnessed from the 1990s onwards: the Bombay riots in 1992–3 followed by the Godhra incident in 2002. The 2002 Godhra riots mark a watershed moment in India's politics. Some Muslims were accused of attacking the Sabarmati Express on 27 February 2002 at the Godhra railway station in Gujarat. A number of the passengers were Hindu pilgrims who were returning from Ayodhya, the site of the Babri Masjid–Ram janmabhoomi conflict. The event sparked attacks against Muslims in Ahmadabad as well as other parts of Gujarat, which were portrayed as retaliatory brutality (Brass, 2008). 'The government told parliament that 790 Muslims and 254 Hindus were killed, 223 more people reported missing and another 2,500 injured' (BBC, 2005). According to Needham and Rajan, the degree and kind of violence committed against Muslims, the similarities between this violence and what was widely considered as a Hindutva tactic employed to garner electoral gains, and the state's role in this violence, all marked out the communal violence in Gujarat 2002 from previous riots (2007: vii). If we look at it carefully, communal violence in recent times has been taking place due to the plurality of Indian society. Historically India has seen different political parties picking up the issue of diversity and using it as an instrument to polarize society. Asghar Ali Engineer critiques inclusivity and plurality as elements of Indian secularism and says the following:

[The] problem of India was pluralism. Different languages, different religion, problem in Europe was church; problem in India was pluralism when democracy came. Secularism here meant the acceptance of all religions. Equal respect for all religion, became [the] essence of our secularism. That is how secularism emerged and when the Indian National Congress was formed in 1885. That is why the first president of the Indian National Congress was from a minority. Badruddin Tyabji was Muslim, then Womesh Chunder Banerjee was a Christian, then Dadabhai Naoroji was a Parsi. Why? Because they [Congress] wanted to convince that we are not a Hindu organization. Pluralism became our secularism. (Personal interview, 8 December 2012)

As Asghar Ali Engineer rightly pointed out, in India pluralism is termed as secularism. However, we can now see that plurality and diversity are no longer celebrated concepts in the country. And this shift is reflected in educational textbooks as well. Recently, the chapters on Democratic Rights, Food Security in India, Federalism, Citizenship, and Secularism have all been dropped by the national education board, The Central Board of Secondary Education's (CBSE), from the Political Science syllabus of Class 11 in 2020 (Kumari, 2020). In the recent past, we have also witnessed how secularism has become a hotly debated topic; the subject has been politicized more by the current ruling party because it perceives India as a monolithic state. In the idea of a Hindu Rashtra, diversity poses a substantial problem. Therefore, secularism has become the biggest challenge for Indian right-wing politics and the ruling dispensation's tackling of the issue has been two-faced. Thus even when Prime Minister Narendra Modi claims to be a Hindu nationalist, for electoral gains he at the same time writes on his Twitter (rebranding to X) handle, 'We are secular not because the word was added in our Constitution. Secularism is in our blood. We believe in *Sarva Pantha Sambhava* [equal respect for all religions]' (Modi, 2014). Uttar Pradesh Chief Minister Yogi Adityanath who vehemently opposes this philosophy of diversity and pluralism says, 'This word "secularism" is the biggest threat to develop India's prosperous traditions and give it a spot on the global stage' (India Today Web Desk, 2021). Additionally, there are supporters and leaders of right-wing politics who have been attempting to change the essence of the word 'secularism' or 'secular' and parodying it as 'sickularism' or 'sickular'. They vehemently oppose the idea of plurality as secularism and this culture is most prominent and popular on social media. Filmmaker Mahesh Bhatt, expressing his idea of the common psyche of the Indian majoritarian people, says:

Political parties only bring out what is there in the hearts of the people. They are very clever. There was a very important saying years back by a man called Bertrand Russell; he said, how long will you blame [the] politician for putting poison in the hearts of the people. He gave an analogy of a cup of coffee with sugar in it and says, if the sugar is not in the coffee, even by stirring it you can't make it sweet; but if it is there, it will become sweet. So, hatred is already there in you. Politicians just stir it up. So-called Islamophobia is not only there as [a result of] the partition of India. It starts way back. That [partition] was the final explosion of what was there in the hearts of the people. To say that it was started at the time of partition or say that it was started at the time of Babri Masjid ... I would say where did it start? The idea of 'them' or the 'other' has always been a part of Indian narrative. (Personal interview, 31 March 2014)

When the BJP won an electoral victory in 2014—the first time since 1984 that a single political party has won a parliamentary majority—majoritarianism became mainstreamed because Hindu-rights ideologues were sponsored by the state. The state no longer stands with the constitution, but is rather the mouthpiece of majoritarianism. As a consequence, we see a rise in the number of controversial policies, laws, verdicts, and Acts, and state activities such as the Citizenship Amendment Act, 2019 (Constitutional Amendment); the abrogation of Article 370 of the Constitution (this article gave special status to the inhabitants of Kashmir, the only Muslim-dominated territory in the country); the anti-religious conversion law (targeting alleged conspiracy theories of 'Love Jihad'); the Supreme Court's verdict on Babri-Ram Janmabhoomi dispute, which clearly points to the chasm between constitutional aspirations of secularism and societal realities favouring majoritarianism.

Apart from these Acts and laws, there is a rise in intolerance because of the cultural nationalism orchestrated by the followers of Hindutva, which refuses to recognize cultural diversity and plurality. Frequent reports have been coming up of people getting lynched due to cow vigilantism and there have been unprecedented attacks against people suspected of injuring cows since 2015. India News of Hindustan Times reports, '86% killed in cow-related violence since 2010 are Muslim, 97% attacks after Modi govt came to power' (Abraham and Rao, 2017); such lynchings and attacks have been directed towards Muslims, who have been targeted based on rumours about them eating beef, or have been seen moving or slaughtering animals, or simply have seemed too Muslim by wearing a beard or skullcap. According to IndiaSpend, a data journalism website, vigilantes attempting to protect cows killed 11 people in 2019, making it the deadliest year since 2010 (Mohan, 2018). Rohini Mohan (2018) mentions in the article, 'A Template for Hate: Polarized Politics and Mainstream Intolerance' that cow protection by Hindu extremists used to populate the fringes of society but has become a part of the mainstream under the BJP; and the fact that the party currently is in charge of not only the central government but also 22 of India's 29 states is an additional factor giving party workers encouragement in this regard. It is no wonder then that 'the Haryana state police has a Cow protection department. Uttar Pradesh launched a cow-ambulance service. The central government funds research to prove that cow urine is a medical miracle. Even some private companies are spending more of their corporate social responsibility requirement on cow upkeep' (Mohan, 2018: 37).

Therefore, Indian secularism and democracy are being questioned in multiple ways. In this regard, Professor Shakuntala Banaji writes, 'Voting—as a marker of democratic citizenship—becomes a masquerade protecting a resurgent far right Hindutva (Hindu fascist) regime under the aegis of Narendra Modi and the BJP. Caste Hinduism's association of cows with deities, and the proscription on meat-eating in certain versions of religious practice, are used as pretexts for unimaginable violence against Muslims, Christians, Dalits, and working class/lower caste Hindus' (Banaji, 2018: 233).

The country recently saw strong anti-CAA protests; now the protesters are being accused of orchestrating the 2019 Delhi riots. In these riots the majority of the casualties were members of the minority population: there were 40 Muslims and 13 Hindus among the 53 people who died. The religious buildings that were demolished (14 mosques and a dargah, but no temple) was yet another sign of the kind of targeted violence that occurred (Jayaprakash, 2020).

Over the past few months, the Delhi Police has arrested several anti-CAA activists for allegedly planning and executing the riots. At the same time, it has been reluctant to pursue allegations against Bharatiya Janata Party leaders like Kapil Mishra, Anurag Thakur and several other Sangh parivar activists who publicly gave inflammatory and communal speeches ahead of the riots. An analysis of the nature of riot cases and charge-sheets filed against multiple accused persons indicates the Delhi police's investigation is marred by selectivity. Many media reports have also shown how a number of riot charge-sheets filed by the police contain little or no evidence about the actual complicity of the arrested persons in the riots (Mahaprashasta, 2020).

The Hindutva ideology has been instrumental in providing the discursive space for Hindi cinema to construct, define, and imagine a particular kind of Muslim identity. The Hindutva ideology of a promised Hindu nation (Hindu Rashtra) made its appearance in popular Hindi cinema in the form of new changes. For example, though the film *Bombay* (1991) received the national award for its theme of national integration, it faced multiple controversies before its release, as different groups sought a ban on the movie. Asghar Ali Engineer has mentioned that Bal Thackeray[8]

> wanted some of the dialogues spoken by the actor Tinnu Anand (playing Bal Thackeray in the film) deleted. The dialogue in question was about wiping out a particular community, which according to Anand, is a direct lift from Thackeray's speeches. There is not a single dishonest statement including the full stop or a comma. Mani Ratnam, the director, however, agreed under pressure to remove this part of the dialogue. (1995: 1556)

Though freedom of speech and expression is an integral part of modern liberal Indian democracy, there are multiple government and non-government agencies that have periodically sought bans on numerous films throughout the history of Hindi cinema. During the last two decades, political parties have garnered more authority to dictate terms to the Censor Board of Film Certification. Hence, from the mid-1990s until today, an increased number of films which are political in nature—such as *Bombay* (1995), *Fire* (1996), *Earth* (1998), *Mr and Mrs Iyer* (2002), *Water* (2005), *Fanaa* (2006), *My Name Is Khan* (2010), *Student of the Year* (2012), *Oh My God* (2012), *PK* (2014), and *Dharam Sankat Mein*

---

[8] Bal Thackeray was the founder of Shiv Sena, the Indian right-wing political party, based in the state of Maharashtra.

(2015)—have encountered bans for critiquing or 'hurting' the sentiments of Hindus. Irfan Engineer reaffirmed this fact:

After the Babri Masjid issue, they [right-wing politicians] were in a position to dictate more. They did not issue threats in every film. However, it acted as an automatic censor. The filmmaker had to keep in mind about the reaction of right-wing party members on every representation because they did not want to get into trouble. They are most vulnerable to their enormous amount of investment in every film. If they had taken a loan, they had to recover it. Moreover, someone requires just 20 goons to stop the screening of the movie, and those 20 people can enter the theatre and throw stones, damage the theatre. The theatre owner will say I am here to make money and not get my theatre damaged. So, it may be automatically playing an important role. (Personal interview, 14 September 2012)

The filmmakers themselves are not necessarily always extremists, nor are they driven by the Hindutva agenda. But because of the prevalent polarized political situation in the country, there is a demand for films with a narrow majoritarian agenda. Sensing the audience's demand, filmmakers have sought to capitalize on the right-wing agendas. Film critic Shiladitya Sen corroborates this sentiment from the perspective of film consumption:

It was not like political party leaders such as Bal Thackeray instructed some of the directors and producers to make communal films. It does not work like that. But producers and directors had the attitude to represent such issues like terrorism, communalism, apprehending that those portrayals would be well appreciated by the audience. (Personal interview, 23 August 2013)

Filmmaker Mahesh Bhatt shared his own experience and personal struggle of getting a clearance certificate for the film *Zakham* (1998) from CBFC (Central Board of Film Certification). The film was written and directed by Bhatt himself, and was based on the Bombay riots:

If you see Zakham, it's an autobiographical film. A person like me gets into the grave and buries his mother and I am proud of that film—it's a part of my mother. That is also an image but I had to fight with the government of India; at that time the NDA government was in power and they were doing everything to create trouble for my film, which finally got the maximum award too. They made me digitally correct those saffron bands which the goons wear. There was a sequence where the hospital was stormed by the goons and they said we will not give you a film certificate if you don't colour that saffron or remove the saffron with any other colour. So, I had to paint each one with black. Though history says that the Babri Masjid was demolished by people who were dressed in saffron and that is reality but in fiction ... you did not want [to show] ... that a particular kind of politics was responsible for the carnage of 1992–93. (Personal interview, 31 March 2014)

During the 1990s and afterwards, Bollywood constructed an imaginary vision of a Hindu nation by fabricating the Muslim 'Other' as an enemy of the nation. Sanjeev Kumar (2013) refers to this hegemonic construct as a 'techno-cultural transmitter'. This refers to the synergy between technology and culture, where the former is used as a pedagogical tool. In his article, Kumar writes, 'The Bollywood film industry has acted as a techno-cultural transmitter in this regard, with its engagement in the production of nationalist cinema that projects in its setting the definition of this Hindu nation' (2013: 459). Consequently, Bollywood adopted different strategies to fuel Hindutva ideology. First, the Hindutva ideology projects India as a land of Hindus and the supporters of this ideology are committed to preserving the cultural and geographical boundaries of the Hindu Rashtra. In films, the stereotypical images of Muslims, defined by attire and strict adherence to codes of Islamic religiosity, were deployed to mark a strong contrast with the progressive and secular projection of Hindus.

The Hindu state (Hindu Rashtra) philosophy of Hindutva ideologues has also made an appearance in Hindi cinema. Although earlier Hindi cinema stereotyped Muslims as 'Other', in recent decades Muslims have been shown as a threat to the nation and as a source of violence within the nation-state. From the early 1990s, Karen Gabriel and P.K. Vijayan (2012), Fareed Kazmi and Sanjeev Kumar (2011), Maidul Islam (2007), S.S. Rajgopal (2011), Amit Rai (2003), Ronie Parciack (2013), and Sanjeev Kumar (2013) have all emphasized the effect of Hindutva nationalism on divisive cinematic representations of Muslims. They argue that Hindu nationalist powers use the media, especially cinema, to instil fear in the minds of the majority population by portraying minorities as terrorists (*jehadis*), religious fanatics, underworld dons, and anti-social elements, who pose a threat to majority culture.

Ideal Image of an Indian Family and 'Hindu-ized' Nation

The 1990s can be considered as one of the landmark periods in the history of Hindi films for two main reasons: first, economic liberalization of India enabled the diaspora community to consume Bollywood texts more widely from 1991 onwards; second, the incident of Babri demolition changed India's sociopolitical landscape forever. In the euphoria of cultural nationalism, Bollywood became an important tool to propagate and create an imaginary identification with the homeland. The divisions in Indian society, whether sexual, religious, or based on ethnic identity, have been more apparent in recent years. But, ignoring that fact, Hindi cinema continues to prioritize a monolithic image of the nation and portrays a 'certain essence of "Indianness"' (Rajgopal, 2011: 240) as 'Indian culture'. Such representations are most popular among the Indian diaspora. The diasporic communities have an important role in forging public culture in India. In the last three decades, the Indian diaspora has been charged with inciting virulent forms of nationalism in the subcontinent. Scholars have pointed out the involvement of the diasporic community in re-imagining the Indian nation within a religious idiom, where they have tried to achieve aggressive 'hyper-masculine' nationalism. According to Sunil Khilnani, towards the end of 1989, a large number of bricks (167,000) were piled up in the pilgrimage town of Ayodhya to build the Ram Temple at the disputed site of the Babri Masjid. These were not ordinary bricks; they were 'Ram shilas', Ram's bricks collected from across India and outside the country. Khilnani points out, 'Each was inscribed with its place of origin, and among the most proudly displayed were those dispatched by 'immigrant' communities in the United States, Canada, South Africa and the Caribbean' (2004: 150). The diasporic community provided an eager market for films which catered to Hindu religion and culture. Films such as *Dilwale Dulhania Le Jayenge* (1995), *Pardes* (1997), *Kabhi Khushi Kabhie Gham* (2001), and *Main Prem Ki Diwani Hoon* (2003) narrate stories of Indian families transported to foreign lands. These films promote Indian culture and rituals 'identified as markers of Hindu tradition, thereby making any other religion or culture appear "Un-Indian"' (Rajgopal, 2011: 242). There are more films such as *Maine Pyar Kiya* (1989), *Hum Aapke Hain Koun ... !* (1994), *Kuch Kuch Hota Hai* (1998), *Hum Saath-Saath Hain* (1999), and *Vivah* (2006) which told stories of Indian Hindu families based in India with the similar tropes of upholding Hindu religious traditions, culture, and rituals. I argue that if Hindu culture and tradition must be portrayed as a national culture, it is undeniable that the 'Others' or cultural elements of other ethnicities and religions would be represented as either less or differently.

All the films mentioned in the previous paragraph glorify the import-ance of marriage, joint family culture, Hindu spiritualism, and nation-alism. Institutionalizing relationships through marriage became one of the important factors in the storylines of those films and the Hindu rituals associated with weddings and marriages get pride of place to be displayed in all their glory. Most interestingly the narratives intertwined Hindu religious rituals and nationalism. As already mentioned, *Kabhi Khushi Kabhie Gham ...* , *Dilwale Dulhania Le Jayenge*, and *Main Prem Ki Diwani Hoon* are set in the background of some foreign land but char-acters rigidly follow all the Hindu religious rituals and traditions to prove their love for their own nation. Even the films which are not set in some foreign land—such as *Maine Pyar Kiya, Hum Aapke Hain Koun ... !, Hum Saath-Saath Hain, Vivah*, and *Kuch Kuch Hota Hai*—incorporate at least one main protagonist who is shown to have just returned from abroad but has/haven't (depending on the need of the script) forgotten Indian Hindu culture, traditions, and values. Javed Akhtar explains the changes in the industry due to liberalization and mentions:

During the 80s and 90s, we have developed the new middle class. This middle class is the result of heavy industrialization and heavy urban-ization. Around 150 million people entered the middle class for the first time; liberalization, which came in the early 90s, brought a kind of huge affluence to the middle class and upper middle class, at least in urban areas. And these industries brought up a whole new middle class, this was the first generation educated or at least the second generation. Unlike the middle class that was there in the 50s, or 40s, they were people who were educated since three or four generations. So the middle class of the 1940s, 1950s, and 1960s was a traditional middle class that was educated and got enough time and generation to develop aesthetics, you see, culture is the last thing to come. When everything is achieved, and everything is available, culture is the last one to enter. So this generation, which found a new affluence, and entered the middle class, hardly had any idea of aesthetics. Then came these multiplexers where the ticket was 300 rupees or 500 rupees or 700 rupees. So, obviously, a particular class was going there. Then the middle class or the upper middle class was coming to the multiplexes paying 500 rupees and these people didn't want to know who is dying of hunger in which village. They want you to show beautiful things. And then there was another big patron sitting outside in the diaspora; they had come out of the country, they were professional, they are living particularly in the USA, Canada, they are doing extremely well. And they want to remember their country and feel nostalgic, but they want to remember the beauty of the country, not what is unpleasant, that will make them feel guilty, that Oh God, here I have six bedroom, seven TV, three cars and an architect's life, and there are people who are dying of hunger. So it will make him feel guilty. So when he will see *Kabhi Khushi Kabhie Gham*, he will feel fine, I'm happy, my country is happy, everybody is living in big houses, and they are wearing beautiful clothes, and so on. So that was good for everybody. (Personal interview, 16 March 2021)

Moreover, one more interesting development took place during the early 1990s when liberalization of the Indian market was initiated. At that time we saw the emergence of a new middle class and due to the existence of multinational or transnational companies, people started migrating aboard and to other big cities within India. Families started getting fragmented into smaller sizes. These films we mentioned earlier are texts that upload the values of joint families on the one hand and try to unite estranged families on the other hand, criticizing characters who advocate the nuclear family concept. These films reflect the conflict between traditionalism and modernity. They not only idealize the joint family, in the name of Indian heritage and tradition, they also glorify bourgeoisie patriarchal culture. Therefore, I argue that on the one hand they propagate traditionalism–Hinduism–nationalism, and on the other hand they try to show their allegiance to modernism–Hinduism–foreignism. On the whole, the films are socially conservative and advocate family traditions, authority, and a hierarchical class structure, all of which aligned well with the authoritarian regime's ideologies. Women had very important roles in this cultural discourse, which was to be the agents to retain the spirituality and traditionalism of 'Indian' culture. Consequently, we see how the above-mentioned films emphasize the purity of women characters, glorify mainstream beauty, and hail docile, submissive, spiritual, straight and traditional women who are at the same time experts in household work—in short they are portrayals of the *sanskari* Indian woman. If we analyse some other films carefully, we will find that during this period sometimes female characters in films were portrayed as modern-day versions of characters from Hindu mythology. For instance, Mani Ratnam's film *Roja* (1992) shows how the Islamist terrorist threat tears apart the lives of a newlywed Hindu couple. The latter part of the film narrates how Roja (the wife) brings back her husband much like the mythological Princess Savitri, who saved her husband from Yama, the God of Death. *Roja* is a symbolic representation of the majority (Hindu) population, who perceived themselves to be under siege from the minority population, embodied by the jihadi terrorists in the film.

As the hegemony of 'Hindu-ized nation' placed significant emphasis on *sanskari* women as the symbol of the homeland, when some filmmakers adopted a 'queer' method to critique the existing majoritarian culture, they were opposed vehemently by right-wing political parties. One such example was Deepa Mehta's *Fire* (1996), which was violently opposed by right-wing Hindu fundamentalists because the film narrates the lesbian relationship of two married women. When the Shiv Sena Chief Bal Thackeray was asked if the censor board would allow *Fire* to be released, he asserted, 'If they pass the film as it is, then I'll welcome the extremists from Pakistan. If you don't have that much respect for the nation, then allow the nation to go to the dogs' (Raval, cited in Kumar, 2013: 463). According to the followers of the Hindutva ideology, the 'queer' status has no place in the Hindu cultural ideal and, by implication, is outside the imaginary of the Hindu nation. Since India belongs to Hindus solely, other groups such as homosexuals, non-Hindus, and any art form that showcases an alternative position cannot be accommodated in India.

As the Hindutva ideology formulated a new version of Hindu nationalism, a new set of films has emerged, which is characterized by family values, Indian culture, and patriarchy. But there is a noticeable absence of Muslim characters as the principal protagonist in such big budget mainstream films. If Muslims are at all depicted they are reduced to minor characters who appear on screen for a very short span of time and are allowed very few dialogues. The films ensure that they are identifiable because of their Islamicate culture. Dr Kaifiya Fatehma (name changed), while mentioning the changing trend of Muslim representation of the Bollywood post-Babri era, mentions:

> Gradually, it started changing from Muslim main protagonist to hero's friend or driver with a Muslim name. Muslim representation was reduced to almost 70 to 80 per cent but still a positive image was maintained. For example, *Hum Aapke Hai Kaun … !* has a Muslim couple who were very badly dressed and at the drop of a hat they tell shayaris. But still there was positive representation, they were welcomed to the house, they were treated as part of the family, they sent a positive image. Then some production houses came up with another film, *Hum Saath-Saath Hai*, where the Muslim character was a driver. From doctor, the Muslim [character] was reduced to driver, still a positive thing. He was very loyal to the family. I think that was the last time I have seen a positive Muslim character in a mainstream movie. (Personal interview, 30 January 2021)

We can locate the most noticeable examples of Muslim characters in Dr Rashid Khan in *Vivah*, Anwar Sheik and Rehana Baig Sheikh as Vivek's friend and his wife respectively in *Hum Saath-Saath Hain*, doctor and his wife Razia Begum in *Hum Aapke Hain Koun..!*, Sayeeda or *Dadijaan*/DJ and her daughter Rukhsaar in *Kabhi Khushi Kabhie Gham…*, and Rahim Chacha in *Maine Pyar Kiya*. In these films the characters are invested with certain attributes of Muslim ethos. The predominant cultural elements such as use of language (Urdu), dress (*sherwani, pathani style, salwar kameez, tabeez*, skull cap), *shayari*, music, and sometimes association with

Arab countries (the case of Rahim *chacha*) were influenced by Islamicate culture. Here their identity as Muslims takes precedence over all other identity markers such as their occupation. In the fabric of these films, Hindus are projected as the norm of the society and Muslims are the 'disrupter of this norm, hence perceived as the Other' (Rajgopal, 2011: 241). Pointing out this trend, Shiladitya Sen mentions:

> After Babri, a lot of films were released, such as *Hum Aapke Hain Kaun, Hum Saath Saath Hai* to highlight the Indian Hindu joint family culture. In those films, there were few Muslim 'side' characters. The representation of those films made it clear that we don't have any problem if you are Muslim, but you have to be subordinate to the majority. For example, you [keep the] head-cap, wear beautiful dresses, sing nice songs and stay like that. We majorities will protect you; we are in a secular state, what we call pseudo-secular. Stay as a subordinate minority; we are there for you. The hegemony is ours. This concept was propagated many times in Bollywood films after the Babri demolition during 1992. (Personal interview, 13 March 2013)

Even Sen locates the family entertainer genre through the lens of 'good Muslims' and 'bad Muslims'. He points out:

> The film, *Hum Aapke Hai Kaun ... !*, is basically a film about Hindu marriage. Krishna does all the miracles in the movie. The Muslim family in the film was depicted as very nice. These types of films brought out two kinds of Muslims: good and bad. Good Muslims as fighting for the state, gelling nicely with Hindu families, sacrificing their lives for the sake of some friends. (Personal interview, 13 March 2013)

Bollywood, thus, becomes an excellent site to examine the complex interplay between culture and politics. The euphoria of cultural nationalism was transmitted to the country's body politic through the cinematic space. Furthermore, this is the first time when Bollywood explicitly started representing Muslims as enemies of society, when a number of films were released where Muslims were depicted as gangsters, underworld dons, and mafia men.

Politics of Portraying Muslim
Gangsters and Mafias

By the late 1970s, there was an emerging trend of making action films based on the lives of Mumbai's underworld dons. These typical Bollywood gangster films fetishize not only crime but also the city, most commonly Bombay/Mumbai, in which they take place. These films include *Dewaar* (1975), *Don* (1978), *Parinda* (1989), *Agneepath* (1990, 2012), *Sadak* (1991), *Satya* (1998), *Vaastav: The Reality* (1999), *Company* (2002), *Ab Tak Chappan* (2004), *Maqbool* (2004), *Sarkar* (2005, 2008, 2017), *Omkara* (2006), *Gangstar* (2006), *Shootout at Lokhandwala* (2007), *Kaminey* (2009, 2011), *Once Upon a Time in Mumbai* (2010), *Saheb Biwi Aur Gangstar* (2011), *Gangs of Wasseypur* (2012), *D-Day* (2013), *Shootout at Wadala* (2013), *Haseena Parkar* (2017), and *Raees* (2017), which were released in the last three decades and portray mafias and gangsters.

Bollywood started connecting Muslims to Mumbai's crime world as underworld dons, mafia men, and gangsters and by the late 1980s Muslims connected to the role of criminals. A number of central protagonists are inspired by real-life Mumbai underworld dons: for example, let us take such creations as Iqbal Seth aka Goldman (based on Dawood Ibrahim) in N. Malik (based on Dawood Ibrahim) in *Company* (2002), Zameer and Feroz in *Ab Tak Chappan* (2004); Miyan Maqbool and Jahangir Khan (Abbaji) in *Maqbool* (2004); Haji Mastan in *Once Upon a Time in Mumbai* (2010); Rauf Lala in *Agneepath* (2012); *D-Day* (2013); Dilawar Imtiaz Haksar (based on Dawood Ibrahim Kaskar) and Haji Maqsood (based on Haji Mastan) in *Shootout at Wadala* (2013); Shoaib Khan (based on Dawood Ibrahim) and Aslam Khan in *Once Upon a Time in Mumbai Doobara* (2013); *Haseena Parkar* (Dawood Ibrahim's sister) and Dawood Ibrahim among others in *Haseena Parkar* (2017); and Raees Alam in *Raees* (2017). There are some exceptions such as Sardar Khan and Faizal Khan among others in *Gangs of Wasseypur*, a film that is set in the backdrop of the Dhanbad coal mafias unlike the earlier mentioned films, which are contextualized in Mumbai. If we critically look at the representational pattern of the text of Muslim gangster films, it is evident that there are two sharp distinctions. First, there are Muslim gangsters who are kind-hearted and compassionate but at the same time run gangs; second, there are hardcore criminal Muslims who are involved in violence and unlawful activities.

As mentioned, Bollywood films have been inspired by the real lives of underworld dons and mafia men of Bombay multiple times. Some films did not use the real names of the men they depicted but the true identity of the character was quite evident from their attributes. Here, we must mention that three most infamous gangsters—Haji Mastan also known as Mastan Haider Mirza from Tamil Nadu, Karim Lala known as Abdul Karim Sher Khan from Afghanistan, and Varadarajan Mudaliar also known as Varadarajan Muniswami Mudaliar from Tamil Nadu—of the 1960s and early 1980s were based in Mumbai (then Bombay). We will find that the initial Bollywood don characters of the 1970s were often shown in a sympathetic light as they were depicted as having a generous and kind nature and were often based on the lives of the above-mentioned three real-life dons. Sher Khan in *Zanzeer* (1973) was glorified for his benevolent nature in spite of the fact that his character was based on Abdul Karim Sher Khan aka Karim Lala, a Mumbai-based mafia don originally from Afghanistan. It is believed that Amitabh Bachchan's character in *Deewaar* (1975) was inspired by Haji Mastan. Vardharajan Mudalier also spawned a lot of similar depictions and the most prominent one is Shakti Velu's character in the film *Dayavan* (1988). All these *bhai* characters were more a copy of existing real-life characters rather than fictional ones. Since there were quite a few well-known dons who happened to be Muslims, these portrayals became common.

Moreover, Hindi cinema often used to be funded by underworld gangsters before filmmaking in Mumbai reinvented itself as an industry in the 1990s. The association of underworld dons with the film industry was spurred on by the fact that government policy made legal sources of funding ineligible for it. Film producers, directors, and actors were required to seek alternative sources of funding in order to complete their projects, which frequently included suspect sources with close ties to gangsters (Desai, 2016). The mafia dons used to finance films either to support their mistress' careers or to convert the black money they earned into white. For example, Haji Mastan was one of the main financiers of Hindi cinema at one time. Senior journalist Abhinash Dey (name changed) mentions:

Bollywood movies were funded multiple times by Haji Mastan, Karim Lala. Funding always had a dark hand, so basically whoever is funding you, you end up portraying that person some way or the other in a positive note, you have to do it; therefore, the glorification of the dons in all those movies as Robin Hood heroes, good-hearted dons, those things came along because those movies were funded by these people. (Personal interview, 14 March 2021)

Once Upon a Time in Mumbai (2010) and *Once Upon a Time Mumbai Doobara* (2013) were based on the real life of Haji Mastan. It has been shown in the film that he gains utmost popularity and is titled as 'sultan' for his work for the poor and needy. All these films tried to depict the gangster in a somewhat positive light by showing a balance between him being a compassionate, benevolent, and kind human and being representative of cruelty, violence, and barbarism. The same trend was noticed in *Haseena Parkar* (2017), which showed Dawood Ibrahim's sister, and in *Raees* (2017), which showed in Raees Alam. Haseena Parkar was portrayed as the underworld don at the same time as the Godmother of Nag pada. The film *Raees* is said to be based on the life of Gujarati gangster Abdul Latif, who is said to be one of Dawood Ibrahim's associates. Though Hasina Parkar and Raees Alam have some connection with Dawood Ibrahim, a mastermind of twelve serial terrorist Bombay bomb blasts in Mumbai, the films show that these characters either did not associate with those attacks or did so unknowingly like Raees. Therefore, at the end of the film, Raees shows his grief and repentance for having caused the blasts. The film glorifies the fact that he sacrificed his wealth and even his life for the sake of the people, though for a great part of his life he engaged in violence and illegal activities. *Raees* justifies his engagement with the violence (Figure 4.2) and illegal activities by repetitive usage of a famous dialogue: '*Koi dhanda chhota nahin hota, aur dhande se bada koi dharm nahin hota*' (No business is small, and no duty is bigger than the business).

In all the above-mentioned films, the gangsters' evil is shown to be born out of desperation, vengeance, or a need for quick cash. The figure of a gangster in Mumbai is a sign of self-made success, and earns our sympathy precisely because of that. Hard work, determination, and a desire to be at the top are rewarded in this city and that gives a certain aura to the personalities of those who do find success. Regarding this kind-hearted

Figure 4.2 *Raees*: Khol-eyed gangster
Source: Nadira Khatun; illustration by Sreeja Burman.

representation of underworld dons, senior journalist Abhinash Dey (name changed) points out:

I think there is a historical reference point there. Because if you go back to the 1960s and 1970s you had these Bombay dons who are quite popular in their own right. For instance, Karim Lala before Dawood came along. They were characters, like dons, like Karim Lala was Afghan, but he went on to rule the Mumbai underworld. Karim Lala had huge Bollywood connections; and he was said to be in real life one of those, you know, you must have seen a lot of movies where an established don is trying to stop the entry of new-age villains, who are trying to introduce drugs or prostitution and the older dog is trying to resist it. I am happy with the smuggling gold and whatever ... murders and everything but I don't want drugs to enter my area of influence. Toh Karim Lala was like one of those characters, old world ... Then you had Yusuf Patel, then Haji Mastan then Vardharajan Mudalier. But Mudalier, of course, was a south Indian; but you know, in terms of big names, who are dons in Bombay, used to be Patel, Karim Lala, and Haji Mastan, they were the inspiration for those movies and later on Dawood and even then these portrayals to my mind were not—not as you know—not an attempt to portray these characters as Muslims, so much as a copy of self, Dawood, Haji Mastaan, or Karim Lala; meaning I don't see a religious angle in this as much as you know Robin Hood type characters. The bhai is a murderer, killer extortionist; the bhai is also a benevolent character who, you know, is helping somebody to get his daughter married. (Personal interview, 14 March 2021)

The negative portrayal of Muslims can be said to have begun after the 1990s when the idea of the terrorist was tagged with the gangster characters, who were then shown as men who could potentially harm the nation. Before that, the audience could make out the identity of the real-life gangsters on whom the don or the *bhai* characters were based, who were also quite stereotyped. Muslims were also shown as villains, living in ghettos and slums; some were portrayed as slum-lords. However, although these were all negative portrayals they did not have much to do with the person's religion. The characters were more like rip-offs from real-life characters who just happened to be Muslim. But in the recent past, there has been a transition from the portrayals of Muslims as compassionate human underworld dons to cruel inhuman gangsters. Echoing this, film critic Syed Ali Mujtaba writes:

Another interesting development in the late 1970s and 1980s was the portrayal of Mumbai's underworld characters as mostly Muslims in Bollywood films. Although they did not bear Muslim names on screen, the spectators knew who the protagonist was in real life. The Muslim characters since then also started becoming negative in Bollywood movies. Smugglers wearing Arab robes, puffing cigar, carrying briefcases became a common sight in the 1980s. This trend became more direct in the late 1980s and 1990s. Movies like *Ghulam-e-Mustafa* and *Angar* could be cited as examples (2006).

Activist Irfan Engineer mentions how the depiction of Muslim characters went from being honest and loyal friends to gangsters and terrorists from the late 1980s onwards. Engineer points out:

Much like Rahim Chacha's character in *Sholay*, you will find a series of Muslim characters who are sort of side characters, marginal characters but portrayed as very honest. But I remember that Bal Thackeray some decades ago issued a threat to Bollywood. He said, 'You portray Muslims as all honest people and Hindus as goons and villains whereas we have Dawood Ibrahim here in our society. Why Dawood Ibrahim is not reflected on the screen?' And then suddenly, the trend changed. Films on terrorism, bad characters and the underworld started getting produced. (Personal interview, 14 September 2012)

Before going into details to discuss the films based on Muslim enemies as terrorist–gangster, I want to reflect on the real-life socioeconomic conditions of the majority of Muslims in India. It has been pointed out multiple times through different reports such as the Sachar Committee Report (2006), the Ranganath Mishra Commission Report (2007), other academic reports such as 'Socioeconomic and Educational Status of Muslims in Mumbai' (Jain and Shaban, 1999) and 'Socioeconomic Profile of Muslims in Maharashtra' (Patel, 2013) that Muslims face huge socioeconomic inequalities in terms of employment, owning property, and loan opportunities which result in a lack of access to health and educational services. Vibhuti Patel has given a detailed account of statistics on the work, employment, and unemployment in her report. She writes: 'About 39.9 per cent marginal workers among Muslim community in rural areas reported as seeking/available for work ... nearly 70.7 per cent engaged in category of work activities such as semi skilled and skilled informal sector work such as carpentry, masonry, electrician, plumber, mechanic, manual labour, coolie job, solid waste management, butchery, weaving, beadwork, *jari* and embroidery work, tailoring, hawking, petty trade, pulling cycle rickshaws and handcarts, driving four wheelers and heavy vehicles' (2013). This economic condition of Muslims had existed even before Independence and in a personal interview Asghar Ali Engineer gave a historical background for it:

The major tragedy of Muslims in India even when Pakistan was not there, there were only two classes of Muslims. Feudal class or landowning class, which was very small, and artisans. They never developed an entrepreneur class except three small communities— Khojas, Boras, and Memons. They are all from Gujarat and their total number does not exceed 5 million. Among Hindus all the upper castes belong to the business class. They control everything and they provide employment to the fellow Hindus. These are historical reasons why Muslims are poor. Who converted to Islam? Dalits and OBCs [Other Backward Castes]. They remained Dalits and OBCs even after becoming Muslims. Muslims never gave them equal status. Feudal lords had much more in common with Hindu feudal lords than Muslim artisans. So, there are two classes though religion may be one. Caste-wise differences [exist], so they felt much closer to Hindu landowners than Muslim artisans. (Personal interview, 8 December 2012)

In the context of this historical economic backwardness, economic liberalization has widened the gap further. After the economic liberalization in the early 1990s, India is experiencing a capitalist system where the means of production are in private hands. Therefore, we see, 'there invariably develops a division between the class that rules (the owners of the means of the production) and the class that is ruled (those who work for the ruling class) creates a substantial amount of crime, often of the most violent sort, as a result of the contradictions that are inherent in the structure of social relation' (Shaban, 2008: 68). Moreover, a major proportion of Muslims live in slums without basic amenities like drinking water, toilets, electricity, and closed drains (Patel, 2013: 69). All these factors make them more vulnerable to getting involved in unlawful and illegal activities. Abdul Shaban in his article 'Ghettoisation, Crime and Punishment in Mumbai' has mentioned the data regarding the crime rate in Mumbai:

> for the year 1999 and 2004 show that people belonging to religious minorities, particularly Muslims ... 'contribute' most of the members of inmates in Indian jails. Muslims constitute about 13.4 per cent of the total population in the country, but their share in total jail inmates is about 21.5 per cent. The share of Muslim prisoners was 28.4 per cent and 22.5 per cent of the total detenues and undertrials, respectively, in jails in 2004. (Shaban, 2008: 70)

After the Mumbai riots of 1992–1993, the situation of Muslims became much more precarious in Mumbai and they started facing increasing social discrimination. Ashutosh Ingle (name changed), who works as a media coordinator at a non-profit organization, shared his own personal account of Muslim ghettoization in the era of post-1992–1993 riots:

> After 1993, we see more ghettoization for self-security of their own community. As I used to shoot in the area, I saw inhabitants of that particular area were not involved in the riots; though very few of them took part in the violence in the flow but that lasted only for 2–3 days. Some anti-social elements came from outside and also some administrative people were involved in the violence. At that time I used to work in a cable channel called Eyewitness. In the riot, the most widespread incident was that a chawl was burnt and 10–12 families were there and all were burnt alive on 7 January 1993; when we enquired later in details and police investigated, four Muslims put the fire to that chawl for a builder named Shetty. Later YUVA (Youth for Unity and Voluntary Action) took the place and made a community centre on that. There were three mishaps in 1984, 1989, and 1992 and it was clear from those that some anti-social elements want issues to do a massacre. After 1993–94, the attitude changed towards other communities for both the communities, Hindus and Muslims. Afterwards, Muslim ghettoization started more and Muslims were denied rent, buying flats from Hindu locality. For example, in my locality one DCP (Deputy Commissioner of Police) wanted to buy a flat but he was denied and later we protested against that. (Personal interview, 4 May 2013)

Along with the data, Shaban has also mentioned in his article that because of social and economic vulnerabilities that Muslims face, it may be easier to jail them and utilize draconian laws and Acts such as TADA (The Terrorist and Disruptive Activities (Prevention) Act, 1987), POTA (The Prevention of Terrorism Act, 2002), MCOCA (The Maharashtra Control of Organized Crime Act, 1999), and so on with regard to their cases. Because of that, following bomb blasts in local trains in the city on 11 July 2006, police rounded up thousands of people living in slums in Bandra and Jogeshwari on suspicion that some of them were involved as mentioned by political scientist Abdul Shaban in his article, 'Ghettoisation, Crime and Punishment in Mumbai'. The suspicion was focused solely on the fact that these slums are predominantly Muslim populated. Hundreds of people were detained and transported to police stations, only to be released following protests and agitation by human rights activists.

We have seen a trend of representing Muslims as criminals and the enemy and this started after the 1993 Bombay blasts. It was then that the portrayal of Muslim as the 'Other' began. As already discussed, though Muslims were represented as villains before that the villainy had hardly anything to do with their religion. Apart from the films we have discussed earlier in the chapter, there are films such as *Ab Tak Chappan* (2004), *Maqbool* (2004), and *Gangs of Wasseypur* (2012) which represent notorious, bloodthirsty, and extremely violent gangsters either based in Mumbai or elsewhere but they were just characters who are Muslims; the religion of the villains did not play an important role in developing the plot. The religious identity of the characters becomes clear mainly from the names or Muslim ethos such as their language, clothing, architecture of their house, and so on. However, this was also a kind of negative stereotypical portrayal of the community. Later, gangster films were not limited to representing Muslims as dons and mafia men involved in organized crimes like money-laundering, kidnapping, smuggling, racketeering, extortion, human trafficking, arms trafficking, murder, gambling, forgery, and so on. After the 2000s the portrayal of Muslims started changing when the subject of terrorism became a common one to be used in Bollywood. *Shootout at Lokhandwala* (2007), *Once Upon a Time in Mumbai* (2010), *Shootout at Wadala* (2013), and *Once Upon a Time in Mumbai Dobaara!* (2013) intertwine the story of gangsters and terrorists. Most interestingly, these films started creating the idea of an enemy who happens to be both gangster and terrorist and can cause harm to the nation—this narrative suited the aggressive Hindutva ideology of the 1990s quite well.

Nationalism, Communal Conflicts, Terrorism, and Geopolitics

The nuanced interplay between culture and politics found an outstanding articulation in Bollywood. Cinematic space was used to communicate patriotism and nationalism to the country's polity. While neo-nationalism became a popular theme in the films of the 1990s, this period also witnessed the rise of films which represented communal conflicts followed by terrorist attacks. I would like to call them 'terroristic films'. In the previous chapter and section, we saw how Hindutva ideology portrays India as a land of Hindus, and how followers of this ideology are committed to maintaining the Hindu Rashtra's cultural and geographical borders. In this section we are going to discuss 'terroristic' films, where Muslims are portrayed as 'Others' who try to harm the nation, while the majority community is often represented as 'victims'. While talking about nuances of terroristic films in Bollywood, filmmaker Kabir Khan mentions:

Islamic terrorism has become in the mainstream cinema a very cool space to deal with. It's cool to have a villain who is a terrorist, mastermind. He is being Mogambo without going into the politics of terrorism, without going into the cause and effect of this global phenomenon. It's just become a character we use in certain films. (Personal interview, 2 November 2013)

Filmmaker Mani Ratnam's *Roja* (1992) opened the floodgates for such films and soon we had *Drohkaal* (1994), *Maachis* (1996), *Dil Se* (1998), *Black and White* (1998), *Sarfarosh* (1999), *The Terrorist* (1999), *Mission Kashmir* (2000), *Fiza* (2000), *Indian* (2001), *Black Friday* (2004), *Fanaa* (2006), *Dhokha* (2007), *Shootout at Lokhandwala* (2007), *Aamir* (2008), *Mission 90 Days* (2008), *Mumbai Meri Jaan* (2008), *A Wednesday* (2008), *Mission Istanbul* (2009), *Sikandar* (2009), *New York* (2009), *Kurbaan* (2009), *My Name is Khan* (2010) *Agent Vinod* (2012), *The Attacks of 26/11* (2013), *Vishwaroopam* (2013), *Holiday: A Soldier Is Never Off Duty* (2014), *Baby* (2015), *Mr X* (2015), *Phantom* (2015), *Neerja* (2016), *Tiger Zinda Hai* (2017), *Omerta* (2017), *Raazi* (2018), *Hotel Mumbai* (2018), *Blank* (2019), *India's Most Wanted* (2019), *Torbaaz* (2020), and many more. In these films, the characters of terrorists are essentialized as Muslims. It is striking and interesting at the same time to note that in the last three decades Bollywood has produced numerous terroristic films in spite of huge box office failures of certain films. These films have connections with the larger political context of the country in the contemporary age which is dominated by Hindutva politics or Hindu Rashtra mission. Sociologist Sitara Shabnam (name changed) mentions:

> I call it a fascist government which has clear-cut fascist tricks. In any fascist government, I feel the role of media and the control over the media is very important because that is how they shape public opinion, that way they generate a particular kind of ethno-nationalism that they want to propagate and the religious nationalism they are trying to instil. In the case of religious nationalism, it is the other religions than yours that need to be constructed as villains, culprit, potential threats and therefore must be removed from the country. So, one of the ways you establish this is through media and when I say media, of course, [I mean the] entertainment industry. Cinema is one of the strongest mediums because it works at the popular level and Bollywood being one of the dominant mediums for capturing popular imagination. Thus, it is important to release a particular kind of movie to sort of reinforce the narrative of Muslims as enemy. This is a very normal mechanism for any fascist government. If you look at German fascist history, the Nazi period had exactly the same trajectory. Capturing media was very important for generating populist opinion. (Personal interview, 31 July 2020)

Though post-Independence India had witnessed much political violence in Kashmir, insurgent movements in the north-eastern states, the Khalistan movement in the Punjab, and Tamil and radical Naxal militancy, these terrorist activities found meagre representation in popular culture. While there were numerous incidents which could be categorized as terrorist acts in world history, such violent acts were never marked by their religion, as is often done with Islam. In this context of the hype surrounding Islamic terrorism, Al-Naseer Zakaria, a professor and politician says:

> If you see historically all over the world, the IRA (Irish Republican Army) gave a hard time to England. England was a superpower at the time. They bombed people in public gatherings, churches, and theatres. So, no one said these are Christian terrorists. In India, do I call Modi a Hindu terrorist? No, he is a terrorist because he terrorizes people. But I won't call him a Hindu terrorist. Media portraying Muslim as terrorist

and Islam as terrorism, they are absolutely wrong. There are some incidents such as suicide attacks, suicide bombing and all. That is against
Islam. Islam never says that you go and kill innocent people. They are
even insulting Islam. (Personal interview, 27 August 2012)

Studies of so-called 'religious terrorism', a topic mostly taken from David
Rapoport's seminal paper from 1984, gave rise to 'Islamic terrorism'.
Later, multiple texts and scholars established a separate discipline called
'terrorism studies' primarily connected to 'Islamic terrorism'. Richard
Jackson mentions:

The discourse is first and foremost founded on a series of core labels,
terms and discursive formations, including, among many others: 'the
Islamic world', 'the West', 'the Islamic revival', 'political Islam', 'Islamism',
'extremism', 'radicalism', 'fundamentalism', 'religious terrorism',
'Jihadists', 'Wahhabis', 'Salafis', 'militants', 'moderates', 'global jihadist
movement', 'al Qaeda', and of course, 'Islamic terrorism'. Crucially, these
terms are often vaguely defined (if at all), culturally loaded and highly
flexible in the way they are deployed textually. In addition, these labels
and terms are organized into a series of dramatic binaries, such as: the
West versus the Islamic world, extremists versus moderates, violent
versus peaceful, democratic versus totalitarian, religious versus secular
and medieval versus modern. (2006: 6)

Terrorism was there even before what is termed as 'Islamic terrorism' and
the most notable examples are the Irish Republican Army, Liberation
Tigers of Tamil Nadu, the Khalistanis, and ULFA (United Liberation
Front of Asom). Moreover, there were Jewish groups and other Muslim
groups in terrorism but religion was never tagged to terrorism at that
time. There are multiple theories on how Islamic terrorism came to be
an established discipline. Activist and professor Ram Puniany reflects on
global politics establishing the idea of Islam as a threat to global security
because of terrorist activities that some Muslims perform in the contemporary age:

The USA always wanted to control the resources as did Russia. They
were the superpowers. So, in America and Britain propaganda was

against authoritarian dictatorial societies and they are trying to promote free world democracy. So, their battle was for the free world; and
in the name of the free world, they supported every despotic dictator.
They align with every retrograde king ruling any particular country.
So that they were clear to control the material. After the demise of
the Soviet Union, they lost the language of opposing socialism. This
is the most dangerous turning point of human history, I would say,
because here for the first time rather than talking of the issues related
to the world, America is criticizing the socialist system. After the demise of the Soviet Union, gradually, they started talking of Islam as
being a threat. Why do I see it as a dangerous turning point of the
world? There was a power competition between Russia and the USA;
Russia collapsed and America survived. Now America uses a language
flag for promoting their goals. If they want to plunder the resources
of India, then they will say we have a civilising mission in the East.
Here they want to control global politics. They say we want freedom.
They are fighting against authoritarianism. Here comes a stage where
the socialist system is out, what do you oppose? Here comes oil—it
is the new wealth and we should control it. (Personal interview, 16
August 2012)

The debate on terrorism is based on a long history and gained more
importance after the 9/11 attacks. The establishing of the discourse of
'Islamic terrorism' was propelled by racial prejudices and extremely hostile media portrayals of Islam and Muslims. The mainstream mass media
has used frameworks centred on brutality, intimidation, extremism,
fanaticism, and terrorism to represent Muslims. Furthermore, these depictions have lasted for decades, perhaps because, as Said argues, they
embody deeper cultural prejudices, anxieties, and perceptions of the
oriental 'Other' that date back to the imperial period (Said, 1978). Media
therefore helped to establish certain narratives more easily than ever before. Richard Jackson mentions a few such narratives:

> Such powerful oppositions function to limit the discursive space for
> more nuanced narratives and to obliterate the multiple and often
> contradictory identities and characteristics of the narratives' cen-
> tral actors. For example, the application of labels such as 'terrorist,'

'Islamist' and 'extremist' to groups like Hamas and Hezbollah func-
tions to obscure and obliterate their simultaneous existence as political
party, social welfare provider, protection force, local association, relief
agency, charity, education provider, bank, guerrilla force and the like.
(2006: 6)

Even though it is often debated that contemporary terrorism is primarily
based on Islamic religious ideologies, filmmaker Kabir Khan holds a very
different opinion about terrorist activities. Being a documentary and feature filmmaker, he has had to travel to different parts of the world and,
most importantly, to terror-prone countries like Afghanistan. He shares
his personal experience of meeting with terrorists and encountering their
ideology:

I met a terrorist in Afghanistan to make *Kabul Express*, and I firmly believe that 95% of these people are not fighting for religion. It is a personal issue; they do not fight for an ideology. In Kashmir, terrorists are
fighting because a fourteen-year-old boy sees that his father is getting
slapped by BSF (Border Security Force) soldiers. Afterwards, the boy is
becoming a terrorist, not because he believes in Jihad. You are the representative of Indian government, and I will shoot you. And these are the
boys very easy to be brainwashed. Kasab[9] came here; it is not because he
hated India, he came here because he was given money. (Personal interview, 2 April 2013)

In the last two decades, the concept of 'enemy images' in Hindi cinema
has been marked with specific political 'signs'. Earlier, the image of the
villain was larger than life, where villains were entertaining, exaggerated, and dramatic figures such as that of Pran (as Sher Khan in *Zanzeer*),
Amrish Puri (as Mogambo in *Mr India*), and Amjad Khan (as Gabbar
Singh in *Sholey*), who plot to take revenge on the hero or his associates.
During the early 1990s and after, films were inspired by real-life villains

---

[9] Ajmal Kasab was a Pakistani militant and a member of the Lashkari-e-Taiba group. He with
other members of the group took part in the 2008 terrorist attacks in Mumbai, Maharashtra
Singh, Harmeet Shah (2009) Pakistani Militant 'Masterminded Mumbai Attacks', Suspect Says.
CNN, 21 July. Available at http://edition.cnn.com/2009/WORLD/asiapcf/07/20/india.mumbai.
trial/ [Accessed 20 October 2022].

or negative characters like terrorists. Sourabh Agarwal, a college student, discusses this:

Nadira: What is your idea of cinematic enemy image?
Sourabh: Whenever I think about an enemy, it always brings to my mind the image of a terrorist imported from Pakistan. (Personal interview, 3 October 2020)

This increasingly became the trend after the terrorist infiltration of Kashmir in the late 1980s. The organization Jammu and Kashmir Liberation Front (JKLF) led the first wave of anti-India violence in 1988–9. It was followed by many other terrorist organizations. Filmmaker Kabir Khan mentions that the Kashmir conflict was one of the early and primary reasons for making films wherein Muslims were represented as terrorists. This is what he says:

> The Kashmir issue is definitely a starting point where Muslim characters were starting to be represented as terrorists, especially Kashmiri terrorists. That is probably one of the turning points because a lot of the films started dealing with Kashmir issues. In comparison, the film *Roja*, I would still say, is more balanced. It had a grey area. Pankaj Kapoor's character was shown in quite a balanced manner. It was not like he was a stock evil terrorist, unlike say in *Mission Kashmir*, where you have a very strong stereotypical [terrorist] character. A few other films were produced later dealing with Kashmir problems and terrorists are shown in those films in a stereotypical black-and-white way. (Personal interview, 2 November 2013)

Manisha Sethi (2002) terms this new set of 'terroristic films' as 'cinepatriotism'. Amit Rai further elaborates the concept and explains, ' "Cinepatriotism" of Bollywood: a set of films, indeed a genre now, that seeks to represent, visualize, and narrativize the sovereignty of the supposedly secular, but in practice upper-caste, Hindu Indian nation. As such, they have critiqued and fuelled the ongoing tensions between Hindus and Muslims that marked India's postcoloniality' (2003: 5). Cinepatriotism is important to discuss here because the films of this period such as *Roja* (1992), *Sarfarosh* (1999), *Mission Kashmir* (2000), and

Fiza (2000) articulate a debate between Muslim identity and Indian nationalism. Film critic Shiladitya Sen sketches out three fundamental characteristics of terrorist films in the post-Babri era:

> After Babri (1992), the politics of representation was to portray Pakistan as the biggest enemy. In the movie *Sarfarosh*, under a Pakistan flag, the terrorists are discussing how they would attack India. It is applicable for the movies like *Border* and *Gadar* as well. When the film represents Pakistan as indulging in terrorism, at the same time, it is implying that the citizens of Pakistan is a single entity. Secondly, in India whoever is doing terrorist acts, all are anti-religious groups and they do not belong to Hindus. Thirdly, the films support state terrorism to kill those terrorists. These are the central messages of those films. (Personal interview, 13 March 2013)

In an attempt to make these films nationalistic and patriotic, 'terrorists' and 'terrorism' are portrayed as Pakistani imports into India. A number of Bollywood films are either directly based on Kashmir or use the place as a cinematic background. On screen, starting with the film *Roja* (1992) in the early 1990s, films started showing a symbiotic relationship between Kashmir, Pakistan, and Muslims. In numerous films such as *Mission Kashmir* (2000), *Roja* (1992), *Yahan* (2005), *Fanaa* (2006), *Sikandar* (2009), and *Lamhaa* (2010), the terrorists or the terrorist training camps were located in Pakistan. Popular culture in India propagates the statist agenda and 'it also treated the issue as a fundamentally affective one, linking it melodramatically and crucially to belongingness, the familial consanguinity and kinship in the context of the nation' (Gabriel and Vijayan, 2012: 300). Unfortunately, these films on Kashmir and Kashmiri militants ignore the sensitive and complex nuances of the Kashmir issue. The statist stance of declaring Kashmir as an integral part of India is represented in these film texts. As a militant, the protagonist is seen engaged in terrorist acts funded and aided by Pakistan, shouting anti-India slogans, and battling for a 'free' Kashmir. I argue that these texts also perpetuate the nationalist agenda by interchangeably portraying Muslims, jihadists, and Pakistanis as the nation's enemies. From the time of the Kashmir crisis in the late 1980s, we can see the gradual shift of representing Kashmir through a nationalistic prism, where the picture of an ordinary Kashmiri is most frequently subsumed by the aggressive char-acterization of militant elements. When I asked a researcher who be-longed to Kashmir about his opinion on the films representing Kashmiris or Kashmir, Mohmad Waseem Malla expressed the following:

> Indeed it is frustrating sometimes to see how these creative minds surrender their consciousness and narrow their lens to portray living people on the screen as shrewdly as possible. One may adhere to a cer-tain political ideology or back up governmental narratives but that doesn't mean [one should] use a powerful medium like cinema to ster-eotype living people in such a narrow lens that their existence becomes perilous. The mediums like cinema, I believe, become a basis for stereo-typical misconceptions and presumptions one comes across while interacting with people from other places in India. Like how does one respond when people ask you how it feels to pelt stones, or there must be Kalashnikov shops in Kashmir or you are an ungrateful lot given 'our job' is every day protecting you and dying for you and other stuff. These all flow from these cinematic representations we have had over the years. (Personal interview, 11 April 2018)

After this interview, I wanted to speak to another Kashmiri because I wanted to capture the emotions of other Kashmiris too on such Bollywood text. Rouf Bhat spoke to me about it:

Nadira: Do you enjoy the Bollywood films representing Kashmir or Kashmiris?

Rouf: I feel angry at the distortion of the agency of Kashmiris in Bollywood. The characters in Bollywood are everything but Kashmiri. They are so alien to me that I sometimes feel whether I am the real Kashmiri or the one portrayed in the movies. It's a misconstruction of a population, which sees multiple onslaughts on its identity. Bollywood with Indian media has been one single factor responsible for casting people of Kashmir as ostracized. (Personal interview, 18 April 2021)

On 5 August 2019, India revoked Jammu and Kashmir's special status under Article 370 of the Constitution, paving the way for the establish-ment of the Union Territories of Jammu and Kashmir, as well as Ladakh.

Article 370 of the Constitution granted special privileges and status to Kashmir, India's single Muslim-majority territory. This new government's stance in this matter has become a source of debate in the Indian public discourse (*Scroll*, 2019). When I spoke to Sandeep Mishra, who works for a corporate firm, about his opinion on the abrogation of article 370 and the state's stance of claiming Kashmir as a part of India, he says:

> That's a very good step. I had a friend whose father was transferred to Srinagar. My friend was so shocked once he was asked by Kashmiris whether he has come from India. In response my friend said that they are also Kashmiris. These Abdulla [Sheikh Mohammad Abdullah] and his clan are multi-billionaires. Why should [it be] hundred rupees for one kg of basmati rice [elsewhere in India] whereas they pay twenty rupees. Why? Why? How long it has to go on? (Personal interview, 28 July 2020)

Here I argue that if a section of ordinary citizens adopts the state's position on abrogation of Article 370, the trope can be well utilized by the filmmakers to exploit the audiences' sentiments. It is important to note that there are exceptional films such as *Haider* (2014) that are also produced by Bollywood. *Haider* was one of the rare films that tried to represent Kashmir from a different and nuanced lens. It had multiple sequences where the text highlights state atrocities visited on ordinary Kashmiris and shows the state taking away the fundamental rights of people of the region. The film is noteworthy primarily for two reasons: first, the depiction of state-based atrocities. What is it to live in a place where the state has taken full control of your everyday life? Your life has no value and you can be dead at any moment. Second are the kinds of vulnerabilities people have to face on an everyday basis. Being a Kashmiri, Waseem connected more to the film *Haider* and says:

> There are though instances when a film like *Haider*, which tries to portray the everyday experiences of common people through the torture scenes at some point and that famous monologue by Shahid Kappor aptly capturing the frustration of people in the middle of happenings whose strings are being pulled by different actors from across the ideological divide, least of those being Kashmiris. A common Kashmiri is

usually docile, often at the mercy of militant characters who are being rescued by the benevolent state apparatus which runs contrary to the realities where state (dominantly) and non-state unleash happenings in the middle trying to navigate the everyday realities. (Personal interview, 11 April 2018)

India witnessed the most vicious communal violence in postcolonial India after the demolition of the Babri Masjid in 1992–3. Mumbai, as we have seen, was worst affected and the deaths there as per official figures were 575 Muslims and 275 Hindus (Shaban, 2006: 71). The gruesome forms of communal conflict are more common in urban areas, as Ashis Nandy pointed out in his book *Creating a Nationality*, with estimates that 'cities with a higher incidence of communal violence appear to have greater proportions of Muslims' (Nandy et al., 1995: 15). Muslims, according to Nandy, can take advantage of dynamic democratic politics because they are numerically powerful in big cities, allowing them to claim their interests. It is easy to mobilize a large segment of the majority population in urban areas against minorities by using prejudices that hold that Muslims are an aggressive ethnic group that poses a significant threat to the state's social structure, which is mostly governed by the majoritarian community. I would like to highlight the country's body politic of the time through the lens of the film *Bombay* (1995), which dealt with the theme of religious harmony and was based on the 1992–3 Bombay riots.

The Babri Masjid demolition and the consequent communal violence throughout India fuelled many other terrorist attacks in different parts of the country. The riots and the terrorist attacks that followed became the theme of many memorable films such as *Khakee* (2004), *Black Friday* (2004), *Dhoka* (2007), *Black and White* (2008), *A Wednesday* (2008), *Mumbai Meri Jaan* (2008), and *Holiday: A Soldier Is Never Off Duty* (2014). These films portray a concern for security or a threat within the majoritarian consciousness. Muslim protagonists of those films are represented as menacing Islamist terrorists who intimidate ordinary citizens. But the films do not incorporate the complex nuances faced by Muslims, who either have to continually prove their allegiance to the nation or protest by engaging in terrorism. Most importantly, these films adopt the state's stance to counter terrorism. During a conversation, film critic Shiladitya Sen shared his own experience and observation of how the audience accepts 'state terrorism'.

> In the film *A Wednesday*, where Naseeruddin Shah as The Common Man is saying that in your house sometimes some insects come in, the way you kill those insects, do the same for these terrorists. For that, you don't need to go to the police or don't have to take any help from the judiciary ... These statements are defying the system of law and order, and *A Wednesday* became popular. I went to a film festival in Goa in 2008 after the blast in Mumbai. They had a special screening of the film and the hall was fully packed. Almost 500–600 people were watching the film and among them were film critics. If you contradict over there, they will beat you to death. (Personal interview, 13 March 2013)

The protagonists of films like *Fiza* and *Fanaa* kill their brother and husband respectively to prove their nationalism; much like Radha (Nargis) killed her own son Birju (Sunil Dutt) in *Mother India*. But the reasons have changed. In the case of *Mother India*, Radha killed to protect the honour of a woman; as she was the Mother India, she was protecting the nation. But in the film *Fiza*, Fiza kills her brother, and in the film *Fanaa*, Zooni kills her husband, to protect the nation from the evil Islamic terrorist. Even the slaughters resemble the killing of Kauravas by Arjuna in the Mahabharata. In the recent films on terrorism, the representations of terrorists are balanced by the existence of a 'patriotic Muslim' who sheds his blood to prove his allegiance to the country. There is a dichotomy between the 'good' and 'bad' Muslim. Cultural theorist Mahmood Mamdani (2004) has theorized this dichotomy and argues that the 'good Muslim' is co-opted by the state and the 'bad Muslim' challenges the status quo. Therefore, we see multiple films on terrorism propagate a similar ideology. Siladitya Sen mentions that there are a number Bollywood films that portray Muslim characters who happen to be the representative of the state, and act as state agents to transform 'bad Muslims' into 'good Muslims' (2018: 68).

Fiza is a Muslim Social film about Fiza, Amaan, and Nishatbi, a middle-class Muslim family whose life is turned upside down during the Bombay riots of 1992–3. It depicts the minority Muslim community as being trapped between opportunistic political figures who mobilize communal agendas on the one hand, and an extremist terrorist organization on the other hand. At the end, Fiza kills her brother, who is a militant. In the film *Fanaa* (2006), Zooni kills Rehaan Qadri, her husband as well as a traitorous militant. Fiza and Zooni defend the state and prove their patriotism and nationalistic zeal, whereas Amaan (Fiza's brother) and Rehan (Zooni's husband) challenge the Indian nation-state. Moreover, in *Fiza*, Rehan Qadri and his grandfather, who struggle for Kashmiri independence, are represented as 'bad Muslims'. Interestingly, Fiza and Faana being Muslim women save the nation from Muslim men who are either terrorists or Pakistani. Inayat Khan, played by Sanjay Dutt, is a Muslim in *Mission Kasmir*, but he proves himself a loyal man by assassinating Muslim terrorists, and his Hindu wife is then kidnapped by Islamic terrorists but still she adopts an orphan called Altaaf. It shows that because of the greatness of her Hindu faith, she forgives the kidnappers and accepts a boy from that community. She is adamant about changing Altaaf's mind, and she succeeds in the end when Altaf realizes his crimes after he executes a series of heinous crimes. Here Siladitya Sen mentions that the film conveys a message that the state legitimizes minorities only if they accept majoritarianism (Sen, 2018: 68) In the film *Drohkaal*, there was a character named Abbas played by Naseeruddin Shah who is a true nationalist and is a police officer. He was shown as being killed by a group of Muslim terrorists. In *Sarfarosh*, Aamir Khan as ACP,(Assistant Commissioner of Police) Ajay Singh Rathod got the maximum help from Muslim inspector Saleem. Saleem is shown saying to Ajay Singh, 'Give me a chance sir, I will show you what I can do for India.' These are the representations that became popular in mainstream cinema. *Hey Ram* is another movie where there was a character named Amjad Ali Khan played by Shahrukh Khan. In *Thakshak* (1999), the character Aslam Khan is shown as killing a Pakistani spy. This is a genre which started after the early 1990s and in this genre films have portrayed many true nationalist Muslim officers. On the other hand, the bad Muslims, basically the terrorists, are shown as killing the good Muslims. *Mulk* (2018) initiates a lot of uncomfortable dialogues related to the current politics of the state, the film narrates the story of a Muslim family struggling to redeem their lost dignity after a family member gets involved in terrorism. The Hindu daughter-in-law becomes the saviour by rescuing the family from the shame. Dr Kaifiya Fatehma (name changed) points out:

> The film *Mulk* is highly condescending and patriotizing. It is like Muslim households need to be reformed; the Hindu daughter-in-law comes to reform the family. The ultimate idea of these films is that Muslims need reform, they are damaged to some extent, and they are backward socially and politically. (Personal interview, 27 February 2021)

Finally, all these 'good' Muslim characters prove themselves to be innocent and thus not anti-national. Thus, we see that the dichotomy between the 'good Muslim' and the 'bad Muslim' is mostly visible in terroristic films.

After the 9/11 terrorist attacks grabbed international attention, the characters of the terrorists received a lot of scrutiny. Soon after, terrorism became the dominant theme in many national and international films. Ronie Parciack points out:

> following the rise of Hindutva in 1990s, rampant communal violence, serial blasts, in different major cities in India (an attack on the Indian Parliament, 2001; serial attacks on Mumbai, 2003, 2006, 2008, 2011; New Delhi, 2008; Varanasi 2006, 2010; Jaipur, 2008; Ahmedabad, 2008 and many more) and, above all, the aftermath of 9/11, the issue of terrorism was brought to the forefront of popular consciousness and to mainstream mass media, resulting in a proliferation of films depicting terrorists and terrorism. (2013: 145)

I contend that there is a relation between world politics and the changing pattern of 'terroristic films'. After the 9/11 attacks and immediately following the American government's announcement of the 'war on terror', a series of films on terrorism such as *DC 9/11: Time of Crisis* (2003), *Fahrenheit 9/11* (2004), *The Sum of All Fears* (2002), *The Path to 9/11* (2004), and *Munich* (2005) were produced in Hollywood. According to Shaheen, with the global reach of Hollywood motion pictures, 'Arab images have an effect not only on international audiences, but on international movie makers as well' (2003: 174). Though Shaheen mentions images of Arabs, his formulation is applicable to the whole of the Muslim world. The convergence of the Western discourse of Islam and the Indian discourse of Islam influenced Indian filmmakers, especially in Bollywood. Filmmaker Vinay Shukla concedes that Hollywood has an effect on Bollywood:

> 9/11 brought a huge change in the way Muslims have been portrayed. The incident had an immediate impact on Hollywood and later in Bollywood. The Muslim terrorist became a stock character that you had to have in any film which is dealing with international politics. He became the stock villain. I think it is a combination of social and historical reasons where things have made the representations of Muslims change but unfortunately 90 per cent portrayals are always being stereotypical. (Personal interview, 26 April 2013)

It is important to note that the changing business models associated with 'increasing corporate links with media houses in the Unites States of America in particular significantly influenced the cinematic treatment of terrorism' (Gabriel and Vijayan, 2012: 301). For example, different international film studios such as Warner Bros, Disney, Fox, and Dreamworks have entered into collaborations with local film production houses to develop Hindi and regional movies. Because of the engagement of these international production houses, there was a need to represent terrorism as an international event that is recognized globally. This resulted in a number of films, based on 9/11 attacks or international terrorism (Figure 4.3), releasing in India for the last decade. The films include *New York*

Figure 4.3 *Torbaaz*: Children are being trained to become terrorists in Afghanistan

Source: Nadira Khatun; illustration by Sreeja Burman.

(2009), *Kurbaan* (2009), *My Name Is Khan* (2010), *Agent Vinod* (2012), *The Attacks of 26/11* (2013), *Vishwaroopam* (2013), *Baby* (2015), *Phantom* (2015), *Neerja* (2016), *Tiger Zinda Hai* (2017), *Omerta* (2017), and *Torbaaz* (2020).

Though the stories in all these films are not directly connected to the 9/11 attacks, except *New York, Kurbaan*, and *My Name Is Khan* (2010), all the other films are vaguely connected to the adventures of RAW (Research and Analysis Wing) agents who are out to accomplish their missions of capturing terrorist leaders or foiling terrorist missions to ensure 'homeland security'. When I enquired about the ideology behind the making of so many films, especially post-9/11, film critic Rajiv Masand provided the following insights on how Bollywood is primarily a profit-making industry that produces whatever sells at a given time:

> As I was telling, filmmakers want SRK [Shah Rukh Khan] and Ranveer Kapoor because their films sell more. Also repeated representation of the same images reinforces the people's belief; why do we show stories in the news repeatedly? Why is the media so obsessed with such kind of stories? There is a term in journalism: 'sexy'. it does not really mean sexy; it means more people would be interested to know Ajmal Kasab's case related to the 26/11 attack than the Swami of Malegaon Blast. We are more interested in urban incidents and that's why 9/11 and 26/11 are more popular incidents because they happened in New York and Mumbai. [Yet] the acts of terrorism are happening all over the world. (Personal interview, 5 February 2013)

The two films *Kurbaan* and *My Name Is Khan* were produced by the same producer but had very different narratives. On the one hand, *My Name Is Khan* narrates the story of a desperate attempt of an Indian Muslim man with Asperger's syndrome to prove that he is innocent and not a terrorist. Thus, he sets out on a cross-country trip to speak to the president of the United States. The film uses the earlier trope of re-affirming that there are Muslims who support the state's stance and do not side with militants, and even has dialogues that put this sentiment into words. On the other hand, *Kurbaan* tells the story of Avantika and Ehsaan who fall in love, marry, and move to the United States, where Avantika learns that Ehsaan's family is linked to Islamic terrorist groups. Later, she is witness to events like the confinement to the house, domestic violence, and murder of a family member Salma. Though the film tried to initiate some discussions at a superficial level in a classroom sequence about how Muslims are stereotypically portrayed in mainstream media, it seems that the filmmakers understand that the brutal image of Muslims has much more impact on viewers. I spoke to the director of *Kurbaan*, Rensil d'Silva, and asked about the conceptualization of the film. He expressed his intentions of portraying the issue of terrorism in a balanced way:

> It was after 9/11 and I wanted to be responsive to the event ... I thought it was a very important issue what Muslims are going through. I wanted the film to be structured as debate. It is structured from two points of view and the classroom sequence which I made as a debate. I wanted to generate a debate because the West is not right nor is the Muslim community. But what do you do when Western society was into what Afghanistan imposes on a culture? What happens to that colonial behaviour? ... That's why I told Karan [Johar, the film's producer], 'I am going to structure my screenplay as a debate.' When you do that there is for and against. (Personal interview, 26 February 2021)

Here, I would like to argue that the impact of debating the discourse of terrorism in a classroom sequence for a few short minutes and portraying the act of terrorism by the lead protagonists for almost half of the film have very different connotations and impact the audience very disproportionately. Filmmaker Kabir Khan raises an important point about Bollywood filmmakers and their political ideology with special reference to *Kurbaan*:

> Karan Johar [the film's producer] is not a communal person. Rensil d'Silva is not a communal person. But *Kurbaan* is a communal film. That's dangerous for me; that's even more dangerous than a communal person making a film with an agenda—he is clear in his mind ... At the end of *Kurbaan*, the message is what? 'Be careful the next Muslim can be a terrorist.' Do you want that? You fell into a trap. I met a person in Delhi named Baikunth Lal Sharma 'Prem' from VHP (Vishwa Hindu Parishad). His constant theory was that 'Muslim boys seduce Hindu women and they make them into terrorists or they become terrorists

and they use them as cover'. This is a ridiculous conspiracy theory. In *Kurbaan*, we fall into that trap. The poor father of the girl is saying, '*Nahi hum log alag hota hai, mat karo shaadi; lekin tum logo ko payaar hai toh kar lo*' ('Don't get married with the guy because we [Hindus] are different, but if you love each other, go for it'). You and his worst fear comes true. So, these things are very sensitive. (Personal interview, 2 April 2013)

Kabir Khan's point become very relevant with regards to the Freedom of Religion Bill, 2020.[10] Fear of threats can help create a bond within a community to counter the enemy; therefore, it is important to induce that terror in the human psyche either by constructing or recreating a threat. I find that Avantika and Ehsaan's characters propagate the modern-day discourse on 'love jihad', which is a 'fake claim by the Hindu right that there is a "Love Jihad" organization which is forcing Hindu women to convert to Islam through false expressions of love' (Gupta, 2001: 13). According to the rumours being spread, some Islamic fundamentalist groups are sponsoring young Muslim boys in order to lure non-Muslim girls into marriage and compel them to convert to Islam. Organizations such as the RSS (Rashtriya Swayamsevak Sangh), VHP (Vishva Hindu Parishad), Sri Ram Sena, Akhil Bharatiya Vidyarthi Parishad, and Hindu Janjagruthi Samiti advocate this belief. To create that psychological fear, 'the female body is utilized as a component to generate that threat' (Khatun, 2018: 8). Therefore, the anti-religious conversion law (targeting the alleged conspiracy theory of 'love jihad') officially known as the Freedom of Religion Bill, 2020, makes religious conversion exclusively for the purpose of marriage illegal; it has been approved as an ordinance by the lower house of the Parliament (Lok Sabha) to follow the lead of two other BJP-ruled states, Uttar Pradesh and Himachal Pradesh, where such laws have already been instituted

[10] The Madhya Pradesh Freedom of Religion Ordinance, 2020 was promulgated on 7 January 2021. The Ordinance specifies the procedure for undergoing religious conversion and prohibits unlawful religious conversion [PRS Legislative Research (N.D) The Madhya Pradesh Freedom of Religion Ordinance, 2020. Available at https://prsindia.org/bills/states/the-madhya-pradesh-freedom-of-religion-ordinance-2020#:~:text=The%20Madhya%20Pradesh%20Freedom%20 of%20Religion%20Ordinance%2C%202020%20was%20promulgated,and%20prohibits%20u nlawful%20religious%20conversion [Accessed 20 October 2022].

(Vishwanath, 2021). The entire discourse of love jihad resonates of right-wing propaganda—Muslims or 'they' are thought to outbreed 'us' Hindus in our own region and outbreeding Hindus in a deliberate effort to achieve electoral superiority (Jeffery and Jeffery, 1997; Rao, 2011). When I asked about the characterization of Avantika and possibilities of recreating the role again because of the whole love jihad controversy, Rensil d'Silva pointed out:

In today's age it would have been tough to create the same characterization but I don't think impossible [pause for few seconds]; it would be tough in the current political climate . . . it is tough now in this political climate [emphasizing], but when I did it a lot of senior people in the industry who were well-wishers, they came and said why do you need to do it. (Personal interview, 26 February 2021)

Amit Rai writes, 'In the wake of the 9/11 attacks on the World Trade Centre, national strategy planning in India and the USA has converged on the dominant theme of "Homeland security"' (2003: 9). We see that the negative image of Muslims was reinforced after the 9/11 attacks and had global impact; therefore, Bollywood started representing Muslims from a particular lens. Film scholar Nasreen Munni Kabir raises certain important concerns on this matter:

but also you have Obama and his father was a Muslim. Can there be any Muslim prime minister in India? In England I don't think there could be a Black prime minister. The whites accepted blacks in America and blacks were [once] slaves. In the 1960s, they got their rights. Can you believe that and 60 years later there is a black president? Since 9/11, all around the world, there is a very negative feeling about Muslims. In India, it was always brooding. Babri Masjit would not have happened if there were not very negative opinions about Muslims. From the early history of India there are key incidents like Kashmir, Pakistan, Partition to show Muslims in a negative light. (Personal interview, 11 February 2013)

Bollywood depicted the 'war on terror' as a holy war. Some of the 'terroristic films' depicted India's ambition to achieve a powerful position among the South Asian countries by aligning itself with the USA. Filmmaker Mahesh Bhatt echoes this further:

Islamophobia is a political tool that was constructed post-9/11 by the USA. The same is responsible for all the tyranny the world has seen, has tremendous support in India too. You are doing the same thing here. You have an enemy outside; you have the homegrown terrorism you talk about, you have an enemy in Pakistan and you say this particular person is an extension of that person. Then all the other communities around have to show that they are different from them and, yes, they are presented all the time with beard and skullcap. (Personal interview, 31 March 2014)

Films like *Mission Kashmir, Faana, Roja,* and *My Name Is Khan* do not incorporate the difficulties faced by Muslims who have to either continually prove their allegiance to the nation or protest by engaging in terrorism. In most of the films, while the active anti-national role of Muslim terrorists becomes clear, we do not get much insight into the ideological conflict and politics behind the terrorist activities. All these films instil the notion of jihad to execute Islamic terrorism in a simplistic way without getting into the details of the politics of the construction of the ideology of jihad, which is a very politicized concept and connected to geopolitics. Dr Ram Puniayani gave a detailed account of the idea of *jihad*:

The word '*jihad*' actually comes in the Koran 42 times. And, jihad basically means striving for the best. Jihad means fight against your own evils, fight against social evils. Now this word Jihad was distorted in the madrasas which were set up by America in Pakistan, through the funding of the CIA (Central Intelligence Agency, USA), ISI (Inter-Services Intelligence, Pakistan) through the relationship between Pakistan and America. Pakistan acted more as a client state, as a satellite. When they had to set up these madrasas, the salafi version of Islam was promoted. Now, this version changed two things. One is the meaning of jihad, second is the word '*kafir*'. *Kafir* in the Islamic context means one who hides the truth. And when new people were getting converted to Islam, people were stabbing in the back the newly converted people; so at that time it was said that these people who were attacking or stabbing you from the back, you can kill them, because they are *kafirs*. The USA has now changed the meaning of the word *kafir* to those who don't believe in Allah. Second, they said that those who are *kafirs*, we had to kill them. So everybody who is not a Muslim, they had to kill them. And if you kill them, this is jihad. So this jihadi terrorist word came from the madrasas set up by America, in Pakistan ... So jihadi basically is a very nice word, but when the word is used in the correct parlance. (Personal interview, 16 August 2012)

Pakistan as Enemy

Bollywood has been producing films in the war genre for a long time. Films such as *Haqeeqat* (1964), *Lalkar* (The challenge) (1972), *Hindustan Ki Kasam* (1973), *Aakraman* (1975), *Border* (1997), *Gadar* (2001), *LOC: Kargil* (2003), *Lakshya* (2004), *Let's Bring Our Heroes Home* (2004), *Tango Charlie* (2005), *Sarhad Paar* (2006), *1971* (2007), *Red Alert: The War Within* (2009), *Mausam* (2011), *The Ghazi Attack* (2017), *Rangoon* (2017), *Raazi* (2018), *Romeo Akbar Walter* (2019), and *Uri: The Surgical Strike* (2019) are examples. Bollywood's war films are most often based on Indo-Pakistan wars and that is reflected in the above-mentioned films too, where most are primarily on Indo-Pak wars. In this section, I will specifically locate and analyse films based on Indo-Pakistan wars or in which Pakistan has been represented as the enemy. As we have already discussed, the 1990s were a period of aggressive communalism and nationalism; showcasing hatred towards 'Islamic Pakistan' through Bollywood films became an important expression of nationalism. Film critic Rajiv Masand says:

Whenever a patriotic film is made, it's unfortunate that either you have to justify being Indian and therefore not being anti-indian or Pakistani Muslims are the villains each time. There has been very rarely a sensitive portrayal of Pakistan. They are also loyal to their country, there has never been that perspective. You always see the other side as the villain. (Personal interview, 5 February 2013)

Apart from Pakistan's role in training terrorists, there have been a number of hugely successful films in the 'war genre' (depicting wars between India and Pakistan) released between 2000 and 2005 in India. Pakistan is considered the biggest enemy of the nation, particularly in the last two decades, despite India and Pakistan being involved in many cross-border confrontations as far back as 1948, 1965, and 1971. The most devastating among these conflicts was the Kargil War in 1999. Between 1997 and 2006, Bollywood produced numerous war films including *Border* (1997), *Sarfarosh* (1999), *Maa Tujhe Salam* (2002), *Pukar* (2000), *Gadar* (2001), *LOC* (2003), and *Lakhsya* (2004). One of the major differences between the pre-1997 and post-1997 films is that earlier Pakistan used to be represented as a nation without any religious assertions, which changed after the Kargil War. Renowned filmmaker M.S. Satyu mentions:

In the 90s, when the communal party was in power [BJP], there were a series of disturbing films. Films like *Gadar, Border, Refugee, Sarfarosh* were highly prejudiced and especially disturbing because, in the guise of being patriotic, they were anti-Pakistan. In the process they also become anti-Muslim. This is a big distortion being purported by these films. They condemn Muslims. (Alagh, 2008: 187)

Commenting on these films, Rauf Ahmed says:

There was a phase in the late 1980s and early 1990s, particularly around the time when Babri Masjid demolition took place—there were some films which were anti-Pakistan at that time, the words 'Pakistan' and 'Muslims' were used as interchangeable words. (Personal interview, 28 August 2013)

In the post-1997 films, the antagonist is an 'Islamic Pakistan' and soldiers are fighting with either Islamic militants or an Islamic army. In the last few years, we saw again the emergence of Indo-Pak war films that adopted much more realistic representations with the help of advanced technicalities to showcase the intricacies of a war. They also carried a message of extreme hate, violence, and revenge. The films *The Ghazi Attack* (2017), *Raazi* (2018), *Romeo Akbar Walter* (2019), *Uri: The Surgical Strike*

(2019) are new-age war films. Most interestingly, audiences have started enjoying these action-packed three-hour films and have started perceiving that they are coming to know of the intricacies of war through them. Sourabh Agarwal mentions:

SA: I watched Uri, it was a fun film. It was pretty informative. The format of the movie was very new.

Nadira: How was Uri informative?

SA: I have seen some National Geographic shows where they have shown how they killed Osama. I compared this to Uri and tried to understand the differences of how these two armies function and both the governments' strategic involvement. Moreover, the airstrike was pretty informative. (Personal interview, 3 October 2020)

I argue that if the reel army operation is perceived with such a great seriousness, it has greater impact on audiences' minds and they start to believe that those screen representations are authentic and real.

The war films of the 1970s—including classics such as *Haqeeqat* and *Hum Dono*—carried the message of peace. However, films produced in the last few decades carry the jingoistic ideology of Hindutva. Similarly, it was no coincidence that films produced immediately after some of the worst communal riots in India portrayed Muslim characters as traitors and villains. The juxtaposition of Muslim–terrorist–Pakistani was crudely done. However, admiring such patriotic films, BJP leader Lal Krishna Advani's daughter, Pratibha Advani, writes:

Patriotic films, as a special and much-admired genre of Indian cinema, have had a tremendous impact on our people, cutting across religious, regional, linguistic, and economic identities. Moreover, they have also proved their unsurpassed power of communicating both to educated and illiterate masses. (Cited in Budha, 2008: 6).

I feel that being a supporter of patriotic films, she also indirectly supports the symbolic relationship of Muslim–terrorist–Pakistani, which is represented in these nationalistic films. Regarding this, one can argue that the rise of right-wing politics during the 1980s and the eventual electoral victory of the BJP in 1998 led to the huge box office success of the film

Border (directed by J.P. Dutta, 1997). The film is inspired by the real-life events based on the 1971 Battle of Longewala. The battle was fought in Rajasthan during the Bangladesh Liberation war. *Border* is considered one of the landmark films of the war genre in India. J.P. Dutta received huge production support for the making of the film from the Indian army. Lyricist Javed Akhtar mentioned a brief background of the sociopolitical situation of the time when the film was made and why it reinforces the Muslim identity crisis.

And then perhaps, at a later stage, when *Border*, which came in 2000, if I remember correctly, was the first film where we call Pakistan as Pakistan. And there are many people to whom it is not clear; even I'm not really clear to differentiate between Indian Muslims and Pakistan. Somewhere their [general people of India] minds are not very crystal clear about it. So, Pakistan was never used in films before. I don't know why, although we had some descriptions and matches earlier also, but after J.P. Dutta made the film *Border* and it was very successful. And these were the times when terrorism had become a common word. And now and then, some people were arrested here, then in Bombay, what happened you know, we in result, we saw a lot of movies where Muslim characters were terrorists. Now, they may be Pakistani, but the fact is that they had Muslim names, and the same kind of names that Indian Muslims had. So, it was not in a watertight compartment. However, even the filmmaker would try to draw a line or make a wall as if they are on that side and they are on this side. But obviously, there was some overlapping. (Personal interview, 16 March 2021)

There is, however, only one Indian Muslim character in *Border*. Film historian and critic Fareed Kazmi points out that the characterization of this person was as 'an archetypical bearded man wearing *achkhan* and cap' (1999: 12). There is a scene where a man is shown standing outside his burning home, which has been bombed by the Pakistan army. He is crying out, '*Mera Quran Sharif bacha lo, andar jal raha hai*' ('Save my copy of the Quran, it is burning inside'). A Hindu army officer, played by Sunil Shetty, rushes inside, brings out the Quran safely and hands it over to the man, who declares in amazement, '*Magar aap to Hindu hain*' ('But you are a Hindu'). The army officer humbly replies, '*Haan hum Hindu*

hain aur Hindu hi apne ko bhool ke doosron ko sambhalte aaye hain' ('Yes
I am a Hindu and Hindus are the ones who at their own expense help
others'). This statement propagates the message of Hindu tolerance.
Mahesh Bhatt corroborates the lack of representation of Muslim army officers in war films:

> Abdul Hamid was the first recipient of India's highest military decor-
> ation, the Param Vir Chakra. He was the Grenadier of the Indian Army,
> who died in the Khem Karan sector during the Indo-Pakistani War
> of 1965. You have the story of an extraordinary Muslim, who fought
> against the enemy and created an icon. But you will hardly find their
> representation in Indian cinema. (Personal interview, 31 March 2014)

J.P. Dutta made his second war drama *LOC: Kargil* in 2003. The film is
based on the Kargil War fought between India and Pakistan. The right-
wing politicians helped J.P. Dutta gain publicity for the film as 'key ministers from the BJP government cabinet, including Prime Minister A.B.
Vajpayee and Deputy Prime Minister L.K. Advani, turned up for the
premiere of *LOC: Kargil*' (Budha, 2008: 8). One of the most prominent
war films is undoubtedly *Gadar* (2001), which was released soon after
the India–Pakistan Kargil War. The film was one of the biggest hits ever
delivered by Bollywood. *Gadar* carried subliminal communal messages, which strengthened the public spirit of hate that prevailed immediately following the Kargil War. Regarding the film, critic Rauf Ahmed
points out:

> If you see *Gadar* I remember I saw the first day, first show till that last
> point where he says that I will go to Pakistan and bring my wife back,
> until that point people get yawning and they are planning to go out
> then suddenly they started throwing coins. (Personal interview, 28
> August 2013)

The film Gadar was appreciated by all strata of Indian society. Manoj
Chaudhury, a security guard, in a residential community who attended
the screening appreciated the movie *Gadar* and Sunny Deol's character,
who is fighting Pakistan. He said:

I liked *Gadar* a lot. I like Sunny Deol's role. I felt very sad for the girl who without doing any crime got harsh treatment. Muslim community in Pakistan was treating her very badly because she fell in love with a Sikh. Without thinking about religion, Sunny Deol saved the girl's life and that's what I liked most. I felt very surprised after seeing so much of fighting between religions. All are human beings. I felt everyone has a heart. I felt Pakistanis have much anger against Hindus. They were not accepting him. I felt that they were trying to convert him into Islam. (Personal interview, 27 June 2013)

Film critic Saba Naqvi Bhoumik, former bureau chief of *Outlook* and freelance author, opines that 'in the film all the Muslim characters—Indian and Pakistani—are fundamentally flawed. It can't be a coincidence that such a film broke all the records at a time when BJP's popularity was at its height. Hindu right's ideology was blatantly propagated' (Bhaumik, 2005: 86). There is a dialogue in the film uttered by a person who represents Pakistan, '*Hindustan, hamse kaatna sikho*' ('Indians learn to kill from us'). As Pakistan and Muslims are used interchangeably, they easily establish that Muslims are butchers. Every Muslim and Pakistani character in the film is portrayed as evil and treacherous. Rauf Ahmed expresses a similar view:

> *Border* became a blockbuster and did very well, much like *Gadar*. Those films were anti-Pakistan but not anti-Muslim. But anti-Pakistan is a subtle way of saying anti-Muslim. Filmmakers are not trying to polarize more but they are cashing in on what is existing in the society. (Personal interview, 28 August 2013)

Another recent spy film *Raazi* (2018) tells the story of a Kashmiri woman Sehmat Syed/Khan. She agrees to marry a Pakistani army officer in order to spy on Pakistan during the 1971 Indo-Pakistan War. She pawns her life to protect the nation. *Raazi* differs from the passive forms of feminist nationalism we have seen in the earlier films through the characters like Zooni, Fiza, and so on in the terroristic films. Generally, women play a passive role in terms of nationalistic fervour. Men are compelled to fight in wars, according to Nagel, because their masculinity is linked to the justification of war, which is expressed in masculine terms such as courage, duty, honour, and freedom (Nagel, 1998: 251–2). In *Raazi*, subversion is at two levels: first, it is a woman who is nationalistic, who has the immense sense of love for her country which is instilled by her father; second, she is Muslim. These two elements play important roles as agents of nationalism. Sitara Shabnam (name changed), a sociologist and academician, mentions:

> The film is a subversion of the nationalism we imagined, the way we image the path to nationalism; she [Sehmat] completely dislodges it, though she is associated with a masculine project in some way because she has all the tactics which are violent in some way. (Personal interview, 31 July 2020)

The expression 'surgical strike' gained special attention after the Indian military intervention against Pakistan in 2016 and entered the public vocabulary. *Uri: The Surgical Strike* (2019) supported the BJP's hypernationalistic electoral campaign for the Indian general election in 2019; moreover, the film painted Prime Minister Narendra Modi in an optimistic light, portraying him as a nationalist hero determined on exacting vengeance on the enemy state (Pakistan) for sheltering terror groups. It was another blockbuster. The film is based on the events of 2016, when India conducted a 'surgical strike' against Pakistan in retaliation for a brutal attack on an Indian army base in Jammu and Kashmir. Even a dialogue from the film has become a very patriotic expression, 'How's the *josh* [energy/enthusiasm for defending the country]?' The iconic phrase was used in official tweets and official government activities by the prime minister, the defence minister, and nearly every other member of the Indian cabinet to project the image of a strong, decisive leadership. A month after the film's release, a militant group attacked an Indian military convoy in Pulwama on 14 February, 2019, killing 40 troops, intensifying the public's need for retaliation. Prime Minister Narendra Modi instantly ordered another 'surgical strike' against Pakistan, this time attacking a military campground allegedly belonging to the Jaish-e-Mohammed (JEM) armed group. Immediately, social media was overwhelmed with the same expression, 'How's the *josh (enthusiasm for and commitment to a particular task)?*' as Indians praised the prime minister for his valour in 'saving' the nation and its pride. Pushpanjali Rath, a schoolteacher, points out:

> I liked the film because the film shows how India took a stand against Pakistan because whatever they have done, we can't sit silent all the time; they can't take it for granted that India is not [going to] retaliate; we can also retaliate. The way they have strategized and how they have done, obviously, we feel those people killed our jawans unnecessarily. I like the film because of the way we take revenge. (Personal interview, 1 October 2020)

The huge success and popularity of war dramas such as *Border*, *LOC: Kargili* and *Gadar* foregrounds the influence of Hindutva ideology on citizens at the time. In an attempt to make these films ultra-nationalistic in nature, filmmakers demonize the 'Other', that is, Muslims to make their films sell.

Conclusion

This chapter attempted to locate the larger connection between the sociopolitical background and the portrayal of Muslims in Indian Hindi cinema by focusing on films released after the Babri demolition. Bollywood, like other forms of mainstream culture, has added to the hegemonic Hindutva debate by portraying the Hindu nation and Muslim minority in a kind of 'Manichean rivalry'. The shift in portrayal represents the fact that Hindi cinema has always projected Hindu narratives to transmit a sense of what it means to be Indian. The portrayal of Muslims in Bollywood is evolving in response to the current political situation, especially in terms of right-wing politics.

The depiction of Hindu culture as hegemonic along with the derogatory portrayal of Muslims as gangsters, jihadists, and Pakistanis has strengthened prejudices already in place. These films' stories deeply challenge the distinction between the self and the Other as Hindu and Muslim. The ultra-nationalist and ultra-violent films released in the last two decades, have provided enough fodder for the radical Hindutva ideology. The theme of 'terroristic films' in different contexts such as

Kashmir infiltration, the scattered terrorist attacks across India, and international terrorism post-9/11 suggests that the persistent reproduction of these stereotypical images in multiple films constitutes Muslims as 'the enemy within'. As a result, Muslims became the victim of vengeful violence within the Hindutva movement as a whole. Further, the symbolic relation between Pakistan, Muslims, and Kashmir engenders a rhetoric of 'Otherization' depending on the intervention of different right-wing political parties. The development of a self-conscious and militant nationalism in Hindi cinema recalls Benedict Anderson's landmark work *Imagined Communities*, in which he described nationalism (1983). Cinema has been a key weapon of propaganda in the hands of nation-builders since its origin. Although the medium was unable to mobilize the nations, it did provide them with a new path. In India's Hindi cinema, some practices and values identified with certain dominant classes are established as the norm, while others are marginalized.

5

The Muslim Modern Genre

From Allegiant to Secular

Figure 5.1 From Allegiant (Rishi Kapoor in *Mulk*) to Secular (SRK in *Chak De! India*)

Source: Nadira Khatun; illustration by Sreeja Burman.

Postcolonial Bollywood and Muslim Identity. Nadira Khatun, Oxford University Press. © Oxford University Press 2024.
DOI: 10.1093/oso/9780198891017.003.0006

In the previous three genres (Muslim Historical, Muslim Social, and Muslim Political), I identified films that dealt with the liminality of the Muslim Other in the national space by stereotyping Muslims or striving to integrate the Muslim Other into the normative Hindu self. After 2005, mainstream films shifted away from traditional depictions of Muslims as the 'enemy' or 'aliens' to one in which Muslims were gradually portrayed as 'pleasant', 'sensible', and 'secular' human beings. The Muslim Modern genre moves away from the clichéd portrayal of Muslims in older popular films and moves towards one in which Muslims are presented as 'good' and 'ordinary' human beings who face everyday issues and challenges. Before going into the details of the Muslim Modern genre, the term 'modern' needs to be theorized. The notion of 'modern', 'modernity', and 'modernism' started in the post-medieval period when technological innovations and industrial development were the primary concerns. Therefore, the term 'modern' seems to have been coined in the nineteenth century to differentiate the 'present' from the 'past' era. But there are multiple arguments by scholars like Jürgen Habermas and Seyla Ben-Habib (1981) and Zygmunt Bauman (1999) attached to the modern era about how to distinguish between what was modern and what was not. There are even debates around whether modernity should be considered a philosophy or just an epoch. Similarly, Foucault (1984) suggested that modernity should be perceived as an attitude rather than as a period of history. He further clarifies what he means by 'attitude of modernity', 'And by "attitude", I mean a mode of relating to contemporary reality; a voluntary choice made by certain people; in the end, a way of thinking and feeling; a way, too, of acting and behaving that at one and the same time marks a relation of belonging and presents itself as a task' (Foucault, 1984: 39). While speaking about modernity, Charles Baudelaire mentions, 'Modernity is often characterized in terms of consciousness of the discontinuity of time: a break with tradition, a feeling of novelty, of vertigo in the face of the passing moment' (Baudelaire, cited in Foucault, 1984: 39). Therefore, in this chapter, I want to adopt modernity as a philosophy that implies 'a break with tradition' rather than a particular historical period. I would like to argue that there is a discontinuity of Muslim representational patterns in the contemporary era because the key Muslim characters are shown without the Islamicate ethos imprinted on them. Muslims are now frequently depicted as ordinary people with mundane dreams or dealing with daily issues. They do not carry any extra baggage of their religious identity but they are very often compelled to show their loyalty to the government or their innocence with regards to the crimes against the state. Regarding this contemporary representation of Muslims, I had a conversation with veteran lyricist Javed Akhtar, who sketched out an all-encompassing change of Bollywood cinema:

> Actually, lots of change has occurred and it happened so slowly that you don't notice but you look back and then you look at the contamination but then you realize how much it has changed, which has changed a lot. In many ways, gradually, traditionally, Indian film used to be near to a novel. And gradually it is coming to words, short story. Slowly but surely, the stories are turning into short stories. While it was generations after generations and the father and the son goes on and so on grandchildren, the stories of generations are going out so it is now in here, here in now. Somewhere the structure is changing; the usage of music into a projection. Now most of the time you'll find the songs in the background. They are not lip-syncing. Certain characters like the mother, the traditional all-sacrificing holy devi-like mother, is shown out of the frame, she is no longer in the film; the villain, *joh eck villain tha smoking karta huya, isme dhuye ke challe banate huya woh kahan hai?* [Where is that villain who used to make smoke rings while smoking?]. That larger-than-life villain has gone out. So somewhere gradually, cinema is becoming more real, sometimes at the cost of dramatic impact, which I don't appreciate. But the dialogue has changed to a great extent. You don't see here any rhetoric in film dialogue anymore. It has become more casual, more conversation-like and so on; characters have become more realistic than what they were, they are not larger-than-life characters. (Personal interview, 16 March 2021)

From the 2000s onwards, one of the most interesting developments which took place in Bollywood cinema was the confluence of mainstream and art-house cinema. We saw the rise of films which had a superstar cast in spite of having an issue-based narrative concerning a marginalized section of the country. *Lagaan* (2001) is one of the earliest examples of this kind of film. In the same year, films like *Dil Chahta Hai* and *Kabhi Khushi Kabhie Gham* were released. All three had different kinds of cinematic languages. *Lagaan* was a big mainstream film because a superstar like Amir Khan was acting in a very sensible big budget movie. *Dil Chahta Hai* had a completely different kind of the glamour of storytelling. *Chandni Bar* (2001) is another film which would have been considered as art-house in previous times but had a mainstream star like Tabu. Along with these films, we also saw the release of a formula film *Kabhi Khushi Kabhie Gham*, which had the old format but was a big blockbuster. Now the line between such different forms of cinema has become blurred. When film critic Rajiv Masand was asked about his opinion about this new change in Bollywood cinema and its impact on Muslim representation, he said the following:

The biggest change is that there is a blurred line between art cinema by Shaym Benegal, Govind Nehlani, Ketan Mehta, and mainstream cinema. Now, there is no distinct two kinds of cinema. Now there is mainstream cinema and new emerging cinema but you can't call it art cinema the way it used to be art cinema, the slow boring stories people use to think. You did not find that the mass audiences are going to watch those films but today mass audiences are going to watch a Shaym Benegal film because Shaym Benegal is making different kinds of movies now. One of the most prominent examples is *Welcome to Sajjanpur*. Is it an art-house movie or a commercial film? It's not an art-house film. It has got songs, also a star like Amrita Rao. Those filmmakers like Shaym Benegal, Ketan Mehta realized that it does not have to be one or the other, you can straddle the middle path. You have started seeing the films more like *Mammo* which speak about identity. As the line began to blur, so a lot of filmmakers who are sensitive started telling stories about Muslim identity, Muslim experience in India; perhaps many of them could not do so earlier in the popular format because you believed that nobody will come and see them in mainstream film and in art-house format; even if they are [making them] but nobody is going to see them. Who went to see *Mammo, Sardari Begum*? These films did not do well. On the other hand, Nagesh Kukunoor's *Iqbal* is a great example, it is such a commercial film. (Personal interview, 5 February 2013)

Iqbal tells story of a physically challenged Muslim boy who belongs to a poor family in rural India. If we look at it critically, we find that the film showcases multiple levels of marginalization for the lead character: the boy is physically challenged, belongs to a minority community, and faces a lack of facilities in rural India. Film critic Nandini Ramnath corroborates this:

> What I like most in *Iqbal* is that, it doesn't make any fuss; you won't realize the guy is Muslim until the end. In fact, it doesn't even matter; he could have been named anything apart from Iqbal. It's a silent film that says you are a Muslim hero. (Personal interview, 5 February 2013)

Consequently, Iqbal can be considered as one of the pioneering films of the Muslim modern genre. The genre contextualizes ordinary Muslims in the present social and political context with their everyday issues and sufferings due to financial constraint, corruption, patriarchy, social conservatism, superstitions, biases, sexuality, love, and greed. Moreover, Muslim modern films focus on current issues which are not only based on Islamic religion. At the same time, the genre examines film narratives that represent Muslim characters without much Islamic religious baggage in spite of using certain Islamic ethos such as language, clothes, and etiquette but these do not mark Muslim identity. For example, Subhash Kapoor's *Madam Chief Minister* (2021), Abir Sengupta's *Indoo Ki Jawani* (2020), Shoojit Sircar's *Gulabo Sitabo* (2020), Ritesh Batra's *Photograph* (2019), Zoya Akhtar's *Gully Boy* (2019), Shelly Chopra Dhar's *Ek Ladki Ko Dekha Toh Aisa Laga* (2019), Abhishek Kapoor's *Kedarnath* (2018), Prosit Roy's *Pari* (2018), Gaurav K. Chawla's *Baazaar* (2018), Advait Chandan *Secret Superstar* (2017), Shivam Nair's *Naam Shabana* (2017), Karan Johar's *Ae Dil Hai Mushkil* (2016), Ali Abbas Zafar's *Sultan* (2016), Gauri Shinde's *Dear Zindegi* (2016), Samar Shaikh's *Bobby Jasoos* (2014), Aanand L. Rai's *Raanjhanaa* (2013), Habib Faisal *Ishaqzaade* (2012), Shaym Benegals' *Well Done Abba* (2009), Shimit Amin's *Chak De! India* (2007), and Nagesh Kukunoor's *Dor* (2006), and *Iqbal* (2005) are the most prominent examples of films in the category of the Muslim modern genre. There are a few more films where Muslims are not the lead characters but play important roles to build the narrative. In recent times, protagonists like Nazia Zaidi in *Pagglait* (2021), Sahil Mirza in *Ek Ladki Ko Dekha Toh Aisa Laga* (2019), Shahida 'Munni' Rauf and Chand Nawab in *Bajrangi Bhaijaan* (2015), Dr Jehangir 'Jug' Khan in *Dear Zindegi* (2016), Kalim in *Ungli* Aslam Sheikh in *Lunch* Box (2013), Imran Qureshi in *Zindegi*

Milegi Nahi Dobara (2011), Farhan Qureshi in *3 Idiots* (2009), Aslam Khan in *Rang de Basanti* (2006), and Ali in *Dhoom* (2004) are some of the characters represented as Muslims. However, none of these are the key protagonists in the film; instead, they are shown as supporting characters, who played important parts in developing the narrative.

I shall now look at some of the other features of the Muslim Modern genre. This chapter has four major sections: (a) 'Modern and Ordinary Muslims' illustrates the everyday life of Muslims; (b) Muslims in Supernatural Cinematic Space; (c) 'Secular, Patriotic, and Self-sacrificing Muslims' demonstrates the accountability of carrying Islamic religious identity; and (d) 'Economics of Filmmaking in the Neoliberal Era' tries to examine the political economy of Bollywood filmmaking to understand the reasons behind the shift in the representational patterns of Muslims.

Modern and Ordinary Muslims

As mentioned earlier, Bollywood rarely depicts Muslims as secular, or-dinary characters in everyday settings; however, now a change can be seen taking place. In this section I am going to analyse these recent changes in representing Muslims. The earliest example of this kind of rep-resentation is comedian Mehmood's slapstick Hyderabadi Muslim char-acter in *Gumnaam* (1965), though after that representation of Muslims slipped into the formulaic mould we have discussed in the previous chap-ters. The films of the Modern Muslim genre are the best examples of films on contemporary ordinary Muslims with mundane struggles. I use the term 'modern' to differentiate the image of Muslims from the earlier lens Bollywood used to imagine Muslim characters. Regarding this new trend of representing modern ordinary Muslim characters who are different than the earlier naïve and self-sacrificing Muslims, Javed Akhtar men-tions the following:

> And there were certain films, which were dealing with this topic, but not in your face, like *Iqbal*. I think that was a very healthy and very good film. Because there is a boy Iqbal who has certain social, cultural, and economic problems and he is a good bowler. And nowhere in the film is his community or his caste mentioned. And some people help him,

some people don't help him, but this [religious] angle is totally absent. I think that's the ideal thing to happen, to show a minority member always holier than others is not necessary. They are ordinary people; some people are good, some people are bad; we should have some kind of a healthy attitude and objectivity, because secularism is not treating the minorities or other community with hate or love; secularism is not bothering about it, not thinking about it. So, I think gradually Indian cinema is coming towards that. This is the time when I will advise that a Hindi filmmaker should always put Muslim characters in their film from back, but the present should be that he may not be a great sacrificing friend, but he can be the old family doctor. He can be the lawyer you have hired and so on. So, this will be healthier. (Personal interview, 16 March 2021)

To contextualize the position of 'ordinary' Muslims, and how contemporary Bollywood accommodates middle-class or subaltern groups in India's neoliberal cultural space, I want to include here a brief account of some of the above-mentioned film texts.

One of the determinants to define 'ordinary', irrespective of religions, is small-town nostalgia in Bollywood contemporary films. Especially in the last two decades, Bollywood has produced an imaginary 'other' to the major metropolitan city through a new set of narratives that is based in small cities—'a counter-utopia which threatens even as it entertains the residual cultural-self trapped in the confident but ill-conceived Indian urbanism' (Kumar, 2013). An important film of the recent era of this type is *Gulabo Sitabo*, a comedy drama. It tells the story of Chunnan 'Mirza' Nawab, who is considered a miserly and greedy old man by the majority of the people he encounters. Fatima Begum is Nawab Mirza's wife who is 17 years older than him. Begum is the owner of Fatima Mahal, a run-down Lucknow mansion, whose rooms are rented out to a variety of tenants. Begum entrusts Mirza with the care of the house; and Mirza can hardly wait for Begum's death so that the mansion can be transferred on to him. Similarly, *Kedarnath* (2018) tells the story Mansoor Khan, a poor Muslim porter, who lives in the valley near the Kedarnath Temple. *Secret Superstar* (2017), a musical drama, tells the story of a teenage girl, Insia Malik, and her journey from Baroda to Mumbai to become a successful singer. One of the five highest-grossing films of all time, *Sultan* (2016), an action drama, narrates the story of Sultan Ali Khan, a middle-aged Jat *pehlwani* wrestler champion in a small town in Haryana. *Lipstick Under My Burkha* (2016) is a dark comedy drama set in Bhopal. In *Bobby Jasoos* (2014) we are told the story of Bilqees Ahmed, alias Bobby, who aspires to be a private detective, and the film is set in Moghalpura, one of the oldest suburbs of Hyderabad. In *Raanjhanaa* (2013), a romantic drama, Zoya Haider belongs to a conservative orthodox family in Benaras. *Ishaqzaade* (2012) is an Uttar Pradesh-based romantic tragic drama. *Well Done Abba* (2009) is a political satire that received a national award for outstanding film on social themes. It narrates the story of Muskaan, the main character, and her battles against bureaucratic corruption with her father Armaan Ali, who seeks a government grant to construct a well to alleviate his village's water shortage. *Dor* (2006), directed by Nagesh Kukunoor, tells the story of Meera and Zeenat Fatima, two women who live miles apart but are linked by fate. Meera is from a village in Rajasthan and Zeenat belongs to a remote place in North-East India. *Iqbal* (2005) follows the struggle of a cricket-crazed hearing- and speech-impaired child from a remote Indian village as he strives to conquer obstacles in order to become a cricketer and play for the Indian national cricket team. All these films are based on local issues that are confined to a place or everyday life of ordinary people who belong to rural or remote places in India. Though we are now seeing such Bollywood texts frequently, it is a fact that the reach of these films is limited to a particular category of audience despite these films using the tropes of mainstream commercial films such as big stars, melodrama, and song-and-dance sequences. Apart from *Sultan*, none of the films we discussed here did very well at the box office. After the introduction of the neoliberal economy in India, there was a huge migration of people from rural India to tier one and tier two cities. This built a new market for a certain kind of Bollywood film—where the audience wanted the place they left behind being represented on screen. They wanted the voyeuristic pleasure of observing the places they once lived in. This demand for small-town nostalgia was supported primarily by the multiplexes and there was a surge of the same from the early 2000s. 'The small town—unlike the idealized residues of the cinematic village that was considered to be the moral axis of Indic civilization until the late 1970s—retains immense potential for an eclectic, quick-witted cinema that could appeal to a range of audiences' (Kumar,

2013). However, despite using certain material signifiers in such kinds of film, such as dialect, language, mannerism, characters of villagers, and village infrastructure, these films hardly ever dealt with the complex and nuanced issues and politics of the place much like the films I discussed in Chapter 4, including M.S. Sathu's *Garam Hawa* (1973), and Saeed Akhtar Mirza's *Salim Langde pe Mat Ro* (1986), and *Naseem* (1995).

On the other hand, most interestingly, *Photograph* and *Gully Boy* situate their plots against the backdrop of a big city, that is, Mumbai. *Gully Boy* (2019) is a musical drama set against the backdrop of Mumbai's Dharavi slums. It narrates the story of Murad Ahmed and his journey to becoming India's most famous rapper. *Photograph* is a romantic drama set against the backdrop of Mumbai and narrates the story of Rafi, a struggling street photographer, who is trying to pay off an old family debt. He meets Miloni, a student from a well-to-do upper-middle-class household. The film mostly focuses on Rafi's background. Both *Photograph* and *Gully Boy* use the stories of members from the subaltern classes who live in Mumbai slums. Like small-town films we discussed in the previous paragraph, even these two films avoid the nuanced complexities of urban sociopolitical space inhabited by Muslim slum dwellers. They instead divert the audiences' attention either to a romantic love story or the narrow customs and practices prevalent within the community.

There are very few films that even superficially address the current crisis of Muslims in the contemporary socioeconomic space. *Kedarnath* is one of the exceptions. In the film, Mukku's fiancé Kullu, an overambitious greedy local businessman, gets to know about the love affair between Mukku and Masoor, a Muslim porter—belonging to a community that is forced to leave the valley because Kullu wants to utilize their land to build a luxurious hotel. The film's subtext propagates the message that a section of people are politicizing religion for their own gain. With the controversy surrounding CAA and CAB (Citizenship Amendment Bill) raging in the country, filmmaker Abhishek Kapoor raises certain uneasy questions through the dialogues used in the film regarding the insecurity faced by Muslims in India. There is a scene where Kullu and Masoor get into an argument regarding the building of a hotel and we find Mansoor opposing the construction. A furious Kullu says, '*Tum Kanha se agaye hamare beech?*' ['From where did you come among us?'] In reply, Mansoor says, '*Hum to hameshasehi yanha hai*' ['I was always here']. Moreover, the

Figure 5.2 *Kedarnath*: Mansoor carrying a pilgrim for Kedarnath pilgrimage
Source: Nadira Khatun; illustration by Sreeja Burman.

film tries to show how such excessive construction work can be detrimental for an eco-sensitive area like Kedarnath. The film is inspired by the 2013 Uttarakhand floods, which many believe were devastating as a result of the illegal construction that went on in the valley making it susceptible to being washed away by floodwaters. But the film does not focus on the intricacies of the problems it portrays in a comprehensive way and rather shifts away the audience's attention to the tragic love triangle depicted in the film. Later, it was alleged that the film hurt Hindu religious sentiments because it had the tagline, 'Love is a Pilgrimage'. Ajendra Ajay from BJP's media relations raised this issue.[1] The film was also accused of promoting love jihad because it depicts the love story between a Muslim porter (Figure 5.2) and a Hindu priest's daughter; later, the film was banned in Uttarakhand.

---

[1] See Press Trust of India (PTI) (2018) BJP Alleges 'Film "Kedarnath" Promoting "Love Jihad"', Demands Ban, *The Indian Express*, 10 November. Available at https://indianexpress.com/article/india/bjp-alleges-film-kedarnath-promoting-love-jihad-demands-ban-5440550/ [Accessed 15 January 2021].

Ishaqzaade (2012) was another film that had tried to challenge the country's contemporary sociopolitical scenario on multiple levels by depicting such issues as premarital sex, marriage outside one's religion, religion, and culture, as well as the very real issue of honour killing. It also upholds how men are glorified if they indulge in premarital sex; however, women who engage in the same are demonized without contextualizing the issues in the larger political discourse.

Another prominent characteristic noticeable in these films is that the romantic leads or even the protagonists are shown as belonging to different religious communities except for a few examples such as *Sultan*, *Gully Boy*, *Well Done Abba*, *Chak De! India*, and *Iqbal*. Sometimes these lead protagonists act as partners or couples, and at other times, they just coexist. One of the best examples of such films is *Gulabo Sitabo* where Ayushmann Khurrana's character is the second lead role, named Baankey Rastogi, a poor tenant in Fatima Begum's mansion. Rastogi lives with his mother and three sisters. Khurrana's role is equally important as Nawab Mirza played by Amitabh Bachchan. In *Ishaqzaade* we see the story of the Chauhans and the Qureshis, two political families with a long history of tension and mutual hostility, against the backdrop of the tragic love story between Zoya Qureshi and Parma Chauhan. As we have seen earlier, Mansoor Khan in *Kedarnath* is a poor Muslim porter in love with Mandakini Mishra, also known as Mukku, the daughter of a Hindu priest who on behalf of the temple council manages the temple's pilgrim guesthouse. In *Raanjhanaa* Zoya Haide is admired by Kundan Shankar, a Tamil Brahmin. As described earlier, *Photograph* tells the story of an unusual bond between Rafi and Miloni, who belong to not only different religions but to altogether different classes. Rafi's grandmother is desperate for him to marry and is relentlessly pressuring him to do so. He placates his grandmother by showing her a picture of Miloni, a timid stranger. As Rafi's grandma presses him to bring his fiancé to meet her, Rafi convinces Miloni to fake their relationship, which she readily agrees to do. Despite their cultural, social, and economic differences, the two form a bond, which transforms both immensely. These films try to blur the line between mainstream and arthouse cinema; there is also an attempt to cater to a large audience by incorporating characters from the majoritarian community so that the films have a much wider reach.

The portrayal of Muslim women is the most strikingly different in the Muslim Modern genre when compared to earlier films. As we have seen in the previous chapters, Muslim women were often depicted as *tawaifs* or were shown as veiled in earlier genres. Now, the female characters are given a crucial role and used to build the narrative—they are the victims of polygamy, sufferers of domestic violence, bearers of conservatism, and so on. In *Gully Boy*, Murad Ahmed, the lead character, stays with his abusive father, Aftab Ahmed, who is not only an abusive husband and parent, but also to the family's dismay brings home a much younger second wife. Criticizing the overused depiction of Muslim polygamy in Bollywood, sociologist Sitara Shabnam (name changed) raises some questions and concerns about the representation:

> Was it really needed to represent two wives of his father? Already people have these negative stereotypes about Muslims. A common assumption people have is that Muslims get married four times, they [Muslims] give birth to twenty children. This is the most usual perception which has been there forever from the post-Independence period. And this narrative has been bolstered by the Hindutva camp. They keep on brainwashing people around the fact that they have four wives and twenty children and therefore [India] would become a Muslim nation at some point in time. I think it's more of a class thing than religion-based issue. I don't think a middle-class Muslim family is going for four marriages. Often in the lower economic class what happens if they are not having a son, they go for a second marriage. This happens across religions in lower classes. It even happens very often among Hindus. So, the presentation in *Gully Boy* reinforces popular perception. As an art form if you are telling a point, if you are arguing for something, you are actually establishing a point. (Personal interview, 31 July 2020)

When I spoke to Rimila Goswami, an audience member, about how Muslims are shown as involved in polygamy in Bollywood films, she expressed her belief and mentioned the following:

> Muslims are generally less educated. The reason behind that is getting married many times. Nowadays, everything is so expensive that it's very difficult to bring up a child properly. As a result, maximum one or two children get proper education. The reason for getting married

many times is because their religion supports that. (Personal interview, 5 February 2021)

On the same matter, Al Nasir Jakaria, who I spoke to, pointed out:

See Prophet Muhammed had four wives. But if you see the reality and you check the 2011 census also you won't find in India that Muslim men are marrying four wives. (Personal interview, 27 August 2012)

Secret Superstar, a musical drama, shows the journey of 15-year-old Insia Malik in becoming a successful singer. She is a talented teenage singer-songwriter living amid domestic abuse in a Gujarati Muslim family. Her father Farookh regularly beats his wife and abuses Insia. She loves to sing, but her father is opposed to her pursuing her dream of being a musician. Likewise, Shabana in the film *Naam Shabana* had been imprisoned as a teenager for assassinating her abusive father, who used to physically assault her mother. This was the incident that brought her to the attention of the intelligence agency. Bilqees Ahmed alias Bobby in *Bobby Jasoos* aspires to be a private detective who lives in a middle-class orthodox family in old Hyderabad. She belongs to a conservative family, and her father does not want her to be a private detective. In *Raanjhanaa*, Zoya Haider belongs to a conservative orthodox family and is not allowed to choose her own life partner. Her family is so conservative that they don't hesitate to kill Jasjeet Singh Shergill who faked his identity as Akram Zaidi to marry Zoya. In *Ishaqzaade*, Zoya Qureshi's family members even get involved in honour killing.

As I mentioned earlier in the chapter, in Shyam Benegal's political satire *Well Done Abba*, Muskaan battles bureaucratic corruption alongside his father. *Well Done Abba* also highlights a few other issues such as polygamy as an Islamic religious practice and the commodification of women through the storyline that shows Muskaan's friend Shakina being married off to a Saudi Arabian Sheikh in exchange for money. Pointing to this historically overused narrative in Bollywood, film critic Rauf Ahmed criticized the practice in contemporary times:

How are we going to stop that because at that time, the Prophet's time, there was a definite need for it because after the Karbala War there were so many widows left. He wanted to do a service. He said, each one of you can pick up three more women, you can have four women, provided you have the capacity to provide equally for all of them. It's impossible; it's a defeat itself. How many people can afford to give four houses to four women and look after them? That defeats the whole purpose, you cannot do it. You can't go and dump them in one room, all four of them, like that. (Personal interview, 28 August 2013)

Most importantly, the female protagonists in these films try to challenge 'traditionalism', which is equated with 'conservatism', and are shown preferring to adopt 'modernity', which is expressed as 'progressive'. Significantly, women in these films existed only within the boundary between tradition and modernity, a binary that has existed from the colonial period. The image of ideal women was represented as 'a judicious blend of traditional qualities of domestic skills, knowledge of religious rituals and practices and modern abilities acquired through education and employment opportunities' (Chaudhuri, 2012: 282). By confining them within the narrow bounds demarcated by 'traditional' and 'modern', I argue, these films choose to ignore larger issues of inequality and exclusion faced by Muslim women in society. The issue of exclusivity becomes more prominent in the case of women of the marginalized section because they face multiple levels of marginalization and also hardly have any agency. But disregarding that very fact, Safeena Firdausi (Murad's love interest) in *Gully Boy*, Shabana in *Naam Shabana*, Insia in *Secret Superstar*, Bilqees Ahmed alias Bobby in *Bobby Jasoos*, and Zoya in *Raanjhanaa* and Zoya in *Ishaqzaade* are shown as trying to seek modernity only to get rid of their current state.

When we talk about the dichotomy between traditional and modern, we need to talk about *Lipstick Under My Burkha* (2016), one of the most important films in recent years that adopts a feminist approach and celebrates women's liberty. The film depicts the hidden lives of four women in pursuit of their independence. Despite all odds and hurdles in their path, they continue to assert their wishes through small acts of bravery. Among these four women, Shireen Aslam and Rehana Abidi are two protagonists who have important roles in the film. Shireen Aslam is a victim of domestic abuse. She is a *burqa*-wearing housewife, a mother of three sons, and also works as a door-to-door salesperson (Figure 5.3).

The last fact she hides from her husband Rahim Aslam because Rahim believes that if women start to earn, they try to dominate their male

Figure 5.3 *Lipstick Under My Burkha*: Shireen Aslam with her sons
Source: Nadira Khatun; illustration by Sreeja Burman.

partners. Due to his male chauvinism, he does not allow Shirin to work. Besides, her husband indulges in marital rape and prohibits the use of contraception; Shireen has had several hidden abortions and is forced to use emergency contraceptives to avoid further pregnancies. Rahim has a harsh attitude towards Shireen and very often physically assaults her. He does not love her and carries on affairs outside his marriage, using Shireen only to satisfy his sexual appetite. Rehana Abidi, a college student, who sews *burqas* for her family's shop, is trying to negotiate with the extremely conservative religious practices that are imposed on her, and trying to adopt modernity in her life. Therefore, she steals make-up to wear to college, where she removes the *burqa* she is forced to wear by her family and turns into a jeans-wearing girl, who loves to sing Miley Cyrus songs. Both the characters not only adopt modernity to get educated and find themselves but they also see modernity as the only solution that can free them from the repressive, orthodox practices of their religion. Dr Kaifiya Fatehma had the following to say regarding the depiction of the subjugation of women in the film:

> The film *Lipstick Under My Burqa* is supposed to be a feminist film, but if you see the film, the way Muslim females are portrayed, literally

they are treated as oppressed. They have no identity of their own other than being a daughter and wife. I am not saying such individuals are not there but when a movie focuses only on that aspect, you are forgetting other women who belong to the same community. The oppressed women, that tag is very much stuck on Muslim women. I don't know where and how it started. You will not find a strong Muslim woman character in Bollywood. (Personal interview, 30 January 2021)

Sometimes, women are not the only ones who are trying to adopt modernity to escape their miseries. Murad Ahmed's character in *Gully Boy* is one example of how men use modernity to their advantage. Being a rapper, his character breaks the stereotype of earlier Muslim representation because that's not the usual profession for a Muslim. At the same time, in the final sequence of the film where he performs in an open forum after becoming an established rapper, he is seen wearing *surma*, which is used deliberately to show that he is wearing his Muslim identity on his sleeve and to reinforce the point the use of *surma* is made.

I contend that in these films we find the point of view of a majoritarian audience looking at minorities. I argue that in a way Hindus become the sole torchbearers of modernity. For most of the Muslim characters, to liberate themselves from their misery and pain help from a representative of the majority community somewhere and somehow is required. There are characters that are not playing the role of a partner but of a second lead who are helping the Muslim characters achieve their dreams and overcome all the hurdles in life. This can be seen clearly in *Gully Boy* and *Iqbal*. Berklee College student Shweta, also known as 'Sky' Mehta, an aspiring singer, contacts Murad and Sher and offers to collaborate on a new album. Later, that collaboration brings Murad fame. Similarly, in the film *Iqbal*, Iqbal enlists the help of a nearby alcoholic, Mohit (Naseeruddin Shah), who was once a great cricketer, and convinces him to serve as his coach. In spite of Iqbal's lack of cricketing experience, Mohit trains him and finds him a spot on the Andhra Pradesh Ranji Trophy squad. In *Pari* (2018), Rukhshana was rescued by Arnab, a young guy running a printing press. They build a close relationship and Rukhshana falls in love with him. In *Secret Superstar*, Insia Malik is able to pursue her dream of being a musician, in spite of facing great odds in life, and she goes on to become a famous singer in Mumbai with the help of music director Shakti Kumar (played by Amir Khan). *Naam Shabana* is an action thriller that tells the backstory of intelligence agent Shabana, and chronicles how she became a spy who was identified as a potential intelligence agent by Ranvir Singh (played by Manoj Bajpayee). By portraying a sidekick or a second lead, such as Sky Mehta, Mohit, Arnab, Shakti Kumar, and Ranvir Singh, film texts propagate the idea of majoritarian supremacy where other religious minorities are to be rescued or uplifted by the representative of the ma-joritarian group. I argue that by upholding the majoritarian imagination these films try to appropriate the Muslim characters in the Hindu self.

Dor (2006), directed by Nagesh Kukunoor, is a slightly different tale about two women separated by distance but connected by destiny. The film begins with Zeenat Fatima, who is desperate to save her husband's life while he is on trial in Saudi Arabia for murder. The only way for him to be released is for the victim's (Shekhar's) wife (Meera) to sign the 'mafi-nama' (statement of forgiveness). Zeenat travels from Himachal Pradesh to Rajasthan in order to obtain Meera's signature. Zeenat's de-meanour demonstrates that she is a self-assured, independent woman, more self-reliant than Meera. She becomes Meera's close friend, and she then receives Meera's signature on the declaration of forgiveness. Later, Zeenat assists Meera in escaping her suffocating and torturous life. Similarly, *Sultan* (2016), an action drama, narrates the story of Sultan Ali Khan, who is a middle-aged wrestler based in a small town in Haryana. The film never projects religion as a highlight of the story. Similarly, in *Ae Dil Hai Mushkil* (2016), a musical romantic drama, the plot revolves around the lead protagonist Ayan Sanger and his journey to become a singer; but it also tells the stories of Alizeh Khan, Saba Taliyar Khan, and MC Ali Khan. Initially the characters of Alizeh Khan and Saba Taliyar Khan were supposed to be Pakistanis. When anti-Pakistan sentiment soared in the wake of the Uri attack, the filmmakers decided it would be safer to turn Lahore into Lucknow, thus changing the Pakistani protag-onists into Indian Muslims. But ultimately that self-censorship did not work and Karan Johar had to pay 5 crore rupees to the Army Welfare Fund as penalty for casting Fawad Khan, a Pakistani actor, in *Ae Dil Hai Mushkil* as demanded by Hindu right-wing movements headed by the Maharashtra Navnirman Sena (MNS). Interestingly, the film was purely a love story free of any religious baggage (except the use of *shayari* through Saba Taliyar's character). Similarly, in *Gulabo Sitabo*, Fatima Begum is one of the most liberated Muslim women characters in Hindi films. Even as an old woman Begum chooses to go away with her lover, another Muslim man, after coming to know that her husband Mirza was going to betray her. Although a conservative Muslim woman from a *nawabi* family, she does not hesitate to dump her husband and goes away with her lover, a man she had been in love with before getting married, because she realizes that she made a mistake by marrying Mirza. Here Begum is navigating modernity through religion. She is adopting modernity though her choice of being liberated and at the same time keeping her spiritual belief intact. Soojit Sircar shared his experience of how organically the character had emerged:

It's absolutely and I think it's also very important about Begum, who was so liberated in her approach in her [outlook] that, just imagine that, still at the age of 98, she ruled that house, and you know, nothing moved … I think it's a very beautiful thing about this film that even he, as a Mirza, couldn't raise his head in front of her until the time she left, so just imagine the power she enjoyed, and she ruled there. So I think that's also very, very, very brave and beautiful, I feel, which I didn't recognize and realize in the beginning, I just went on with a mood of the film, but later I realized, no, she, she was so liberating. (Personal interview, 5 March 2021)

In the Muslim modern genre, Muslim characters are not shown as carrying any kind of religious baggage, and are not marked out by religious problems and issues. Unlike films of the yesteryears, Islamicate culture is not exaggerated in any of these newer films. Furthermore, most fortunately the films do not portray Muslims as gangsters or Islamic terrorists; rather, the protagonists of these films battle the justice system, bureaucracy, and biases that prevail in our culture. However, regardless of these points, I argue that the Muslim characters in the films do bear certain Islamic religious connotations to reaffirm their religious identities; I even go so far as arguing that these characters continue to be represented as the 'cultural other' in relation with the majority community. Sartorial choice is one of the most distinct markers of creating the identity of the 'cultural Other'. In all the films we have discussed so far, the Hindu women are most often depicted wearing a sari, whereas none of the Muslim characters are shown wearing a sari; they are mostly seen wearing salwar kameez, headscarves, *burqa* or Western outfits. *In Secret Superstar*, Insia Malik and her mother Najma Malik wear *burqas* and salwar kameez, and cover their heads with scarves. Shabana Khan in *Naam Shabana*, Zoya in *Ranjhnaa*, Zoya in *Ishaqzaade*, and Zeenat in *Dor* are all seen in salwar kurta with dupatta. Maybe they style their dupattas in different ways but they invariably wear dupattas. Zoya in *Ishaqzaade* wears a waistcoat on her salwar kameez instead of a dupatta. In *Gully Boy*, Safeena Firdausi wears kurta and jeans but is always seen as covering her head with a scarf. In *Lipstick Under My Burqa*, both the Muslim women characters Shireen Aslam and Rehana Abidi are seen in *burqas* as that is the dress accepted by their family members; on the other hand, the character of Usha 'Rosy' Buaji is generally seen in a saree and another character Leela wears either Western clothes or kurta-pyjama sets. Most interestingly, these films use the salwar kurta to denote modern middle-class Muslim women and their choice of clothing is utilized differently with different styles to mark a class identity. For examples, in *Photograph*, Rafi's *dadi* Farrukh Jaffar is seen wearing traditional salwar kameez and her head is covered with a dupatta. In the same way, in *Gully Boy*, Murad's mother Razia Ahmed also wears traditional salwar kameez and keeps her head covered using a dupatta. In *Kedarnath*, Mansoor's mother Ameena Khan and in *Well Done Abba* Muskaan Ali along with all other Muslim women dress in a similarly traditional way and wear a head covering. *Gulabo Sitabo* uses Lucknow as its context and Begum is identified using certain markers of Islamicate ethos—she speaks in Urdu and wears kurta-pyjamas. The contrasting binary of dressing Hindu women in saris and using the kurta-pyjama and *burqa* as a Muslim attire is itself a politicized narrative. This is more so because the sari is further associated with the images of Hindu goddesses. 'Traditional Indian garb, like the sari—communicate positive attributes of "honesty", "obedience" and represent the nation' (Hussein and Hussain, 2015: 295). Therefore, in Bollywood films, women's sartorial depictions indicate 'Muslim women's choice of rejecting the sari [and] becomes representative of rejecting the nation' (Hussein and Hussain, 2015: 295). In India, women's clothing is produced, used, and read through a conflict between the ostensibly 'Hindu', that is, the Indian sari, and the ostensibly 'Muslim', i.e., the un-Indian veil (Osella and Osella, 2007).

The practice of using attire to mark Muslims as 'cultural Other' is not only restricted to women in these films. Men also play an equally important role. For example, wearing of *tabeez* is a commonly used signifier to show Muslim identity. Iqbal in the film *Iqbal* and Mansoor in *Kedarnath* are the most prominent examples of this. In *Gully Boy* Murad's character is identified by vesting him with certain Islamic religious markers such as beard, kohl-rimmed eyes, and kurta-pyjama. Nawab Mirza's kurta-pyjama, beard, and skull cap add markers to the identity of Muslims as the 'cultural Other'. Regarding the characterization of the protagonists of the film, director Soojit Sircar says the following:

> See, he is what you call Mirza. So I know when he is Mirza and the way his get-up is, what his look is, we know that he is a religious man. It doesn't matter whether he is a religious man or not, what matters is what his actions are. So, I don't think anybody has thought the way I have presented the film, I think that never comes across in anybody's mind. I think you go with the characterization, then after a point whoever has liked the film, they start owning Mirza and Begum and [their] world. So that world becomes and if you go to Lucknow you will find they are all coexisting in these kind of *havelis*. There is one there who is Jain, there is one Hindu, there is one Muslim. If you hear the soundtrack in one hour, you know, *azaan* is coming, and the other hour the arti you can hear, the bells are coming in. So I think Lucknow city is like that, you know, where you can, if you go there, it's such a beautiful amalgamation and a coexistence of religions out there, has always been. And on the other side there is a church also … I think everything is coexisting and Lucknow is such a walled city that you can hear everything all around. I didn't have to force that into it. We knew that you know, as a character … they do their own rituals all the time. So I think it's never shouted out that okay, that I'm playing a Muslim family you know, or you know, or Hindu owners. I think it's very common in our old cities like Old Delhi or Kolkata or Lucknow—wherever you go this kind of family you will find where everybody is coexisting. (Personal interview, 5 March 2021)

However, what is important also to note is that these elements do not become the most dominant factors in the films, and thus the narrative does not make use of heightened Islamicate culture as was done in the Muslim Social genre.

There are films in which Muslims play sidekicks where they are not required to prove their loyalty or innocence. Ali Akbar Fateh Khan in *Dhoom* (2004), Farhan Qureshi in *3 Idiots* (2009), and Aslam Khan in *Rang de Basanti* are just a few such characters. *Dhoom* (2004) is about a robbery spree which is being carried out by a mysterious gang of bikers. In the film Ali Akbar Fateh Khan, a mechanic, is one of the important protagonists who is a member of a motorcycle gang. He assists ACP Jai with the investigation into the robberies. With the clock ticking, they must catch the thieves in the act. Ali has a flamboyant image and wears a bandana, leather jacket, jeans, neck chains, and wristband. These ornaments and clothes immediately break the image of the archetypical Bollywood Muslim characters. *3 Idiots* is a story of three friends who are aspiring to see the world differently. Farhan Qureshi is one of them. In the case of Farhan Qureshi the only indicators that he is a Muslim are his parents' clothing and his name. Aslam Khan is a liberal and patriotic character in *Rang de Basanti*. He has made it his life's mission to rid the country of corruption. Despite the fact that he is not prejudiced and dresses in the same manner as his other friends, he is shown as belonging to a conformist family.

I find that such non-lead Muslim characters carry even less religious baggage in films such as Zoya Akhtar's *Zindagi Na Milegi Dobara* (2011), Ritesh Batra's *The Lunchbox* (2013), Rensil D'Silva *Ungli* (2014), Gauri Shinde's *Dear Zindagi* (2016), Gaurav K. Chawla's *Baazaar* (2018), Subhash Kapoor's *Madam Chief Minister* (2021), and Umesh Bist's *Pagglait* (2021).

Imran Qureshi in *Zindagi Na Milegi Dobara* is a flamboyant man who wears fedora hats and has a scarf wrapped around his neck; his colourful clothes do not mark out a particular religious identity. Aslam Sheikh, an orphan, is sort of the sidekick of Saajan Fernandes in *The Lunchbox* (2013) and is his colleague. This film doesn't project Aslam's character through an Islamic religious lens; Aslam does not carry religious symbols either in terms of clothes, language, or gesture. Aslam Sheikh is a typical middle-class clerk whose only concern is to save his job.

Ungli tells the story of five friends, Kalim among them, who are struggling against corruption. As the film has nothing to do with religion,

Kalim's character is free of any religious references. However, in one scene we see Kalim offering *namaz*, praying before going out to one of his assignments to punish the people who are involved in corruption. This is in contrast to the absence of any reference to praying or any other religious activity on the part of the other characters belonging to other religious communities. When I quizzed the director on the issue, Rensil D'Shilva had the following to say:

Nadira: How did the *namaz* shot add more significance to the scene and overall storyline of the film?

Rensil D'Shilva: (a long pause) I don't know. I just felt that he [Kalim] is just a happy-go-lucky guy in the gang. But we have never seen his spiritual side but I don't think there is anything more. Because I always found that Muslims pray on Fridays and irrespective of their age, economic differences, they all pray on Fridays but that's not true for Christians. Look I don't go to church for many years and that is very true for Hindu friends who have not gone to temple for many years but they call themselves Hindus … whether a young person from another religion may or may not pay that much attention to spiritual life or his religious life but a Muslim boy of that age will. So that's the only reason. (Personal interview, 26 February 2021)

Shah Rukh Khan as Dr Jehangir 'Jug' Khan, in *Dear Zindagi*, who helps Kaira overcome depression and find an aim in life, is one of the most interesting and remarkable Muslim characters depicted on screen in recent times. He not only breaks all the stereotypes associated with any Muslim character, what is more remarkable is that Shah Rukh Khan performs a supporting role in a women-centric film in spite of being one of the biggest stars in the country. This shows that both content and Indian filmmaking practices are taking a different direction. *Baazaar* (2018) is a thriller where Rizwan Ahmed, a small-time young stock trader from Allahabad who has big aspirations, works as a stockbroker for a well-known businessman after relocating to Mumbai. Apart from his name, Rizwan Ahmed is not given any sort of religious identity.

Danish Rehman Khan in *Madam Chief Minister* (2020) is a second lead character. The film is set against the backdrop of Uttar Pradesh politics and uses Lucknow as its primary context. The main narrative of the film showcases the caste atrocities in the state. The film does not focus on Danish's religious identity as a separate trope. Like any other ordinary man, Danish is also greedy for political power and when an opportunity presents itself, he betrays his wife Tara Roopam, who is the lead protagonist of the film. Earlier, the film showed his opportunistic side when we find him marrying Tara in spite of being engaged to Shazia Ahmed. To the credit of the filmmakers, there is no fuss around the inter-religious marriage of Tara and Danish.

Muslims in Supernatural Cinematic Space

We see one more interesting development and trend in representing Muslims in recent times—that is of identifying the character with a demonic spirit. This trend was never seen in Bollywood films before. *Pari* (2018), a supernatural horror film, centres on the demon Ifrit and Auladhchakra, a satanic sect in Bangladesh dedicated to advancing Ifrit's bloodline. They torment ordinary innocent women and summon the demon to sexually assault them in order to impregnate them with the demon's spawn. Rukhsana is the daughter of one of these women, who was a survivor of the satanic ritual and managed to escape before her child was killed. Another film, Ashok G.'s *Durgamati: The Myth* (2020) also uses Arabic as an Islamic signifier. The film is not about Muslim stories or Muslim characters; yet when Chanchal, the lead protagonist, is shifted to the Durgamati Bungalow, she is possessed by Rani Durgamati who was the Queen of the house before India's Independence. After being possessed, Chanchal starts chanting in Arabic from one of the books kept in the house. There was no clear indication or reason why suddenly an Islamic language is used in the film. Regarding the film, Dr Kaifiya Fatehma (name changed) says:

Recently I watched *Durgamati*. It's a horror movie and has nothing to do with Muslims; [but] it has a Muslim character, introduced in between to create a kind of bigger than the character thing. (Personal interview, 30 January 2021)

Hardik Mehta's *Roohi* tells the story of a ghost that possesses brides. Roohi is one such bride who is possessed by a demonic spirit. Bhawra Pandey, a kidnapper, is infatuated with Roohi; on the other hand, Kattanni Qureshi, another kidnapper, falls for the spirit who has possessed Roohi and who identifies herself as Afza. At the end, Roohi accepts Afza and rejects both Bhawra and Kattanni. Thus, we see that *Pari* uses the reference of a powerful spirit of Islamic mythology; *Durgamati* utilizes Arabic, which is considered the secret language of Islam; and Roohi becomes an imaginary ghost image of a Muslim girl. One interesting fact to note here is that all three are women-centric films that celebrate women's strength, power, and freedom. I argue that in the films, when these women characters are unable to counter the social evil, they resort to using a sort of demonic spiritual power. As women are considered to be *sanskari*, and who obey the patriarch, the films introduce subtexts to subvert that by implying that women have to shed that subservient and 'good' image and embrace a demonic one belonging to the 'Other' if they wish to find respite from social evils.

The films discussed in this section show Muslims as modern, secular individuals who deal with everyday challenges. However, there are a few films of this genre where Muslims are forced to prove their innocence and patriotism. I'll go into more detail about that in the following section.

Secular, Patriotic, and Self-sacrificing Muslims

I have discussed in the earlier section that there is a discontinuity of representing Muslims in the Muslim Modern genre from the earlier genres; the newer films carry images of liberal, contemporary, and secular beings. I argue that in the contemporary political discourse, whenever we attribute the terms like 'liberal' and 'secular' to Muslims, we must also acknowledge that there is a prerequisite which is attached to that image— they must show their allegiance either to the nation or to majoritarianism. This theme is observable in quite a few films such as *Kedarnath* (2018), *Pari* (2018), *Indoo Ki Jawani* (2021), *Chak De! India* (2007), *Iqbal* (2005), and *Rang De Basanti* (2006). I categorize these films into two categories, namely those showing (a) sacrificing Muslims and (b) loyal Muslims.

In the previous section, we have already looked at *Kedarnath* where the eponymous protagonist Mansoor encounters the charming and rebellious Mukku, and his life is turned upside down as he is swept up in a vortex of intense love. At the end of the film, Masoor sacrifices his life to save Mukku from a flood. Mansoor's sacrifice can be interpreted in two ways. Mainstream Bollywood is still not prepared to represent an inter-religious relationship; supporting that assumption is the fact that the film was accused of promoting love jihad. Second, the film shows Mansoor's mother recounting that her husband was a noble man who had died helping someone else. She warns Mansoor not to follow in the same path. However, at the end of the film, Mansoor too choses the same fate as his father and proves himself to be a sacrificing noble human being. In *Pari* Rukhshana and Arnab build a close relationship and Rukhshana falls in love with Arnab. At the end, it is shown that she could have harmed Arnab to save herself but she chose to sacrifice her life for Arnab.

While in the Muslim Political genre we saw how Pakistan is depicted as the biggest enemy, we will now look at *Indoo Ki Jawani*, which questions that narrative and tells the story that shows that all Pakistanis are not terrorists. The film cleverly keeps terrorism from becoming the primary narrative of the film. A comedy drama set against the backdrop of Pakistan-imported terrorism, the film is the story of Indira Gupta, also known as Indoo, who is a Ghaziabad-based Indian teen. She accidentally meets Samar on a dating application. Samar is a sensible Muslim young guy from Hyderabad, Pakistan, but Indoo assumes that he is from Hyderabad, India. Later, she comes to know that Samar is Pakistani and assumes that he is a Pakistani whom she has seen on television and throws him out of her home. On the way back Samar realizes that Indoo is actually trapped in her house with Pakistani terrorists. In spite of knowing that he is risking his life, he rushes to save Indoo from the extremists and finally he saves her. Though the film breaks the stereotype associated with Pakistanis, it does not completely abandon that trope. The film uses the binary of Pakistani terrorists and Pakistani noble Muslims who are fighting against those terrorists. I argue that to prove his good nature Samar has to fight terrorists; only then can he prove his worth.

India is currently going through a phase where one can be considered an ideal citizen of the country by adopting a nationalistic mindset. In

India sports is one of the most important cultural events to showcase someone's true sense of nationalism. Because of that, the nationalism of Indian Muslims is most appreciated when they support the Indian cricket team and reject the Pakistani team during an India–Pakistan cricket match. Here I discuss some films that show the allegiance of Muslims towards the nation through sports. We again look at *Iqbal*. The film has a scene in which the titular character dreams of winning a match against Pakistan. A sports fan from the stadium also holds a poster that reads, 'If Zaheer can, Irfan can, Iqbal can too,' referring to the Muslim cricketers Zaheer Khan and Irfan Khan, who have both played for the Indian national team. The importance of winning a match versus Pakistan while being a Muslim player is subtly emphasized in this moment.

The other important film in this regard is *Chak De! India*, directed by Shimit Amin and released in 2007. The story is mostly inspired by Mir Ranjan Negi's real-life narrative as the goalkeeper of the Indian men's hockey team for the 1982 Asian Games final. In that match, India was beaten by Pakistan by a score of 7–1. Negi was held responsible for the defeat. He faded into obscurity as a result of the humiliation, only to resurface many years later as the coach of the Indian women's hockey team. He coached them and guided them to victory in the 2002 Commonwealth Games. In *Chak De! India*, Negi's character is transformed into that of Kabir Khan to cash in on the public sentiment that would arise out of watching a Muslim character redeem himself. Kabir Khan's loyalty was a more consumable narrative in the then-sociopolitical space. Khan is not marked with any Islamic symbols, yet it is shown that his faith provides him with strength. He is finally able to reclaim his dignity by coaching the national women's hockey team. Regarding Kabir's loyalty towards the nation, Mahesh Bhatt says the following:

In *Chak De! India*, Kabir Khan had to prove his nationalism and patriotism [and that] is a concept which is generally approved by the majority. A Muslim can't criticize this bogus patriotism and be patriotic. A Hindu can; Tagore used to criticize because he said, I love my country, that's why I criticize it. We have got away with it because he was Rabindranath Tagore. I feel there is a need to present a new [long pause and thinking] moderate Muslim or which is distinct from the hardliner Muslim. (Personal interview, 31 March 2013)

The film starts with an India–Pakistan match in the men's hockey world championship, where India loses the game when the captain (Kabir Khan) decides to take the last shot himself and misses the goal. He shakes hands with and hugs a Pakistani player (Zamir) after the game. A journalist captures this moment in a photograph. Later, other journalists question Kabir Khan, 'Are the Pakistani players good friends of yours? You are the only one to have congratulated them after the match.' They also approach him and directly accuse him afterwards, asking, 'Do you believe we lost because someone sold out?' When Kabir hears this, he pushes the journalist and attempts to hurt him in order to communicate his annoyance. 'Now Kabir has played dirty with the country or not, you will have to decide', the journalist adds in the news bite, describing the sportsman's rage and sadness as an eruption of his disloyalty. In the following scene, the print media (newspapers in several languages) label Kabir Khan as a 'traitor captain'. Later in the film, the same rhetoric is uttered by Khan's neighbours and an anonymous voice from the crowd says, '*Aise logon ko to partition ke time hi Pakistan chale jana chahiye*' ('These people [Muslims] should have migrated to Pakistan during Partition').

In the rest of the film, through multiple dialogues and visuals, director Shahid Amin proceeds to establish Khan as a nationalist hero. For example, on the day before the women's hockey World Cup final, Kabir Khan is seen appreciating and enthralled by a situation in which a foreigner raises the Indian flag. Captain Vidya Sharma is taken aback by the image, and she asks Khan, 'What are you staring at?' Probably, the filmmaker was attempting to show Khan as a more nationalist figure than Vidya Sharma, who is a member of the majoritarian community. In the end, India wins the World Cup with the assistance of Kabir Khan. Everyone is ecstatic with the triumph, and Kabir is the man of the moment. His reputation is redeemed and he is accepted by the nation. As he demonstrates his innocence, he is hailed as a national hero. After proving himself, Kabir Khan goes home, where he is greeted warmly by his neighbours. When a youngster erases the word '*gaddar*' (traitor) that was inscribed on his wall seven years ago, the acceptance becomes complete.

Rang De Basanti is a story of five friends whose life's mission is to free the country of corruption. Aslam Khan is one of them. He plays a liberal and patriotic character in the film. Aslam's family is highly orthodox, despite the fact that he has no prejudice and lives like his other friends. On the other hand, his friends in the film are members of a modern, liberal Hindu family who are dealing with their own problems. While speaking to an audience regarding Aslam and his conflict within himself to join in the group and work for the country, Rimila Goswami points out:

> I have never seen in a Bollywood movie that a Muslim guy is fighting for the country. I have noticed that there is a much lower number of [Muslims] in the army because Indian Hindus still believe that a Muslim can't fight to death for India. I have seen such a scene in *Rang De Basanti* where a guy is saying, 'I will fight for the country' but his neighbourhood and family members are saying, 'This is not our country. Why are you going for it?' Probably. Probably, we will but some time we can't think that Muslims can do so much for this country. (Personal interview, 5 February 2021)

I questioned Kamlesh Pandey, the writer of *Rang De Basanti*, on why he described Aslam's family members as orthodox during a personal interaction. He irately retorted:

> That was my choice. Why should I represent them as modern? As a writer, I have the right to choose. I am not an idealist. I cannot make everybody happy. I choose my own story, I choose my own characters. I wanted to use a very typical Muslim family which gives Aslam a dilemma between family and friends. So it was a contemporary Muslim's dilemma to choose between family and country. And he went to work for the country. An educated Muslim would have been weak and meaningless in my story. I had to have the lowest common denominator possible as a Muslim family. So he goes against his family. And not only that ... he goes against his family and follows his own heart, he dies for the country. (Personal interview, 29 March 2013)

The above viewpoints of the audiences and the directors raise two concerns: Does Aslam's decision to choose his family over his country depend on his religion? How does Islam become an obstacle there? Is it really a modern issue for Muslims to prioritize nation before family? Historically, these kinds of dilemma were more prevalent during the Independence struggle irrespective of religions and was not specific to any one faith.

If Muslim nationalism is a recent phenomenon, how can we explain the emergence of numerous Muslim freedom fighters in India including Rafi Ahmed Kidwai, Khan Abdul Ghaffar Khan, Khan Bahadur Khan, Abul Kalam Azad, and Ashfaqulla Khan, who fought in the country's freedom struggle?

We may deduce from the discussion in this section that the Muslim Modern films depict Muslims like any other ordinary people who suffer daily economic and social challenges. The term 'Muslim' is not even used once in most of these films. Muslims are not portrayed as the nation's enemies in this genre, as they are in Muslim Political films, but they must establish that they are nationalists, patriots, and harmless in most circumstances. The films where Muslims play an important role—*Iqbal*, *Chak De! India*, *Rang De Basanti*—depict that they must demonstrate their loyalty to the nation. All of the heroes are stereotyped in some way since they are meant to establish themselves as good human beings by constantly asserting their patriotism and innocence.

Economics of Filmmaking in the Neoliberal Era

After liberalization of the Indian economy, we can see a considerable change in the filmmaking practices of Bollywood, which had an influence on the content of the films being produced. As we have seen in the last two sections, Muslims are less stereotypically portrayed in the Muslim Modern genre; though there are representational politics attached to the narratives and images, at least there is a discontinuity in the representational scheme from the earlier genres. During my interviews with various filmmakers and film critics, I asked them to explain their opinion on the change, but they were unable to provide a definitive response. Almost all of them said that the shift is attributable to a younger generation of filmmakers who are less interested in stereotypical portrayals. Because these independent filmmakers have no prior filmmaking experience, they were able to avoid falling into the trap of crafting formula films. The trend started with very few directors such as Anurag Kashyap (*Gangs of Wasseypur*), Nagesh Kukunoor (*Dor, Iqbal*), and Shyam Benegal (*Well Done Abba*), who are among the most well-known filmmakers of recent times to take on small-budget projects without using superstars. Nagesh

Kukunoor used the money he earned as an engineer to finance his debut film, *Hyderabad Blues*. He could make the film autonomously since he was also the producer and did not have to cater to the demands of an external producer. Kamlesh Pandey said the following:

> Somewhere perhaps, educated filmmakers and writers came into the industry. For example, Jaideep Sahni, who wrote *Chak De! India*, is a very intelligent and educated writer. I think more educated and enlightened writers and filmmakers came into the business and when they started writing and making films, the quality of films began changing. (Personal interview, 2 March 2013)

I asked Shyam Benegal about his initiative of portraying Muslims in their everyday persona in several of his films, such as *Mammo*, *Sardari Begum*, *Well Done Abba*, and *Zubeida*, and how he managed to accomplish that. This is what he had to say:

> In my case, there was a conscious effort on my part. See, you have to look beyond the self-definition we might have because there is a common humanity, so you are concerned about that common humanity. There is an innately secular character among Indians. So *Sardari Begum* was successful for it. So was *Mammo*, so was *Zubeida*. What's the problem with it? (Personal interview, 29 June 2013)

Liberalization also enabled new-age filmmakers and a section of the audience to access international content and world cinema. With the economy opening up, filmmakers gained exposure to world cinema. The audience also gained access to international channels, foreign-language films, and new content through the Internet, which had a huge impact. These factors played a big role in helping filmmakers evolve. Film critic Rajiv Masand believes:

> Once the liberalization happened and once you had access to the content from all over the world, stereotyping [became] difficult. Now audience has access, if you are reinforcing stereotypes everywhere then there would be definitely certain audience [who will] tire of it . . . I think now more options are available. Filmmakers are deciding to make more

varieties in the cinema. It is hard to assume whether a matured audience pushed filmmakers to go beyond their comfort zones. Some of that laziness went away and ... some part of the audience got exhausted with that kind of storytelling and that's why a new generation of filmmakers has been allowed to blossom in this industry. (Personal interview, 5 February 2013)

There are a number of filmmakers who have followed this new path. When discussing the new developments in Bollywood film content, it is important to recognize that it is not only new-age filmmakers and exposure to international content that has fostered the change in content and characterization in Bollywood cinema. We also need to understand how Bollywood film financing has a significant impact on filmmaking. There are five most prominent emerging financing trends that can be tracked in the filmmaking industry in recent times: (a) corporatization of Bollywood; (b) multiplex culture; (c) stars turning producers; (d) promotion strategy; and (e) OTT (over the top) platforms. I contend that although these factors may not be directly influencing Muslim representation, they definitely have an indirect effect on the overall representational pattern. Therefore, in this section, I am going to discuss these points and try to locate the effect of these factors.

The most noticeable change that is taking place in the industry is that it is getting more and more corporatized. On the other hand, there are studios which originated in India and are operating as multinational companies; on the other hand, there are international studios and production houses that are collaborating with different Bollywood production houses. Regarding this J.P. Singh and Kate House (2010) point out that India is the world's leading film producer. Rather than Hollywood films governing the Indian market, Hollywood studios such as Disney, Sony, Miramax, and Warner Bros are creating Bollywood-style films in Mumbai in regional languages. Indian media companies, on the other hand, like Reliance Entertainment, are financing Hollywood projects and co-producing films abroad. Hollywood directors like Woody Allen are casting prominent Bollywood stars in their films, while Hollywood producers and executives are instructing their Mumbai counterparts on production, distribution, and marketing strategies (Singh and House, 2010: 3). UTV Motion Pictures is a leading production house in India, jointly owned by Walt Disney India and UTV Software Communications. Ronnie Screwvala and Siddharth Roy Kapur are the heads of UTV Motion Pictures. Among the films which I have mentioned in the earlier sections, *Rang De Basanti, The Lunchbox, Haider,* and *Shahid* along with many other high-grossing films were co-produced by UTV. Viacom18 Studios, a division of Viacom 18, which is a joint venture between Viacom and Network18, was established in 2007. *Gangs of Wasseypur, Manto,* and *Bazaar* are among their co-produced works. Since 2011, Viacom 18 Motion Pictures also distributes Paramount Pictures films in India, Bangladesh, and Sri Lanka. The Japanese conglomerate Sony has established a production company called Sony Pictures India. *My Name Is Khan, Ae Dil Hai Mushkil,* and *Ek Ladki Ko Dekha Toh Aisa Laga* are among the films Sony has produced. Warner Bros is another big Hollywood production house with a presence in India from 2008. In addition to collaborating with UTV to produce films, Walt Disney has also established its own independent entity in India.

Second, multiplexes began to appear in Indian metro cities as a result of the neoliberal economy. Because the neoliberal economy does not just impact India's tier one cities but tier two cities as well, multiplexes are also sprouting in the those cities. From 925 screens in 2009 to 3,200 screens in 2019, India's multiplexes have grown dramatically.[2] Because of this drastic growth in the number of multiplexes, many single-screen theatres are shutting down. Tejeswini Ganti (2012) in her seminal ethnographic work has mentioned how exhibitors were excited about this new multiplex phenomenon but the owners and managers of the single-screen theatres were threatened by this new development. As a result of this phenomenon, silver screens gradually became extinct over time, ultimately being replaced by newer and shinier multiplexes. When we talk about film viewing in multiplexes, we must discuss audience mapping which is divided into a binary—classes and masses—which is connected to class hierarchy and taste. Assumptions about class and taste are common in the development of this framework, where taste is most notably represented

---

[2] Basuroy, Tanushree (2021) Number of Multiplex Screens across India from 2009 to 2019. *Statista Research Department,* 17 May, available at https://www.statista.com/statistics/731215/number-of-multiplex-theatres-india/ [Accessed 12 July 2022].

as an aversion for particular aesthetic norms, narrative styles, and thematic concerns (Bourdieu, 1984).

The ladies, family, Overseas Territory, and (sometimes) city categories
make up the larger audience category known as the 'classes', whose other
is the 'masses' ... Members of the industry define the masses vaguely
in terms of occupation—domestic workers, manual laborers, rickshaw
drivers, taxi drivers, factory workers—implicitly gendering them as exclusively male and characterizing them as either illiterate or having had
very little formal education. Other terms for the masses are 'laboring
classes' or 'the common man' in English, or 'janta' (people) in Hindi.
(Ganti, 2012: 295)

Audiences from metropolitan cities patronize such modern representations due to the cosmopolitan atmosphere they belong to. A subset of individuals in any metro belongs to a multicultural society and works for
multinational corporations (MNCs), where the individuals interact with
people from other religions, ethnicities, and cultures. As a result, when
they see someone who looks like him on the screen, they quickly identify
with that individual. Sayan Kundu, an engineer who works for a multinational corporation, remarked as follows:

I like to watch films on contemporary themes, so naturally the protagonists of the films are also contemporary. I can relate with them more.
I go to the office where in my project account we have three Muslims
within the total population of forty. So, no one can point out those three
people separately. But, I find the way Muslims are represented in a few
old films like *Mughal-E-Azam, Pakeezah* ... very absurd in the modern
context. (Personal interview, 7 August 2012)

Until the introduction of multiplexes in 2001, the masses were the primary patrons of Bollywood. It is believed that the masses were trying to
escape from the harsh realities of their often difficult lives while watching
films. On the other hand, 'The classes are defined as the exact opposite of
the masses: educated men and women; usually English-speaking; sophisticated; preferring realism; able to handle a slower-paced film; open to
innovation in subject matter; and more likely to view films in the comfort

of their homes' (Ganti, 2012: 297). From the theorization of class and mass, and by linking this binary to multiplexes, it automatically becomes clear that due to ticket prices and the class hierarchy, there was created a demand for alternative kinds of cinema through the multiplex culture. But completely ignoring these facts, director Kabir Khan thinks that the multiplex culture is just a special issue rather than an issue inherently rooted in class.

> The whole multiplex phenomenon honestly to me is very confusing and I don't understand that. I don't know how a multiplex audience is different from a single-screen audience but people keep saying it's different. I guess that certain segmentation has happened. Maybe you can make a film, which caters to a small section of people, and find success in the multiplexes because of the higher ticket price. I don't know whether it's a class divide or big city and small city divide. I don't think multiplex is a class issue, rather it's a big city and small city divide. You will not get multiplex in small cities. Aurangabad is very affluent but I don't know how many multiplexes would be there, maybe one or two. Multiplex culture mainly affected A [tier one] cities. (Personal interview, 2 November 2013)

Film researchers Tejaswini Ganti (2005) and Sangita Gopal (2012) mention that, after the introduction of economic liberalization, satellite television and multiplex theatres were introduced, and there was an increasing demand of a new kind of film from the middle classes that led filmmakers to adopt new filmmaking techniques and practices (Ganti, 2005). Filmmakers could conveniently distribute and market their films with the emergence of multiplex theatres. In the same vein, Rakesh Omprakash Mehra, director of *Rang De Basanti*, believes that 'the distribution platforms have changed in the country and that has helped new age story lines to develop and deliver' (Charles Acland, cited in Gopal, 2012: 126). Teesta Setalvad mentioned:

> I must say things are changing now. I think that is because of multiplexes or whatever. Now cinema is going in many directions. We have very positive examples. People are trying to show things of complex identity, complex realities. (Personal interview, 4 September 2012)

Nandini Ramnath has doubted the phenomenon and points out:

> No, but I didn't make a misconception that multiplex's film is art-house films, that's bullshit. There are no figures to support it. Most of these films don't do well in multiplexes. They will do well only if you let them sit in a multiplex for three months and earn your money over time. That's not considered by the industry standard. No, I think films find their audience. So, I am not too perturbed about that, but yeah, so sometimes you have to consciously make a film around Muslim characters to counter archetypical traits. (Personal interview, 5 February 2013)

The third big change is the emergence of a large number of independent producers. Many stars are producers now. As they are extremely conscious of their own image, therefore, they are themselves conveying the message that they want to send out to society by financing certain kinds of films. In 2003, actor Shah Rukh Khan and his wife Gauri Khan founded Red Chillies Entertainment, an Indian visual effects, production, and distribution firm. Aamir Khan Productions (AKP) is a Mumbai-based film production and distribution firm founded by Aamir Khan in 1999. Salman Khan Films was founded in 2011 and Salman Khan Being Human Productions was formed by Bollywood star Salman Khan as a film production and distribution firm in India. Similarly, Akshay Kumar's Hari Om Entertainment and Grazing Goat Productions make Bollywood films. Priyanka Chopra, an actor and producer, founded Purple Pebble Pictures, an Indian film production firm. Actor Ajay Devgn founded FFilms, an Indian film distribution and production firm, in 2000. Actor Saif Ali Khan and producer Dinesh Vijan established the Mumbai-based film production firm Illuminati Films in 2009. Anushka Sharma and her brother Karnesh Ssharma founded Clean Slate Filmz, a film production and distribution company, in October 2013. In 1999, Ritesh Sidhwani and Farhan Akhtar established another production firm, Excel Entertainment. John Abraham's JA Entertainment also made a mark in the industry. Even independent directors such as Soojit Sircar, Anurag Basu, Zoya Akhtar, Farhan Akhtar, Imtiaz Ali, and Sanjay Leela Bhansali have started producing films. Because these actors and directors have become producers and financers, they are more liberated to make films that convey certain messages; at the same time, they are desperate to earn a profit to survive in the industry. Therefore, we can locate here the trend of making films that are a blend of mainstream and alternative cinema. Moreover, some filmmakers are focusing on making certain kinds of films. Soojit Sircar is one of the most celebrated filmmakers of recent times, who deals with unconventional topics in his films. When he was asked about his mechanism of dealing with the unconventional subjects and how he manages to finance his films, he had the following to say:

> See, first, to answer your first question is that my stories are different, I wouldn't, I mean, it's maybe different. But you know, for me, they are not different, they're all issues going on in my head. And if you think you're talking about the moral values of film, you know, every story has a moral value. So, I mean, you know … there is a moral of the story. And it's the moral of the story or could be, could be anything, you know, so, and art basically is, is the mirror, you know, of what you see in terms of around in the world and the society as such; your presentation maybe, you know, varies from director to director, but it's the what you feel around and that will be very clearly seen in your cinema. If your conscience is not seen in your cinema, then I think there's something wrong with the director, I feel personally. So, [how is] what you say different? Or what do you see as a possible message or something under, you know, undercurrent in the film? It's surely my conscience. And that's what you see. Yes, I had a lot of problems in getting a lot of funders. So, then you will have to find your way through and make films because it's an expensive medium. And so nowadays, whatever I earn from various sources of my filmmaking, and making and expertise, I put it in all my films, and I make my own films. (Personal interview, 5 March 2021)

The fourth change is the promotional strategy in contemporary times due to the presence of social media. A lot of films are in the spotlight long before the film's release. One can get to know each step about the film from the initial conception until the release from multiple stakeholders like actors, directors, production house, producer, and so on through their personal social media handles. Regarding this phenomenon, Nandini Ramnath points out:

New movies ... are in the limelight so much from the beginning and now-
adays a movie is tracked from the time it is announced to the time of its release ... now the whole world is involved in your conversation. You open
the film out to every[one] ... all scrutiny, every Tom, Dick, and Harry
on Twitter is putting out his views and how our trailer is and the poster
should have been of this colour. You don't know what everybody wants
and you have to be very careful. (Personal interview, 5 February 2013)

The last change that occurred in Bollywood film production is the phe-
nomena of exhibiting and releasing films on the OTT platforms. Initially,
filmmakers used to sell their product and earn profit from three main
sources: (1) Theatrical release; (2) Satellite rights; and (3) OTT platforms. Because of the rising influence of digital platforms, the entire marketing strategy during the post-production phase has changed. Earlier
filmmakers were forced to spend more on marketing and promotions for
the theatrical releases of the film. In the case of OTT, the cost for promotion is much less because films can be promoted digitally. Therefore, the
cost of overall filmmaking is getting reduced these days. Moreover, due
to the advent of OTT platforms, the overall risk of loss is also reduced
because filmmakers are able to quote their prices to OTT buyers keeping
certain margins in mind, and now profit does not solely depend on the
footfall in the theatres. Added to this is the fact that filmmakers can now
avoid the hassles of vying for theatre slots. Earlier, a serious concern for
small-budget films was to get slots in the multiplexes if there happened to
be a big-budget film release at the same time.

After analysing all of these aspects, it is possible to say that aspiring
filmmakers who are willing to advocate for new types of content will have
less of a predisposition to portray stereotyped images because such content is not aimed at the lowest common denominator. This has led to the
breakdown of the superstar culture in Bollywood. As some of the newer
films do not have a tremendously broad canvas and are only meant for a
particular category of audience, a superstar image is not needed to sell
them to a large target audience. Satish Munda, a new-age filmmaker who
has just started his journey in Bollywood, points out the following:

Before the popularization of OTT platforms, I think, audiences had
started accepting actors like Ayushman Khurana, Raj Kumar Rao,

who have gradually become stars. Until 2005, there was a monopoly of superstars like the Khans. These new actors started entertaining people with a message and audiences started accepting them. (Personal interview, 30 July 2020)

However, others disagree. Soojit Sircar has a completely a different opinion on OTT platforms and he says:

See, frankly speaking, the OTT platform doesn't change anything [pertaining to] filmmaking. It is another medium of displaying your films. Right? Exhibiting your films. The day any medium or any, you know, or method or any platform affects your filmmaking then that's not filmmaking, that's not a cinema. Cinema is you make cinema the way cinema is. (Personal interview, 5 March 2021)

Conclusion

In summary, in neoliberal India, the country is adopting and at the same time going through a lot of changes in public policy, cultural identity, development, and globalization. Moreover, communalism and nationalism, which became inextricably linked in the postcolonial Indian political landscape, persist to this day. India is witnessing one of the worst phases of communal hatred in contemporary times; the reasons are many, a major one being the fact that Indian right-wing political parties have implemented and proposed certain Acts such as the CAA and NRC, advocated for the abrogation of article 370 and banning of cow trade in multiple states, promoted the sporadic lynching based on religion, and lent their support to movements like 'ghar wapsi'[3], 'bahu lao, beti bacho',[4]

---

[3] *Ghar Wapsi* (Back to Home) is a series of reconversion efforts organized by the Indian Hindu organizations Vishva Hindu Parishad (VHP), Rashtriya Swayamsevak Sangh (RSS), and Hindu Makkal Katchi to assist Christians and Muslims convert to Hinduism and Sikhism. Rajeshwar, Y. and Amore, R.C. (2019) Coming home (Ghar Wapsi) and going away: Politics and the mass conversion controversy in India. Religions, *10*(5), p. 313

[4] *Bahu Lao, Beti Bachao* is a campaign organized by Bajrang Dal, the Vishva Hindu Parishad's youth wing. The motto of the campaign is to encourage young Hindu men to marry non-Hindu females and to raise awareness about Love Jihad among Hindu girls. Hussein, N. and Hussain, S. (2015) Interrogating Practices of Gender, Religion and Nationalism in the Representation of

and so on. At such a turbulent time, most interestingly, we are seeing a range of diversified representations of caste, religion, gender, and region in Bollywood cinema as has never been witnessed before. Bollywood is going through a transformation in terms of film narratives, filmmaking techniques, and film exhibition; in the process, Muslims are being represented differently from the usual stereotypical forms we had come to expect. As we have seen through the discussion in this chapter, Muslims are being represented without any religious baggage except in a very few films; however, there is still a small degree of stereotyping. On the surface, the growth of new types of films may be seen as a response to changing needs of a certain film-watching demographic, which has progressively evolved over two decades following the deregulations of the early 1990s. However, we still cannot claim this as a mainstream trend as it is until now merely a superficial development in the industry.

Muslim Women in Bollywood: Contexts of Change, Sites of Continuity. *Exchanges: Warwick Research Journal.*

Epilogue

The Representation of the 'Other'

At the time of writing, a recent case of the inter-faith marriage between Manmeet Kaur (a Sikh girl) and Shahid Bhatt (a Kashmiri Muslim) has created a massive uproar and become the topic of discussion on a few primetime television channels. It is being discussed how Hindus are forced to convert to Islam and how 'love jihad' is one of the biggest threats now for Hindus in India. One more incident has recently become the centre of political debate: Abdul Samad Saifi, 72, claims that on 5 June 2021 in Ghaziabad district's Loni region, he was kidnapped in an autorickshaw by some men and held captive in a remote place. Saifi claims he was beaten up and made to shout '*Jai* Shri Ram'. He further said that the attackers shaved his beard and forced him to view films of Muslims being attacked. Scroll.in, a digital news production house, mentions that the Ghaziabad police denied there was any communal angle to the case later; in a strange twist the police in Uttar Pradesh filed a case against Rana Ayub, Twitter, news website The Wire, journalists Saba Naqvi, Mohammad Zubair, Congress leaders Salman Nizami, Masqoor Usmani, and Sama Mohammad because it was believed that they had sent out tweets in order to incite communal strife in relation to the incident.[1]

I began my research with the goal of gaining a broader insight into how Muslims are portrayed in Hindi films, as well as to understand the reactions of audiences, film reviewers, and filmmakers to such depictions.

---

[1] See Scroll Staff (2021) Ghaziabad assault video: Journalist Rana Ayyub gets protection from arrest for four weeks. *Scroll.in*, 21 June. Available at https://scroll.in/latest/998114/ghaziabad-assault-video-journalist-rana-ayyub-gets-protection-from-arrest-for-four-weeks. [Accessed 22 July 2022].

Postcolonial Bollywood and Muslim Identity. Nadira Khatun, Oxford University Press. © Oxford University Press 2024.
DOI: 10.1093/oso/9780198891017.003.0007

The motivation for this study was a concern with the 'homogenized' and 'caricatured' portrayal of Muslims in Hindi movies. The idea of reading an imaginative Muslim identity from depictions in Bollywood films was conceived a long time ago and I started the work as my doctoral topic in 2010. The debate and discussion around this topic is most relevant in our contemporary time, more than ever before, as now Salman Khan, Amir Khan, and Shahrukh Khan tower over the cinematic space of Bollywood; this is starkly in contrast to the stars of yesteryear who felt the need to hide their religious identity such as Yusuf Khan (as Dilip Kumar), Mumtaz Jehan Begum Dehlavi (as Madhubala), and Mahjabeen Bano (as Meena Kumari) in the post-Partition era. That the three Khans are the most popular stars of Bollywood cinema becomes evident from the fact that they have starred in the highest-grossing films in Bollywood history where they have been playing the role of heroes for the last thirty years. Even after being the favourite stars for almost the last three decades, in recent years they have been hideously trolled for expressing their views on contemporary sociopolitical issues. For instance, Amir Khan was very badly trolled for raising concerns about the growing religious intolerance in contemporary India. There were several orchestrated attacks against Shahrukh Khan and his film *Dilwale* (2015) after his comment on 'extreme intolerance' witnessed against minorities in the country. Similarly, Saif Ali Khan faced vehement protests after he and his wife Kareena Kapoor named their first son Taimur. All these controversies, protests, and attacks appeared mostly in the last decade. These actors' sense of loyalty towards their nation was doubted through multiple protests with a section of protesters even proposing to send them to neighbouring Pakistan, an Islamic country. Dr Kaifiya Fatehma (name changed) mentions the recent change that has become visible in audiences.

In my generation, we have grown up watching these three Khans [Shahrukh Khan, Amir Khan, Salman Khan]. The kind of fandom they had, nobody realized they are Muslims, but the attitude of my friends even got changed now. Now Shahrukh Khan is looked [upon as a] Muslim movie actor. (Personal interview, 30 January 2021)

Along with the real-life controversies associated with Muslim actors, we have discussed in the earlier chapters how contemporary Bollywood films have been encountering multiple controversies for hurting religious sentiments of certain sections of people.

Earlier Muslim actors and stars changed their name to hide their religious identity due to post-Partition trauma, but the film texts of the period spread the message of unity, integrity, and secular ethos in spite of representing Muslims in a stereotyped way. Cinema is a reflection of society and, therefore, when Muslims are often lynched for not chanting 'Jai shree Ram' or are killed based on the suspicion that they consumed beef, it becomes obvious that only those texts will be accepted which conform to the majoritarian political discourse. The 'Khans' are among the biggest stars of the current Bollywood film industry, and when Shahrukh Khan acted as Rahul, Salman Khan as Prem, and Aamir Khan as Bhuvan, they did not carry any special affiliation with the name and there was no hindrance in their playing mostly Hindu characters. On the other hand, if they portrayed Muslim characters on screen—such as Rizwan Khan in *My Name is Khan* or Rehaan Qadri in *Fanaa*—they were portrayed as either terrorists or forced to prove that they were not terrorists. Though their religious identity never intervened in their stardom, they still faced the compulsion to perform within the framework of the state apparatus to make their films more acceptable to the masses. I think this phenomenon reinforces larger social narratives of prioritizing majoritarian religious faith; other religious groups are only accepted and welcomed if they can shed their religious identity or accept the majoritarian religion and don't make their own religious identity publicly obvious.

On the one hand, there has been a decline in the number of Islamic terrorist attacks across the country, apart from the 2019 Pulwama attack and 2019 Jammu bus stand grenade, in the last five years. These two attacks were allegedly carried out by Pakistan-based militant groups Jaish-e-Mohammed and Lashkar-e-Tayiba respectively. On the other hand, during this same period, we've witnessed the triumphant march of aggressive Hindu religious nationalism in the country. I have already mentioned the two most recent examples of controversies on the basis of religious politics in the country; similarly, we are witnessing multiple cases of communal violence such as riots, lynchings, and also multiple debates associated with 'love jihad'. As a result, the secular concept of nationhood as propagated in the Nehruvian period has come to be in jeopardy. In the post-Partition Nehruvian period, India witnessed a slew of communal riots. While ignoring the realities of lifelong exile, miseries caused by communal tensions, and the newly created identity crisis of the post-Partition period, Bombay Hindi cinema depicted inter-community connections as a composite culture. It created and made possible a plural imagining of a collective identity. In a way, the duty of mending the awful memories of bloodshed of that time was given to the film industry. As a result, filmmakers praised syncretic tales, and films about Muslims emphasized positive qualities such as their rich culture and language. Muslims were typically shown as wise rulers and devoted lovers—in the process, Muslims were positively stereotyped. The portrayal of Muslims in films has evolved throughout time and gradually their on-screen image has been transformed into negative stereotypes because they are mostly represented as terrorists and criminals. Regarding a quite similar phenomenon in Hollywood cinema, Jack Shaheen points out that films depict 'Islamic faith with the male supremacy, holy war, and acts of terror, depicting Arab Muslims as hostile alien intruders, and as lecherous, oily sheiks intent on using nuclear weapons' (Shaheen, 2009: 15).

Drawing from the introduction of this book, where we saw Javed Akhtar (sahab) mention that Bollywood was always indifferent when it came to representing the mayhem of Partition and completely ignored the incident until M.S. Sathyu's *Garam Hawa* (1974), we can say that, quite similarly, Bollywood has failed to represent the communal violence and the religious politics of contemporary times. Most critically, Bollywood continues to produce films based on Islamic terrorism and ignores the incidents of communal violence directed against minority communities. It can be argued that Bollywood as a mass art form has responded to selective historical moments of the past and present. Through these selective ultra-nationalist and ultra-violent representations of the notion of the Hindu nation and Muslim Other, Bollywood has contributed to the hegemonic Hindutva discourse. Film scholar Sanjeev Kumar HM phrases this as 'Manichean rivalry'. Though we have discussed the representation of modern Muslim characters in the Muslim Modern genre where Muslims are comparatively free from the positively or negatively stereotyped representations, we have to agree that even these films ignore the realities of Muslims in contemporary India, and instead portray a superficial understanding of the community. There are some recent developments in terms of viewing films and series on OTT platforms.

The texts presented in these platforms do raise some critical questions on contemporary sociopolitical developments in India, sometimes also critiquing present conditions and honestly depicting minority issues.

The research in this book may be expanded to look at the relationship between politics, production, audience, and text, as well as how all of these elements are interconnected in a broader sociopolitical context. Many elements may be investigated in more depth, such as various groups' cinema-viewing patterns, class and national awareness, and political parties' intervention in filmmaking and the ensuing effect on representation. Above all, it is critical to dig further into how Bollywood texts about Muslims shape audience perspectives. One may concentrate more explicitly on how cultural materials create stereotyped views of certain ethnic and religious communities. I hope the scholarship in this book gives rise to more in-depth investigation into these facets.

Interview Schedule/Questionnaire

Interview Schedule for Audience

Personal Details:

- Age:
- Gender:
- Marital Status:
- Education:
- Occupation:

Family Background Details:

- No. of Total Family Members:
- Average Income of the Family:
- Occupations of Family Members:

Questions:

1. How many movies do you watch in a week/month?
2. You prefer to watch movies at home or at theatre?
3. With whom do you generally watch a film?
4. What type of movies do you prefer to watch? Genre and Language.
5. Do you like to watch old Hindi movies or new ones?
6. Do you like to watch a film many times? Quote some of the film names which you watched many times.
7. Have you seen the movies like *Mughal-e-Azam, Taj Mahal, Mehboob, Nikah, Bazar, Chaudhvin ka Chand, Garam Hawa, Umrao Jaan*? If yes tell something about those movies. Give your opinion in terms of image, characterization, and plot.
8. Have you seen the movies like *Roja, Anger, Bombay, Naseem, Gulam-e-Mustafa, Fiza, Pukar, Mission Kashmir, Fanna, New York, My Name is Khan, Road to Sangam, Bajirao Mastani* (2015), *Padmaavat, Manikarnika: The Queen of Jhansi, Panipat, Kesari, My Name is Khan, Parzania, Fanaa, Vivah, New York, Road to Sangam, Gangs of Wasseypur, Ishaqzaade, Shahid, Ek Tha Tiger, The Attacks of 26/11, Shootout at Wadala, D-Day, Baby, Haider, Bajrangi Bhaijaan,*

Phantom, Neerja, Haseena Parkar, Secret Superstar, One Less God, Lipstick Under My Burkha, Naam Shabana, Raees, Tiger Zinda Hai, Raazi, India's Most Wanted, Uri: The Surgical Strike, Hotel Mumbai, Shikara, and *Tanhaji*?

9. Did you see the movies which were based on Muslims produced after the Babri Masjid demolition?

10. What type of themes and images are the films trying to portray?

11. Is there any stereotype associated with the community?

12. If yes, what are they?

13. What are the factors behind representing those stereotype images? Your opinion.

14. What are the differences in the pattern of representation between the earlier phase and current phase?

15. If yes, why have you watched those films? From whom did you get the reference?

16. Do you recall any film which represented terrorism? If yes, what do you think about the ideological conflict between the nationalist victim and the jehadi terrorist in the film? What was the political statement of the film?

17. In most of the cases, Muslims were represented as 'Other' and they are demonized as we have seen in the movies just discussed. Is the representation justified in that manner? Or, is there any other political reason behind that?

Interview Schedule for Film Critics

Personal Details:

- Age:
- Gender:
- Education:
- Occupation:

Questions:

1. What is the difference between Hollywood and Bollywood in representating Muslims?
2. Do you think that commercial cinema has a more active role in representing Muslims in a stereotyped manner?
3. What kind of role do you feel that Hindi cinema plays in representing Muslims from its early age? Give your opinion in terms of image, characterization, and plot.
4. Did you see the movies which were based on Muslims produced after the Babri Masjid demolition?
5. Do you think that there is a shift in representation of Muslims after the incident of Babri?
6. What type of themes and images are the films trying to portray?
7. Is there any stereotypes associated with the community?
8. If yes, what are they?
9. What are the factors behind representing those stereotype images? Your opinion.
10. What are the differences in the pattern of representation between the earlier phase and current phase?
11. What is your perspective on the representation of the history in the historical films during post-Independence films and the recently released ones?
12. Do you think political history of the country does have any influence on Bollywood films?
13. Why do recently released Bollywood films represent aggressive nationalism in most of their films?
14. In most of the cases, Muslims were represented as 'Other' and they are demonized as we have seen in the movies just discussed. Is the representation justified in that manner? Or is there any other political reason behind that?

Interview Schedule for Filmmakers

Personal Details:

- Age:
- Gender:
- Education:

Questions:

1. What are the things which you keep in mind while writing a film or making a film?
2. Do gender, caste, class, religion play an important aspect to make a film more sensitive? Do you keep in mind the sentiments of human beings while writing a plot or making a film? Or do you only believe to make the film a box office hit?
3. Why are the films based on rural issues necessarily small-budget movies and without any superstar and are considered as parallel cinema?
4. Do you think that cinema has a power to reinforce human belief?
5. While writing a movie plot, do you go deep into an issue? Or do you write a plot based on superficial stories? Do you research the issue?
6. How do producers play an important role to mould a story of a film?
7. How does majority/religion play an important role to mould a story of a film?
8. What is the difference between Hollywood and Bollywood in representing Muslims?
9. Do you think that commercial cinema has a more active role in representing Muslims in a stereotyped manner?
10. What kind of role do you feel that Hindi cinema plays in representing Muslims from its early age? Give your opinion in terms of image, characterization, and plot.
11. Why did the sudden shift happen between Muslim Historical and Muslim Social?
12. Which of the following movies focusing on Muslims produced after the Babri Masjid demolition have you seen?
13. What do you think are the major differences in representation of Muslims in cinema produced before and after the Babri Masjid demolition? Elaborate.
14. What type of themes and images are the films trying to portray?
15. Are there any stereotypes associated with the community?
16. If yes, what are they? Elaborate.

List of Movies Forming the Universe of the Study

The Muslim Historical

1. *Tansen* (1943)
2. *Mumtaz Mahal* (1944)
3. *Humayun* (1945)
4. *Shahjehan* (1946)
5. *Baiju Bawra* (1952)
6. *Anarkali* (1953)
7. *Mirza Galib* (1954)
8. *Mughal-e-Azam* (1960)
9. *Taj Mahal* (1963)
10. *Jahan Ara* (1964)
11. *Norrjehan* (1967)
12. *Taj Mahal: An Eternal Love Story* (2005)
13. *Jodha Akbar* (2008)
14. *Bajiro Mastani* (2015)
15. *Padmaavat* (2018),
16. *Manikarnika: The Queen of Jhansi* (2019)
17. *Paanipat* (2019)
18. *Kesari* (2020)
19. *Tanhaji* (2020)

The Muslim Social

1. *Pukar* (1939)
2. *Qaidi* (1940)
3. *Najmu* (1943)
4. *Elaan* (1947)
5. *Chaudhvin Ka Chand* (1960)
6. *Mere Meheboob* (1963)
7. *Benazir* (1964)
8. *Gazal* (1964)
9. *Bahu Begum* (1967)
10. *Palki* (1967)

11. *Mere Huzoor* (1968)
12. *Mehboob Ki Mehndi* (1971)
13. *Pakeezah* (1972)
14. *Garam Hawa* (1973)
15. *Umrao Jaan* (1980)
16. *Nikah* (1982)
17. *Bazaar* (1982)
18. *Salim Lange Pe Mat Ro* (1989)
19. *Sanam Bewafa* (1991)
20. *Angaar* (1992)
21. *Muhafiz* (1994)
22. *Mammo* (1994)
23. *Gulam-e-Mustafa* (1997)
24. *Zubeida* (2001)
25. *Elaan* (2005)
26. *Fitoor* (2016)

The Muslim Political

1. *Amar Akbar Antony* (1977)
2. *Roja* (1992)
3. *Anger* (1992)
4. *Bombay* (1995)
5. *Naseem* (1995)
6. *Border* (1997)
7. *Zakham* (1998)
8. *Sarfarosh* (1999)
9. *Fiza* (2000)
10. *Pukar* (2000)
11. *Mission Kashmir* (2000)
12. Gadar (2001)
13. *LOC: Kargil* (2003)
14. *Black Friday* (2004)
15. *Dev* (2004)
16. *Ek Tha Tiger* (2012)
17. *Naam Shabana* (2017)
18. *Veer Zara* (2004)
19. *Parzania* (2005)
20. *Fanna* (2006)
21. *New York* (2009)
22. *Road to Sangam* (2010)
23. *Gangs of Wasseypur* (2012)
24. *Ishaqzaade* (2012)
25. *Neerja* (2016)
26. *Haseena Parkar* (2017)
27. *Raees* (2017)

28. *Tiger Zinda Hai* (2017)
29. *Raazi* (2018)
30. *India's Most Wanted* (2019)
31. *Uri: The Surgical Strike* (2019)
32. *Hotel Mumbai* (2019)
33. *Shikara* (2020)

Muslim Contemporary Films

1. *Iqbal* (2005)
2. *Dor* (2006)
3. *Chak De! India* (2007)
4. *Secret Superstar* (2017)
5. *Lipstick Under My Burkha* (2017)
6. *Amir* (2008)
7. *Well Done Abba* (2009)
8. *My Name is Khan* (2010)
9. *Madam Chief Minister* (2021)
10. *Indoo Ki Jawani* (2020)
11. *Gulabo Sitabo* (2020)
12. *Photograph* (2019)
13. *Gully Boy* (2019)
14. *Ek Ladki Ko Dekha Toh Aisa Laga* (2019)
15. *Kedarnath* (2018)
16. *Pari* (2018)
17. *Baazaar* (2018)
18. *Secret Superstar* (2017)
19. *Naam Shabana* (2017)
20. *Ae Dil Hai Mushkil* (2016)
21. *Sultan* (2016)
22. *Dear Zindegi* (2016)

Demographic/Brief Biography of the Participants

Filmmakers

Javed Akhtar: One of the most successful and renowned lyricists, Indian political activists, and screenwriters. He is well known for his contributions to Hindi film and he has won five National Film Awards as well as the Padma Shri and Padma Bhushan, two of India's prestigious and highest civilian award honours, in 1999 and 2007, respectively. With the 1973 film *Zanjeer*, Akhtar made his name with the Salim–Javed duo and achieved success as a screenwriter. He subsequently went on to pen the 1975 films *Deewar* and *Sholay*.

Shoojit Sircar: Indian filmmaker, director, and producer Shoojit Sircar was born in or around 1967 and is best known for his work in Hindi cinema. He has earned a Filmfare Award and two National Film Awards, among other honours. He is best known for his films like *Gulabo Sitabo* (2020) and *Madras Café* (2013).

Shyam Benegal: Shyam Benegal is an Indian director, screenwriter, and documentarian. He is frequently hailed as the father of parallel cinema and is regarded as one of the greatest directors of the post-1970s era. He has won numerous honours, including a Filmfare Award, a Nandi Award, and eighteen National Film Awards. He received the Dadasaheb Phalke Award, India's top honour in the art of cinema, in 2005. He received the Padma Shri, the fourth-highest civilian honour bestowed by the Indian government, in 1976. For his services to the arts, he also received the Padma Bhushan, the third-highest civilian honour, in 1991.

Kabir Khan: Hindi-language film director, screenwriter, and cinematographer Kabir Khan is an Indian national. He began his career as a crew member for documentaries before directing *Kabul Express* in 2006, his feature film directing debut. Civil recognition for his contributions to the arts. He is known for his films like *Ek Tha Tiger* (2012) and *Bajrangi Bhaijaan* (2015), among many others.

Shibani Bhathija: Shibani Bathija is an Indian screenwriter known for her work in Bollywood films such as *My Name Is Khan* (2010) and *Fanaa* (2006).

Mahesh Bhatt: Mahesh Bhatt is an Indian film producer, screenwriter, and director best known for his work in Hindi cinema. *Saaransh* (1984), which was presented at the 14th Moscow International Film Festival, is a standout movie from his early career. It was then designated as India's official entry for the Best Foreign Language Film category of the Academy Awards.

Kamlesh Pandey: Kamlesh Pandey is an Indian screenwriter and best known for writing the script of *Rang De Basanti* (2006).

Ashutosh Gowarikar: Ashutosh Gowariker is a Hindi-language film producer, actor, screenwriter, and director from India. He is best known for his historical *Lagaan* (2001), *Swades* (2004), and *Jodhaa Akbar* (2008). He became a voting member of the Academy Awards when his movie Lagaan was nominated for the 74th Academy Awards' Best Foreign Language Film category (Thomas, 2005).

Vinay Shukla: Vinay Shukla is an Indian film writer, producer, and director. He is best known for his film *Godmother* (1999), which won the National Film Award for Best Feature Film in Hindi in 1999.

Amit Khanna: An Indian film producer, director, writer, and journalist with the name of Amit Khanna. He served as the first chairman of Reliance Entertainment, the first trustee of the Mumbai Academy of the Moving Image, and the former president of the Producers Guild of India. Khanna is also a producer and songwriter who has earned three National Film Awards. He is credited with creating the word 'Bollywood' (Dey, 2019).

Haider Ali: An Indian actor and screenwriter for film and television, Haidar Ali is also known by the names Hyder Ali and Haider Ali. The storyline for Ashutosh Gowarikar's historical film *Jodhaa Akbar* (2008) was afterwards written by Haidar Ali.

Rensil D'Silva: Rensil D'Silva is an Indian film director, screenplay writer, ad film maker. He is best known for his films *Kurbaan* (2009) and *Ungli* (2014).

Satish Munda: Satish Munda is a new age filmmaker. He is a film writer and director. *Chakki* (2022) and *Dansh* (2016)

Film Critics/Public Intellectuals

Mayank Shekhar: Indian author, journalist, and film critic Mayank Shekhar has worked for *Hindustan Times* as both a film reviewer and a national cultural editor.

Nasreen Munni Kabir: Kabir a renowned television producer based in the UK and a well-recognized Indian film historian. Also a director and author, she was born in India. She is best known for producing an annual season of Indian movies for Channel 4 in the United Kingdom.

Nandini Ramnath: Currently employed by Scroll.in, Nandini Ramnath has written extensively on cinema. She has formerly worked for the Mint.

Rauf Ahmed: Ahmed is a well-known film critic and former editor of publications such as *Filmfare*, *Screen*, and *Zee Premiere*.

Rajiv Masand: Rajeev Masand is the Entertainment Editor of CNN-IBN. In his weekend show 'Now Showing', he typically analyses Hollywood blockbusters and Bollywood movies that have been released in India.

Shiladitya Sen: Film critic and journalist who has worked as a journalist with Ananda Bazar Patrika for several years.

Dr Ram Puniyani: Ram Puniyani is an author, academician, and activist. He has held the positions of senior medical officer at the Indian Institute of Technology Bombay and also Professor of Biomedical Engineering. Currently serving as the President of the Executive Council of the Centre for Study of Society and Secularism (CSSS). He is involved in human rights work and campaigns to counter Hindu extremism in India.

Teesta Setalvad: Teesta Setalvad is a journalist and civil rights activist from India. She serves as the secretary of Citizens for Justice and Peace (CJP), a group established to support the Gujarat riot victims in 2002.

Asgar Ali Engineer: Asgar Ali Engineer is an Indian reformist author and social activist. He is the leader of the Progressive Dawoodi Bohra movement and is well known internationally for his work on liberation theology in Islam. His writings mostly deal with communalism, ethnic conflict, and violence against minorities in South Asia and India.

Irfan Engineer: Irfan Engineer is a prominent voice in the fight for secularism and a champion of minority rights. Author, activist, and managing editor of the *Indian Journal of Secularism*, Irfan Engineer is also the director of the Centre for Study of Society and Secularism.

Audiences

Sitara Shabnam (name changed), a sociologist and academician

Abhinash Dey (name changed), a senior journalist

Al Nasir Jakaria, an activist and politician

Dr Kaifiya Fatehma (name changed), a doctor and blogger

Sunita Misra, an entrepreneur

Sourabh Agarwal, an undergraduate student

Pushpanjali Rath, a schoolteacher

Sandip Misra, a middle-aged manager in a multinational corporation

Diviya Kodoth, a research scholar doing her PhD on gender studies

Ashutosh Ingle (name changed), a media coordinator at a non-profit organisation.

Mohmad Waseem Malla, a researcher who belonged to Kashmir

Rouf Bhat, a researcher and academician

Manoj Chaudhury, a security guard in a residential society in Mumbai

Pushpanjali Rath, a schoolteacher

Rimila Goswami, an engineer who works for a multinational corporation

Sayan Kundu, an engineer who works for a multinational corporation

References

Online Sources

Abraham, Delna, and Rao, Ojaswi (2017). 86% killed in cow-related violence since 2010 are Muslim, 97% attacks after Modi govt came to power. *The Hindustan Times*, 16 July. Available at https://www.hindustantimes.com/india-news/86-killed-in-cow-related-violence-since-2010-are-muslims-97-attacks-after-modi-govt-came-to-power/story-w9CYOksvgk9joGSSaXgpLO.html [Accessed 25 October 2021]

Athavale, Sanika (2019). Bollywood, A Propaganda Tool: Mughals Were Bad, Hindutva Is Great, But These Movies Are Historically Wrong. *The Logical Indian*, 11 December. Available at https://thelogicalindian.com/exclusive/bollywood-propaganda-mughals-hindutva/ [Accessed 21 January 2021]

BBC (2005). Gujarat Riot Death Toll Revealed, 11 May. Available at http://news.bbc.co.uk/2/hi/south_asia/4536199.stm [Accessed 18 November 2021]

BBC (2018). Padmaavat: Why a Bollywood Epic Has Sparked Fierce Protests, 25 January. Available at: https://www.bbc.com/news/world-asia-india-42048512 [Accessed 17 April 2021]

Bhardwaj, Ashutosh (2016). Bharat Mata: From Freedom Struggle Metaphor to Patriotism's Litmus Test. *The Indian Express*, 21 March. Available at https://indianexpress.com/article/explained/in-fact-bharat-mata-from-freedom-struggle-metaphor-to-patriotisms-litmus-test/ [Accessed 25 February 2021]

Brass, Paul (2004). The Gujarat Pogrom of 2002. *therearenosunglasses.wordpress.com*, 26 March. Available at https://therearenosunglasses.wordpress.com/2008/12/01/the-gujarat-pogrom-of-2002/ [Accessed 6 May 2015]

Desai, Ronak D. (2016). Bollywood's Affair with the Indian Mafia. *Forbes*, 3 March. Available at https://www.forbes.com/sites/ronakdesai/2016/03/03/bollywoods-affair-with-the-indian-mafia/?sh=6d39696f4aa6 [Accessed 5 March 2021]

Deshmukh, Arunkumar (2014). Umangen dil ki machlin. *Atul's Song A Day—A Choice Collection of Hindi Film & Non-Film Songs*. [blog] 25 July. Available at https://atulsongaday.me/2014/07/25/umangen-dil-ki-machlin/ [Accessed 16 January 2021]

Engineer, Asghar Ali (2000). Maintenance for Muslim women. *The Hindu*, 7 August. Available at https://archive.ph/20150902123704/http://www.thehindu.com/2000/08/07/stories/05072524.htm#selection-219.1-219.301 [Accessed 22 February 2021]

Express News Service (2017). On Yogi's Website: 'Women Power Does Not Require Freedom, But Protection'. *The Indian Express*, 18 April. Available at https://indianexpress.com/article/india/on-yogis-website-women-power-does-not-require-freedom-but-protection-4617177/ [Accessed 9 April 2021]

FE Online (2018). Manikarnika: The Controversies that Kept Kangana Ranaut and Her Film in the News. *The Financial Express*, 19 December. Available at https://www.financialexpress.com/entertainment/manikarnika-the-controversies-that-kept-kangana-ranaut-and-her-film-in-the-news/1418973/ [Accessed 28 April 2021]

HT Correspondent (2019). Amit Shah Says Lok Sabha Elections Third Battle of Panipat, Mocks Rival. *The Hindustan Times*, 11 January. Available at https://www.hindustantimes.com/lok-sabha-elections/amit-shah-says-lok-sabha-elections-third-battle-of-panipat-mocks-rival/story-h5RHzCRX8aVa6dWRaUzRtI.html [Accessed 16 March 2021]

India Today Web Desk (2021). Secularism Biggest Threat to India's Tradition on Global Stage, Says Yogi Adityanath. *India Today*, 8 March. Available at https://www.indiatoday.in/india/story/yogi-adityanath-secularism-biggest-threat-to-india-tradition-on-global-stage-1776752-2021-03-08 [Accessed 12 September 2022]

Jayaprakash, N.D. (2020). Delhi Riots 2020: There Was a Conspiracy, But Not the One the Police Alleges. *The Wire*, 15 July. Available at https://thewire.in/communalism/delhi-riots-2020-there-was-a-conspiracy-but-not-the-one-the-police-alleges [Accessed 27 May 2021]

Kumari, Anisha (2020). Federalism, Secularism among Chapters Dropped from CBSE School Courses. *NDTV* (ndtv.com), 8 July. Available at https://www.ndtv.com/education/cbse-removes-chapters-on-federalism-citizenship-secularism-from-political-science-syllabus [Accessed 5 January 2021]

Mahaprashasta, Ajoy Ashirwad (2020). How Delhi Police Turned Anti-CAA WhatsApp Group Chats Into Riots 'Conspiracy'. *The Wire*, 3 August. Available at https://thewire.in/communalism/delhi-riots-police-activists-whatsapp-group [Accessed 7 Aug 2021]

Masud, Iqbal (2005). Muslim Ethos in Indian Cinema. *Screen Weekly, The Indian Express (web archive)*, 4 March. Available at https://web.archive.org/web/20050308204743/http://www.screenindia.com/fullstory.php?content_id=9980# [Accessed 17 November 2014]

Modi, Narendra (2014). We are secular not because the word was added in our Constitution. Secularism is in our blood. We believe in Sarva Pantha Sambhava. *Twitter*, 28 April. Available at https://twitter.com/narendramodi/status/460685920652390400?lang=en [Accessed 29 September 2021]

Mohan, Rohini (2018). A Template for Hate: Polarized Politics and Mainstream Intolerance. *Harper's Magazine*, 337(2020), pp. 34–40. Available at https://harpers.org/archive/2018/09/india-bharatiya-janata-party-intolerance-bjp-muslim-hindu/ [Accessed 4 February 2021]

Mujtaba, Syed Ali (2006). Bollywood and the Indian Muslims. Indian Muslims (indianmuslims.info web archive), 21 November. Available at https://web.archive.org/web/20070601175254/http://indianmuslims.info/articles/syed_ali_mujtaba/articles/bollywood_and_the_indian_muslims.html [Accessed 16 October 2014]

Pillai, Manu S. (2017). Manufacturing the Fable of Padmavati. *The Mint*, 10 February. Available at https://www.livemint.com/Leisure/DuN5tsGGpEtkVnuIW6pcFN/Manufacturing-the-fable-of-Padmavati.html [Accessed 8 May 2021]

Press Trust of India (PTI) (2018). BJP Alleges Film 'Kedarnath' Promoting 'Love Jihad', Demands Ban., *The Indian Express*, 10 November. Available at https://indian

express.com/article/india/bjp-alleges-film-kedarnath-promoting-love-jihad-demands-ban-5440550/ [Accessed 15 January 2021]

Puniyani, Ram (2021). Is Secularism a Threat to Traditions of India? *coastaldigest.com*, 18 March. Available at http://www.coastaldigest.com/column-top-story/secularism-threat-traditions-india?page=1 [Accessed 20 August 2022]

Rajan, Benson (2018). Gendered Sufi Music: Mapping Female Voices in Qawwali Performance from Bollywood to YouTube Channels. *MAI: Feminism & Visual Culture*, 12 September. Available at https://maifeminism.com/gendered-sufi-music-mapping-female-voices-in-qawwali-per-formance-from-bollywood-to-youtube-channels/ [Accessed 8 December 2021]

Rao, Rarsa V. (1997). A Review of Shyam Bengal's *Sardari Begum*, Premiered Recently on the Television. *Biblio: A Review of Books*, 2(5). Available at http://biblio-india.org/showart.asp?inv= 12&mp=M97 [Accessed 2 August 2014]

Sanghvi, Vir (2008). Counterpoint: Age of Intolerance. *The Hindustan Times*, 2 April. Available at https://www.hindustantimes.com/columns/counterpoint-age-of-intolerance/story-YNuCqYaG8HGkE8LATI7yTK.html [Accessed 13 December 2013]

Scroll Staff (2019). Scrapping of J&K Special Status against People's Will and Unconstitutional, Petitioners Tell SC. *Scroll.in*, 11 December. Available at https://scroll.in/latest/946483/abrogation-of-j-k-special-status-against-peoples-will-and-unconstitutional-petitioners-tell-sc [Accessed 29 May 2021]

Sen, Debarati S. (2017). 'Bollywood Is Soaking in the Sufi Spirit'. *The Times of India: Entertainment*, 17 January. Available at https://timesofindia.indiatimes.com/entertainment/hindi/music/news/Bollywood-is-soaking-in-the-Sufi-spirit/articleshow/55354195.cms [Accessed 4 August 2021]

Sen, Sonali Ghosh (2004). The Embers Refuse to Die. *hardnewsmedia.com*, N.D. October. Available at https://web.archive.org/web/20080616183213/http://www.hardnewsmedia.com/oct2004/bio.php [Accessed 15 September 2007]

Sharma, Devesh (2020). Filmfare Recommends: Top Bollywood Historical Films of This Decade. *Filmfare.com*, 12 April. Available at https://www.filmfare.com/features/filmfare-recommends-top-bollywood-historical-films-of-this-decade-40148.html [Accessed 12 December 2021]

Sharma, Kalpana (2007). Remembering Roop Kanwar. *The Hindu*, 23 September. Available at https://www.thehindu.com/todays-paper/tp-features/tp-sundaymagazine/remembering-roopkanwar/article2275587.ece [Accessed 6 May 2021]

Tantray, Shahid (2019). Day before Ayodhya Verdict, RSS Holds Meeting with Muslim Professionals. *The Caravan (caravanmagazine.in)*, 8 November. Available at https://caravanmagazine.in/politics/day-before-ayodhya-verdict-rss-holds-meeting-muslim-professionals [Accessed 23 April 2021]

Times Now Digital (2021). 'Beti paraya dhan hoti hai': Babul Supriyo's Twitter Meme on Mamata Banerjee Draws Ire. *Times Now News (timesnownews.com)*, 28 February. Available at https://www.timesnownews.com/india/west-bengal/article/beti-paraya-dhan-hoti-hai-babul-supriyo-s-twitter-meme-on-mamata-banerjee-draws-ire/726227 [Accessed 7 March 2022]

Tripathi, Rahul (2020). Who Are Members of 'Tukde Tukde Gang': RTI. *The Economic Times*, 15 January. Available at https://economictimes.indiatimes.com/news/politics-and-nation/who-are-members-of-tukde-tukde-gang-rti/articleshow/73263876.cms?from=mdr [Accessed 15 January 2021]

Tully, Mark (2017). 'How the Babri Mosque Destruction Shaped India. *BBC News*, 6 December. Available at https://www.bbc.com/news/world-asia-india-42219773 [Accessed 22 October 2022]

Vishwanath, Apurva (2021). 3 States, 3 Anti-Conversion Laws: What's Similar, What's Different. *The Indian Express*, 3 January. Available at https://indianexpr ess.com/article/explained/religion-conversion-bill-bjp-7129285/ [Accessed 10 September 2022]

Vyas, Shvetal (2012). *The Disappearance of Muslim Socials in Bollywood. Muslim and Non-Muslim Understanding.* Commentary, International Centre for Muslim and Non-Muslim, University of South Australia. Available at https://www.unisa.edu. au/siteassets/episerver-6-files/documents/eass/mnm/commentaries/vyas-mus lim-socials.pdf [Accessed 9 December 2014]

Reports

Jain, Ranu, and Shaban, Abdul (1999). *Socio Economic and Educational Status of Muslims in Mumbai. A Research Report, Submitted to the Maharashtra State Minorities Commission.* Mumbai: Government of Maharashtra.

Justice Nanavati Commission Report (2005). Justice Nanavati Commission of Inquiry (1984 Anti-Sikh Riots). [Pdf] A Report: Ministry of Home Affairs, Government of India. Available at https://www.mha.gov.in/sites/default/files/Nanavati-I_eng_0.pdf [Accessed 3 March 2014]

Justice Ranganath Misra Commission Report (2007). *Report of the National Commission for Religious and Linguistic Minorities.* [pdf] Ministry of Minority Affairs, Government of India. Available at https://www.minorityaffairs.gov.in/sites/default/files/volume-1.pdf [Accessed 19 November 2013]

Pew Research Centre (2009). *Mapping the Global Muslim Population: A Report on the Size and Distribution of the World's Muslim Population.* [pdf] The Pew Forum on Religion and Public Life. Available at https://www.pewresearch.org/relig ion/wp-content/uploads/sites/7/2009/10/Muslimpopulation-1.pdf [Accessed 6 March 2012]

Rao, Mohan, Mishra, Ish, Singh, Pragya, and Bajpai, Vikas (2013). *Communalism and the Role of the State: An Investigation into the Communal Violence in Muzaffarnagar and Its Aftermath.* [pdf] A Report: Economic and Political Weekly. Available at https://www.epw.in/system/files/pdf/2014_49/2/Muzaffarmagar%20Report%20-%20Final%20(1).pdf [Accessed 17 November 2021]

The Registrar General of India (2011). *Census 2011 Data on Population by Religious Communities. Ministry of Home Affairs, Government of India.* Available at https://pib.gov.in/newsite/printrelease.aspx?relid=126326 [Accessed 31 October 2022]

Sachar Committee Report (2006). *Social, Economic and Educational Status of the Muslim Community of India. [pdf] A Report: Prime Minister's High Level Committee. Government of India.* Available at https://www.minorityaffairs.gov.in/sites/default/files/sachar_comm.pdf [Accessed 4 March 2012]

Books, Articles, Unpublished Thesis

Aapola, Sinikka (1997). Mature Girls and Adolescent Boys? Deconstructing Discourses of Adolescence and Gender. *Young*, 5(4), pp. 50–68.

Abbas, S.B. (2003). *The Female Voice in Sufi Ritual: Devotional Practices of Pakistan and India*. University of Texas Press.

Ahmed, A.S. (1992). Bombay Films: The Cinema as Metaphor for Indian Society and Politics. *Modern Asian Studies*, 26(2), pp. 289–320.

Alagh, Tavishi (2012). Guftagu: M.S. Sathyu, Javed Akhtar, Mahesh Bhatt. In: Bharat, M. and Kumar, N. (Eds), *Filming the Line of Control: The Indo–Pak Relationship through the Cinematic Lens*. New Delhi: Routledge.

Ambedkar, Bhimrao Ramji (2014). *Annihilation of Caste. The Annotated Critical Edition*. Verso Books.

Amin, Shahid (2003). 'Representing the Musalman: Then and Now, Now and Then', in Shail Mayaram, M.S.S. Pandian and Ajay Skaria (eds), *Muslims, Dalits and the Fabrication of History: Subaltern Studies*, vol. 12. New Delhi: Permanent Black and Ravi Dayal Publishers, 2005, pp. 1-35. *Subaltern Studies*, 12(1).

Anderson, Benedict (1983). *Imagined Communities: Reflections on the Origin and Spread of Nationalism*. Verso Books.

Bacchetta, P. (1994). Communal Property: On Representations of Muslim Women in a Hindu Nationalist Discourse. In: Hasan, Z. (Ed.), *Forging Identities: Gender, Communities, and the State in India*. Boulder, CO: Westview Press, pp. 188–225.

Bacchetta, P. (2000). Sacred Space in Conflict in India: The Babri Masjid Affair. *Growth and Change*, 31(2), pp. 255–84.

Bacchetta, P. (2004). *Gender in the Hindu Nation: RSS Women as Ideologues*. New Delhi: Women Unlimited.

Banaji, Shakuntala (2018). Vigilante Publics: Orientalism, Modernity and Hindutva Fascism in India. *Javnost-The Public*, 25(4), pp. 333–50.

Banerjee, Sikata (2012). *Make Me a Man!: Masculinity, Hinduism, and Nationalism in India*. SUNY Press.

Banerjee, Sikata (2016). *Gender, Nation and Popular Film in India: Globalizing Muscular Nationalism*. Taylor & Francis.

Barnouw, Erik K. (1963). *Indian Film*. Madras: Orient Longman.

Basu, Anustup (2010). *Bollywood in the Age of New Media: The Geo-televisual Aesthetic*. Edinburgh University Press.

Bauman, Zygmunt (1991). *Modernity and Ambivalence*. Cambridge: Polity Press.

Bauman, Zygmunt (1999). *Culture as praxis*. Sage.

Beckerlegge, Gwilym (1997). Followers of 'Mohammed, Kalee and Dada Nanuk': The Presence of Islam and South Asian Religions in Victorian Britiain. In: Wolffe, John. (Ed.), *Religion in Victorian Britain, vol. 5, Culture and Empire*. Manchester and New York: Manchester University Press, pp. 222–67.

Bell, Kelly J. (2009). Who Makes a Nation? An Examination of Nationalism, Gender, and Membership in the Nation. *Inquiries Journal*, 1(12). Available at http://www.inquiriesjournal.com/a?id=80 [Accessed 16 September 2018]

Benegal, Shyam (2007). Secularism and Popular Indian Cinema. In: Needham, Anuradha D. and Rajan, Rajeswari S. (Eds), *The Crisis of Secularism in India*. New Delhi: Permanent Black, pp. 225–28.

Berger, J. (1985). *Ways of Seeing*. Harmondsworth: Penguin.

Bharat, Meenakshi, and Nirmal Kumar (Eds.) (2012). *Filming the Line of Control: The Indo–Pak Relationship through the Cinematic Lens*. Routledge.

Bhaskar, Ira (2005). *The Persistence of Memory: Historical Trauma and Imagining the Community in Hindi Cinema*. PhD Thesis. New York: New York University.

Bhaskar, Ira, and Allen, Richard (2009). *Islamicate Cultures of Bombay Cinema*. Tulika Books.

Bhatia, Nandi (2010). *Acts of Authority/Acts of Resistance: Theater and Politics in Colonial and Postcolonial India*. University of Michigan Press.

Bhaumik, Saba Naqvi (2005). Politics of Indian War Films. *South Asian Journal*, 10, pp. 116–26.

Brass, Paul R. (2005). *Language, Religion and Politics in North India*. iUniverse.

Booth, G.D. (2007). Making a Woman from a Tawaif: Courtesans as Heroes in Hindi Cinema. *New Zealand Journal of Asian Studies*, 9(2), pp. 1–26.

Bose, R. (2009). Writing 'Realism' in Bombay Cinema: Tracing the Figure of the 'Urdu Writer' through Khoya Khoya Chand. *Economic and Political Weekly*, 44(47), pp. 61–66.

Bourdieu, Pierre (1984). A Social Critique of the Judgement of Taste. In: *Traducido del francés por R. Nice*. London: Routledge.

Budha, K. (2008). Genre Development in the Age of Markets and Nationalism: The War Film. In: Bharat, Meenakshi and Kumar, Nirmal (Eds.), *Filming the Line of Control: The Indo-Pak Relationship through the Cinematic Lens*. New Delhi: Routledge, pp.3-20.

Butalia, U. (2017). *The Other Side of Silence: Voices from the Partition of India*. Penguin UK.

Cameron, Deborah, and Panovic, Ivan (2014). *Working with Written Discourse*. Sage.

Chada, Kalyani, and Anandam, P. Kavoori (2008). Eroticized, Marginalised, Demonized: The Muslim 'Other' in Indian Cinema. In: Kavoori, P. Anandam and Punathambekar, Awin (Eds.), *Global Bollywood*. New Delhi: Oxford University Press, pp. 131–45.

Chakravarty, Sumita (2000). Fragmenting the Nation: Images of Terrorism in Indian Popular Cinema. In: Hjort, M., & MacKenzie, S. (Eds.). *Cinema and nation*, London and New York: Routledge, pp.209-223.

Chakravarty, Sumita (2011). *National Identity in Indian Popular Cinema, 1947–1987*. University of Texas Press.

Chatterjee, Partha (1989). Colonialism, Nationalism, and Colonialized Women: The Contest in India. *American Ethnologist*, 16(4), pp. 622–33.

Chaudhuri, Maitrayee (2012). Indian 'Modernity' and 'Tradition': A Gender Analysis. *Polish Sociological Review*, 178(2), pp. 281–93.

Chhabra, G.S. (2005). *Advance Study in the History of Modern India (Volume 2: 1803–1920)*. Vol. 2. Lotus Press.

Daniels-Yeomans, F. (2017). Trauma, Affect and the Documentary Image: Towards a Nonrepresentational Approach. *Studies in Documentary Film*, 11(2), pp. 85–103.

Das Gupta, Chidananda (1980). New Directions in Indian Cinema. *Film Quarterly*, 34(1), pp. 32–42.

Dingwaney, Anuradha N., and Rajan, Rajeswari S. (2007). *The Crisis of Secularism in India*. New Delhi: Permanent Black Publications.

Dudrah, Rajinder K. (2006). *Bollywood: Sociology Goes to the Movies*. New Delhi: Sage Publications.

Duff, J.G. (1873). *A History of the Mahrattas*. Published at the Times of India Office.

Dwyer, Rachel (2006). *Filming the Gods: Religion and Indian Cinema*. Abingdon: Routledge.

Dyson, T. (2018). *A Population History of India: From the First Modern People to the Present Day*. Oxford University Press.

Eisele, John C. (2002). The Wild East: Deconstructing the Language of Genre in the Hollywood Eastern. *Cinema Journal*, 41(4), pp. 68–94. University of Texas Press.

Elison, William, Novetzke, Christian Lee, and Rotman, Andy (2016). *Amar Akbar Anthony: Bollywood, Brotherhood and the Nation*. Cambridge, MA: Harvard University Press.

Engineer, Asghar Ali (1991). Remaking Indian Muslim Identity. *Economic and Political Weekly*, 26(16), pp. 1036–38.

Engineer, Asghar Ali (1995). Communalism and Communal Violence in 1995. *Economic and Political Weekly*, 30(51), pp. 3267–69.

Foucault, Michel (1984). *The Foucault Reader*. Pantheon.

Gabriel, Karen, and Vijayan, P.K. (2012). Orientalism, Terrorism and Bombay Cinema. *Journal of Postcolonial Writing*, 48(3), pp. 299–310.

Ganti, Tejaswini (2004). *Bollywood: A Guidebook to Popular Hindi Cinema*. New York: Routledge.

Ganti, Tejaswini (2005). Shoveling Smoke: Advertising and Globalization in Contemporary India. *Visual Anthropology Review*, 2(1&2:Spring/Fall), pp. 181–83.

Ganti, Tejaswini (2012). *Producing Bollywood: Inside the Contemporary Hindi Film Industry*. Duke University Press.

Gilmartin, Sophie (1997). The Sati, the Bride, and the Widow: Sacrificial Woman in the Nineteenth Century. *Victorian Literature and Culture*, 25(1), pp. 141–58. Available at https://doi.org/10.1017/S1060150300004678 .

Gledhill, C. (2009). Recent Development in Feminist Criticism. *Journal Quarterly Review of Film Studies*, 3(4), pp. 457–93. Available at: https://doi.org/10.1080/10509207809391419.

Gopal, Sangita (2012). *Conjugations*. University of Chicago Press.

Gupta, Charu (2001). *Sexuality, Obscenity, Community: Women, Muslims and the Hindu Public in Colonial India*. New Delhi: Permanent Black.

Gupta, Charu (2009). Hindu Women, Muslim Men: Love Jihad and Conversions. *Economic and Political Weekly*, 44(51).

Gupta, Charu (2016). Allegories of 'Love Jihad' and Ghar Vāpasī: Interlocking the Socio-Religious with the Political. *Archiv Orientalni*, 84(2).

Habermas, Jürgen, and Ben-Habib, Seyla (1981). Modernity versus Postmodernity. *New German Critique*, 22, pp. 3–14.

Hodgson, Marshall G.S. (1974). *The Venture of Islam, Volume 1: The Classical Age of Islam*. University of Chicago Press.

Hubel, T. (2012). From Tawaif to Wife? Making Sense of Bollywood's Courtesan Genre. In: Roy, A.G. (Ed.), *The Magic of Bollywood: At Home and Abroad*. New Delhi: Sage, pp. 213–34. Available at: https://dx.doi.org/10.4135/9788132113 966.n12.

Hussein, Nazia, and Hussein, Saba (2015). Interrogating Practices of Gender, Religion and Nationalism in the Representation of Muslim Women in Bollywood: Contexts of Change, Sites of Continuity. *Exchanges: The Interdisciplinary Research Journal*, 2(2), pp. 284–304.

Islam, Maidul (2007). Imagining Indian Muslims: Looking through the Lens of Bollywood Cinema. *Indian Journal of Human Development*, 1(2), pp. 403–22.

Islam, Maidul (2018). Imag(in)ing Indian Muslims in Post-liberalization Hindi Cinema. *Indian Muslim(s) after Liberalization*. Oxford University Press, pp. 91–149.

Jackson, Richard (2006). Religion, Politics and Terrorism: A Critical Analysis of Narratives of 'Islamic Terrorism'. *Centre for International Politics Working Paper Series*, 21, pp. 1–22.

Jeffery, R., and Hall, I. (2020). Post-conflict Justice in Divided Democracies: The 1984 Anti-Sikh Riots in India. *Third World Quarterly*, 41(6), pp. 994–1011.

Jeffery, Roger, and Jeffery, Patricia (1997). *Population, Gender and Politics: Demographic Change in Rural North India*. Cambridge University Press.

Jha, Dwijendra Narayan (2002). *The Myth of the Holy Cow*. Verso.

Kaplan, E. A. (2005). *Trauma culture: The politics of terror and loss in media and literature*. New Brunswick, New Jersey and London: Rutgers University Press.

Kaul, A., and Sen, M. (2014). Manifesto of the New Cinema Movement (India, 1968). In: MacKenzie, S. (Ed.), *Film Manifestos and Global Cinema Cultures: A Critical Anthology*. Berkeley, CA: University of California Press, pp. 165–68.

Kavoori, P. Anandam, and Punathambekar, Awin (2008). *Global Bollywood*. New Delhi: Oxford University Press.

Kazmi, Fareed (1999). *The Politics of India's Conventional Cinema: Imaging a Universe, Subverting the Multiverse*. SAGE Publications Pvt. Limited.

Kazmi, Fareed, and Kumar, Sanjeev (2011). The Politics of Muslim Identity and the Nature of Public Imagination in India: Media and Films as Potential Determinants. *European Journal of Economic and Political Studies*, 4(1), pp. 171–87.

Kesavan, M. (1994). 'Urdu, Awadh and the Tawaif: The Islamicate Roots of Hindi Cinema'. In: Hasan, Zoya (Ed.), *Forging Identities: Gender, communities and the state in India*. Delhi: Kali for Women, pp. 244–57.

Khatun, Nadira (2016). Imagining Muslims as the 'Other' in Muslim Political Films. *Journal of Arab & Muslim Media Research*, 9(1), pp. 41–60. Available at https://doi:10.1386/jammr.9.1.41_1.

Khatun, Nadira (2016). *Imagining Muslim Identity: An Interpretive Study of Hindi Cinema*. PhD Thesis. Tata Institute of Social Sciences.

Khatun, Nadira (2018). 'Love-Jihad' and Bollywood: Constructing Muslims as 'Other'. *Journal of Religion & Film*, 22(3).

Khatun, Nadira (2020). Conceiving the Discourse of Compassion through the Lens of Media. *Social Action (special issue on Morality, Public Compassion and Other-directedness)*, 70(1:January–March), pp. 17–31.

Khilnani, Sunil (2004). *The Idea of India*. Penguin Books India.

Kumar, Akshaya (2013). Provincialising Bollywood? Cultural Economy of North-Indian Small-Town Nostalgia in the Indian Multiplex. *South Asian Popular Culture*, 11(1), pp. 61–74.

Kumar, Sanjeev (2013). Constructing the Nation's Enemy: Hindutva, Popular Culture and the Muslim 'Other' in Bollywood Cinema. *Third World Quarterly*, 34(3), pp. 458–69.

Laine, J.W. (2003). *Shivaji: Hindu King in Islamic India*. Oxford University Press.

Lane-Poole, S. (1896). *Aurangzib, and the Decay of the Mughal Empire (Vol. 5)*. Clarendon Press.

Louis, P. (2000). *The Emerging Hindutva Force: The Ascent of Hindu Nationalism*. New Delhi: Indian Social Institute.

Mamdani, Mahmood (2005). *Good Muslim, Bad Muslim: America, the Cold War, and the Roots of Terror*. Harmony.

Master, Natasha (2009). *Representing the Unrepresentable: The Bollywood Partition Film*. Master of Arts. Unpublished Thesis. Carleton University. Available at https://curve.carleton.ca/4e9725cf-2294-402e-a263-00cd7b8d49d9 [Accessed 15 August 2022]

Mayne, Judith (1993). *Cinema and Spectatorship*. London: Routledge.

Merivirta, Raita (2016). Historical Film and Hindu–Muslim Relations in Post-Hindutva India: The Case of Jodhaa Akbar. *Quarterly Review of Film and Video*, 33(5), pp. 456–77.

Mubarki, Meraj Ahmed (2014). Exploring the 'Other': Inter-Faith Marriages in *Jodhaa Akbar* and Beyond. In *Contemporary South Asia*, 22(3:July), pp. 255–67. Available at https://doi:10.1080/09584935.2014.930419 .

Mukhopadhyay, Urvi (2013). *The 'Medieval' in Film: Representing a Contested Time on the Indian Screen (1920s–1960s)*. Orient Blackswan.

Mulvey, L. (1975). Visual Pleasure and Narrative Cinema. *Screen*, 16(3), pp. 6–18. Available at: https://doi.org/10.1093/screen/16.3.6 .

Nagel, Joane (1998). Masculinity and Nationalism: Gender and Sexuality in the Making of Nations. *Ethnic and Racial Studies*, 21(2), pp. 242–69.

Nandy, Ashis, Trivedy, Shikha, Mayaram, Shail, and Yagnik, Achyut (1995). *Creating a Nationality: The Ramjanmabhumi Movement and Fear of the Self*. New Delhi: Oxford University Press.

Nandy, Ashis (1980). Woman versus Womanliness in India: An Essay in Cultural and Political Psychology. *At the Edge of Psychology: Essays in Politics and Culture*. Delhi: Oxford University Press, pp. 32–46.

Nandy, Ashis (2006). Nationalism, Genuine and Spurious: Mourning Two Early Post-nationalist Strains. *Economic and Political Weekly*, 41(32), pp. 3500–504.

Nayyar, A. (1988). *Qawwali*. Lok Virsa Research Centre.

Needham, Anuradha Dingwaney, and Rajan, Rajeswari Sunder. (2007). *The Crisis of Secularism in India*. Duke University Press.

Nehru, Jawaharlal (2008). *Discovery of India*. New edition (1 February 2008). Penguin UK.

Norman, Daniel (2009). *Islam and the West: The Making of an Image*. Oneworld Publications

Oldenburg, V.T. (1990). Lifestyle as Resistance: The Case of the Courtesans of Lucknow, India. *Feminist Studies*, 16(2), pp. 259–87. Available at https://doi.org/10.2307/3177850.

Osella, Caroline, and Osella, Filippo (2007). Muslim Style in South India. *Fashion Theory*, 11(2–3), pp. 233–52.

Pandey, Gyanendra (1990). *The Construction of Communalism in Colonial North India*. Delhi: Oxford University Press.

Pansare, Govind (2018). *Shivaji Kon Hota?* Lokayat Prakashan.

Parciack, Ronie (2013). Terror as Cinematic Desire: Discourses of Citizenry and the Challenge of the 'Non-Statist'. *South Asian Popular Culture*, 11(2), pp. 145–55.

Patel, Vibhuti (2013). Socio-economic profile of Muslims in Maharashtra. *Social Change*, 43(3), pp. 481–93.

Prasad, Madhav M. (1998). *Ideology of the Hindi Film: A Historical Construction*. New Delhi: Oxford University Press.

Prasad, Madhav M. (1998). The State in/of Cinema. In: Chatterjee, Partha (Ed.), *Wages of Freedom: Fifty Years of the Indian Nation-State*. Delhi: Oxford University Press.

Puniyani, Ram (2010). Deconstructing Communalism in India: Striving for Harmony. *All India Secular Forum*. Mumbai.

Puri, B. (1993). Indian Muslims since Partition. *Economic and Political Weekly*, XXIX(40), pp. 2141–49.

Qureshi, R.B. (1999). His Master's Voice? Exploring Qawwali and 'Gramophone Culture'in South Asia. *Popular Music*, Cambridge University Press, 18(1), pp. 63–98. Available at https://doi.org/10.1017/S0261143000008734.

Rai, Amit (2003). Patriotism and the Muslim Citizen in Hindi Films. *Harvard Asia Quarterly*, 7, pp. 4–15.

Rajeshirke, A.B. (1981). Political and Economic Relations between the Portuguese and the Marathas (1630–1680). *In Proceedings of the Indian History Congress*, Indian History Congress, 42, pp. 233–240.

Rajgopal, Shoba Sharad (2011). Bollywood and Neonationalism: The Emergence of Nativism as the Norm in Indian Conventional Cinema. *South Asian Popular Culture*, 9(3), pp. 237–46.

Ramaswamy, Sumathi (2001). Maps and Mother Goddesses in Modern India. *Imago Mundi*, 53(1), pp. 97–114. Available at: https://doi.org/10.1080/03085690108592940.

Ramaswamy, Sumathi (2008). Maps, Mother/Goddesses, and Martyrdom in Modern India. *Journal of Asian Studies*, 67(3), pp. 819–53.

Rao, Mohan (2011). Love Jihad and Demographic Fears. *Indian Journal of Gender Studies*, 18(3), pp. 425–30.

Roy, Baijayanti (2018). Visual Grandeur, Imagined Glory: Identity Politics and Hindu Nationalism in Bajirao Mastani and Padmaavat. *Journal of Religion & Film*, 22(3), p. 9.

Sarkar, T. (1999). The Gender Predicament of the Hindu Right. In: Panikkar, K.N. (Ed.), *The Concerned Indian's Guide to Communalism*. New Delhi: Penguin Book India, pp. 131–59.

Said, Edward W. (1978). *Orientalism*. New York: Vintage.

Said, Edward W. (2001). *Orientalism: Western Concepts of the Orient*. Penguin.

Said, Edward W. (2008). *Covering Islam: How the Media and the Experts Determine How We See the Rest of the World*. Fully revised edition. Random House.

Sardar, Ziauddin (1992). Terminator 2 Modernity, Postmodernism and the 'Other'. *Futures*, 24(5), pp. 493–506.

Schulze, B. (2002). The Cinematic 'Discovery of India': Mehboob's Re-Invention of the Nation in Mother India. *Social Scientist*, 30(9–10), pp. 72–87.

Sen, Siladitya (2018). *Sankhadhikkher Chalachitra Asahishnutar Khatiyan (An Account of Intolerance in Majoritarian Cinema)*. Kolkata: Priyabrata Deb.

Sengupta, Roshni (2020). *Reading the Muslim on Celluloid: Bollywood, Representation and Politics*. Delhi: Primus Books.

Sethi, Manisha (2002). Cine-Patriotism. *SAMAR: South Asian Magazine for Action and Reflection*, 15.

Shaban, Abdul (2008). Ghettoisation, Crime and Punishment in Mumbai. *Economic and Political Weekly*, 43(33), pp. 68–73.

Shaheen, Jack G. (2003). Reel Bad Arabs: How Hollywood Vilifies a People. *The ANNALS of the American Academy of Political and Social Science*, 588(1), pp. 171–93.

Shaheen, Jack G. (2009). *Reel Bad Arabs: How Hollywood Vilifies a People*. Northampton: Olive Branch Press.

Singh, J.P., and House, Kate (2010). Bollywood in Hollywood: Value Chains, Cultural Voices, and the Capacity to Aspire. In: *APSA 2010 Annual Meeting Paper*.

Singh, V.P. (2014). From Tawaif to Nautch Girl: The Transition of the Lucknow Courtesan. *South Asian Review*, 35(2), pp. 177–94. Available at https://doi.org/10.1080/02759527.2014.11932977.

Smith, V.A. (1966). *Akbar the Great Mogul, 1542–1605*. Dalcassian Publishing Company.

Soherwordi, Syed Hussain Shaheed (2013). Hindu Nationalism and the Political Role of Hindu Women: Ideology as a Factor. *South Asian Studies*, 28(1).

Somaaya, B., Kothari, J., and Madangarli, S. (2012). *Mother Maiden Mistress: Women in Hindi Cinema*. New Delhi: Harper Collins.

Srivastava, S.P. (2001). *Jahangir, a Connoisseur of Mughal Art*. Abhinav Publications.

Stein, B. (2010). *A History of India (Vol. 9)*. John Wiley & Sons.

Stubbs, Jonathan (2013). *Historical Film: A Critical Introduction*. Bloomsbury Publishing.

Taylor, Lisa, and Willis, Andrew (1999). *Media Studies: Texts, Institutions and Audiences*. Wiley-Blackwell.

Thapar, Romila (2007). Secularism, History, and Contemporary Politics in India. In: Needham, Anuradha Dingwaney and Rajan, Rajeswari Sunder (Eds.), *The Crisis of Secularism in India*. Duke University Press, pp. 191–207.

Thapar, Romila, et al. (2016). *On Nationalism*. New Delhi: Aleph Spotlight.

Vasudevan, Ravi S. (2015). Film Genres, the Muslim Social, and Discourses of Identity c. 1935–1945. *BioScope: South Asian Screen Studies*, 6(1), pp. 27–43. Available at https://doi.org/10.1177/0974927615586930.

Ward, L. (2008). *Images of Decolonising India: Bollywood's Tawai'f and the Postcolonial Muslim*. New York: Columbia University.

Wolpert, Stanley (2006). *Encyclopedia of India*. Scribner.

Zaidi, S. Hussain (2012). *Dongri to Dubai: Six Decades of the Mumbai Mafia*. New Delhi: Roli Books.

Zubedi, Irfan, and Sarrazin, Natalie (2016). Evolution of a Ritual Musical Genre: The Adaptation of Qawwali in Contemporary Hindi film. In: Beaster-Jones, Jayson and Sarrazin, Natalie (Eds.), *Music in Contemporary Indian Film: Memory, Voice, Identity*. New York: Routledge, pp. 162–76.

Index

For the benefit of digital users, indexed terms that span two pages (e.g., 52–53) may, on occasion, appear on only one of those pages.
Figures are indicated by *f* following the page number